Praise for U

"Deb Ozarko's splendid book won't tell you hc
society. Instead, it will help you find the pov   ......purpose that lie
within you. If you want to live an authentic and compassionate life, if you want
to be connected to the wellsprings of life, you'll find inspiration here."

—**JOHN ROBBINS**, author of *Diet for a New America*, and President of the
Food Revolution Network

"Pulsating with a visceral aliveness, Deb Ozarko's book is a stunning choir of
global voices that jolts us up and out of our collective numbness, awakening
what she accurately describes as our 'primal spiritual instinct.' An instinct that
will feel like a stir deep in the body, a restless agitation that is designed to redirect our attention out of our mindless habituated ways and deep into the present
moment … the only place where authenticity and the emergence of a new world
can live. Trust what awakens inside you as you read. It is your gateway HOME."

—**NAOMI IRONS**, co-author of *Guardians of the Vision: Parenting for the
Birthright of Potential*, and co-creator of the Rural Consciousness Project

"A compelling wake-up call to a deeper life, a life largely catalyzed by turning
toward our pain and the pain of others, step by increasingly compassionate step.
Down-to-earth, as direct as it's caring, a book infused with the power to turn
inspiration into needed action."

—**ROBERT AUGUSTUS MASTERS**, author of *Spiritual Bypassing,
Transformation through Intimacy*, and *To Be a Man*

"Deb's book, *Unplug*, captures the beauty and essence—the up-side—of the
changes taking place in our world. Amongst the chaos and confusion that often attracts our attention, through the stories in this book, we instead see the
magnificent unfolding of the human spirit. *Unplug* is an inspiration for all of us
to see and experience the potential for a new consciousness that brings about a
new world."

—**HOWARD MARTIN**, co-author of *The HeartMath Solution* and
Executive Vice President, HeartMath

"Deb Ozarko's work is something I can resonate with as a filmmaker. I am also drawn to the pulsating humanity of the human heart, and draw inspiration from change-makers, activists, and artists who often risk their own lives to bring about social justice and love in dark places. Thank you, Deb, for your piercing contribution."

—**LIZ MARSHALL**, filmmaker, *The Ghosts in Our Machine*

"Filled with infectious joy and a grab-your-attention passion for life, this book, like Deb, leaves no room for passive or apathetic thinking. Instead, it will fill your heart with a love for all of life, and a desire to do more to protect and celebrate all of the world's citizens.

Deb has brilliantly gathered others who share her passion and compassion to tell their stories of awakening and action. It will be impossible to read this book and not have your compassion and awareness expand. Be ready to be filled with the desire to take action and unplug from the status quo. We will all be better for it. It's a must read for anyone who loves the planet and wants all of the life found within it, and on it, to thrive."

—**BECA LEWIS**, professional how-to-shift trainer and author of *Living in Grace: The Shift to Spiritual Perception*

"Deb Ozarko's *Unplug* is a beautiful tapestry that embodies the Rig Vedic verse, "Ekaṁ sat, viprā bahudhā vadanti. Truth is one, the wise call it by many names." As Deb skilfully threads through the journeys of 26 different seekers of the Truth, you are bound to find a strand that resonates with your own and inspires you to seek harder."

—**SAILESH RAO**, author of *Carbon Dharma: The Occupation of Butterflies* and founder of Climate Healers

"In an unfeeling world, Deb Ozarko is a powerful force who has the courage to feel—and to speak what she feels. She inspires us to rise up and experience the potential we have to simply love. *Unplug* is a manifestation of her gift to unite purpose with compassion. You, the reader, will be taken on a journey that will awaken and inspire the expression of the perfection of your gifts."

—**SYLVIE GOUIN**, author of *Inspired Living: A Guided Yoga Journal*

"This book is dangerous. It breaks the status quo, inoculates our hearts, and rips asunder the terrified and unyielding voice of the ego. *Unplug* will become one of the most tweeted, shared, and quoted sources of our times. It is inspiring, cathartic, and opens our eyes to what lies within us all."

—**SEAN HOWARD**, author of *Creators 2.0: How to Find Your Purpose, Build Sustainable Growth and Change the World*

"Deb Ozarko is a force of nature and force FOR nature. She is a passionate voice for all things precious: life, love, our imperiled planet, and all its creatures, both small and large. As someone who has interviewed environmental leaders for more than a decade, I recognize a skilled and subject-savvy questioner when I hear one. Whether through her passion-filled podcasts or her concise yet deeply insightful writing, Deb gets it! What *Unplug* brings to us is nothing short of brilliant, necessary, and just what our weary and disillusioned world needs most right now. As a longtime activist for a better world, Deb walks the walk, talks her walk, and perhaps best of all … she listens … deeply. Deb Ozarko is one of my she-roes!"

—**BETSY ROSENBERG**, Green Radio Host/Producer, Eco-Solutionary, Speaker, Writer

UNPLUG

26 PEOPLE SHARE HOW THEY RECHARGE AND RECONNECT
TO PASSION, PRESENCE AND PURPOSE

DEB OZARKO

Published by: Deb Ozarko Publishing, debozarko.com
Front Cover Photography: Valentin Russanov (iStockphoto)
Back Cover Photography: Deb Gleason
Cover and book design: Deb Ozarko
Edited by: Marilyn Burkley
Printed by: CreateSpace, an Amazon.com company

Cover photo: The lighthouse is an inspired metaphor. It guides us with its inner light and helps us stay on course in all external conditions. It remains solid in itself, even when pounded by the fury of the waves that come from all directions. We are all powerful like the lighthouse when we claim our voice, our heart, and our light.

ISBN 978-0-9949845-0-0

Available from Amazon.com and other online stores.

Dedication

To Gaia
My heartbeat, my breath, my soul.
Mother of us all.
We are not separate.
May you forgive us for forgetting …

To my birth mother, Christine
You left the Earth too soon, but your love, humor, and
compassion remain the ever-present wind beneath my wings.

To my father, Michael
You gave me the strength to speak my truth
and stand tall with conviction.
Your courage and fire live on in my heart.

To the animals. All of them.
The purest gurus of all who've shown me
humility, compassion, humor, integrity, fortitude,
courage, and a limitless expanse of love.
You inspire me to make the world a better place.

To my rock, Deb Gleason
My life partner, my best friend, my deepest love.
Thank you for your unwavering belief in me.
Thank you for your belief in a kinder, more compassionate world.
May we continue our passionate quest to transform this world together!

To you
This book is dedicated to all of the soul-connected,
purpose-driven, action-oriented Earth lovers who
know that a better world is our birthright.
I salute you.

Contents

From the Elders of the Hopi Nation
Oraibi, Arizona June 8, 2000

TO MY FELLOW SWIMMERS

We have been telling the people that this is the Eleventh Hour
Now you must go back and tell the people that this is the Hour
And there are things to be considered.

It is time to speak your truth.
Create your community.
Be good to each other.
And do not look outside yourself for the leader.

There is a river flowing now very fast.
It is so great and swift that there are those who will be afraid.
They will try to hold onto the shore.
They are being torn apart and they will suffer greatly.

Know the river has its destination.
The elders say we must let go of the shore, and push
off and into the river, keep our eyes open,
and our head above the water.

See who is in there with you and celebrate.
At this time in history, we are to take nothing personally,
least of all ourselves, for the moment that we do,
our spiritual growth and journey comes to a halt.

The time of the lone wolf is over.
Gather yourselves.
Banish the word struggle from your attitude
and your vocabulary.

All that you do now must be done in a
sacred manner and in celebration.
For we are the ones we have been waiting for.

Introduction
Reclaiming the Human Spirit

"Every renaissance comes to the world with a cry,
the cry of the human spirit to be free."

– ANNE SULLIVAN

We're born to the world as pure potential—radiant, innocent, untarnished. A fresh slate ripe for expansion; eager to learn what it means to be human. Without the awareness to fend for ourselves, the next several years are shaped by an external world of hand-me-down belief systems. Conformity, consumption, judgment, fear, and indifference fragment our consciousness and rob us of *all that matters in life*: truth, joy, presence, purpose, love, and our intrinsic need to better the world. We're indoctrinated into the paradigm of separation, adulterated by beliefs that silence the voice of our hearts.

It's been said that the indoctrination process is complete by the tender age of five. The unexamined belief systems of a culture in a trance so deeply installed that we are markedly altered: anesthetized byproducts of a consumptive machine. We conform, we consume, we comply, we compete.

We normalize the abnormal to preserve what we know. At great expense to our souls, we're taught to make choices that cause harm to so many—including ourselves.

The blind acceptance of what we know in our hearts to be untrue has caused irreversible damage: wanton violence; global oppression; rampant greed; rapacious consumption; runaway climate change; unbridled overpopulation; and widespread unhappiness. As a species, we've become an indomitable infestation of destructive parasites paving the way for our own demise as the sixth great mass extinction event currently plays out. Many have lost their capacity to care. Culture rules. No questions asked. This is the collective mindset we've fatuously assumed. This is status quo—a ruthless predator that destroys our souls.

The unconscious masses will never be free from the cultural inertia that holds their minds captive. Without conscious awareness, they acquiesce to half-lives built on antiquated stories, conditioned by beliefs with immune systems that hold them intact. Many remain lost as they aimlessly grasp at a false sense of hope or illusory solutions in an external world. At best, they remain trapped in low-grade unhappiness—a self-created purgatory. At worst, they succumb to life-numbing addiction—a self-created hell.

The collective consciousness of humanity has flat-lined. We live in a world that appears mindlessly committed to its own demise. In many ways, the twenty-first century has morphed into the second coming of the Dark Ages. But we can no longer lay claim to the blind ignorance of this dark time in history. Instead, we are guilty of something far more sinister: willful ignorance—the arrogant choice to consciously disregard truth. This marks a truly dangerous choice, provoked by the voracious consumptive patterns that have the immense potential to end life on Earth as we know it.

So what's the deal? Have we really lost our way?

Ceaseless wars. Mass shootings. Starvation. Tsunamis. Cyclones. Droughts. Flooding. Oil spills. Wildfires. Superstorms. Fracking. Clearcutting. Tar sands. Overfishing. Terrorism. Unending poverty. Rampant judgment, depression, anxiety, addiction, obesity, homophobia, racism, sexism, and species-ism. Unfathomable violence toward billions of "food" animals annually. All of this is destroying us, both literally and figuratively. There is little doubt that something has gone seriously awry with species *homo sapiens*. The planet is burning up with the fever of human exploitation as our minds simultaneously burn up with the fever of spiritual disconnect. It's proving to be an ugly sight with widespread repercussions that beg the question: Are we single-handedly destroying life on this planet?

As Louise LeBrun writes in her provocative blog post "Evolution by Intention: New Beginnings for Weary Souls"[1]: "We go about our lives, every cell in our body bathed in and formed by the numbing effects of generations of mindless, habituated thinking, asleep to that which crumbles around us, hoping that someone else will take care of it all. What will it take to awaken the giants that we are from the intergenerational slumber that has now become a coma? What will it take for us to call up the courage to find out?"

Humans are a hybrid species of flesh and spirit, ego and soul. For thousands of years, ego has ruled with an imbalanced stranglehold on reason, logic, excuses, opinions, comparison, competition, blame, reactivity, advice, justification, projection, impatience, cynicism, and denial. We continue to experience the fallout of this oppressive intellectual dominance through escalating violence, selfishness, addiction, conformity, consumption, compliance, judgment, fear, indifference, and outright apathy. Many have resigned themselves, while others lash out.

The root cause of every problem facing us today is as simple as it is complex. Regardless of magnitude, all problems stem from a dumbed-down consciousness that inflates ego at the expense of the soul. This is the consciousness that perpetuates the dangerous Myth of Separation.

The Myth of Separation supports an anthropocentric worldview that implies we are separate from animals, from nature, from one another, and most frightening of all, from our true Selves. Separation has alienated the masses from the natural world, the body, intuition, creativity, authenticity, truth, compassion, purpose, and love. On a collective scale, separation sickness has left us feeling worthless, empty, and isolated.

We sustain the epidemic of separation through our thoughts, choices, behaviors, and actions. We know more about the celebrity-du-jour than we do our own neighbors. We have more free will, abundance, and freedom than at any other time in history, yet we're more depressed, unhappy, fearful, and unfulfilled than ever before. With more than seven billion humans inhabiting Earth, we should feel anything but separate, but the widespread epidemic of loneliness clearly shows the extent of our collective insanity.

What does this tell us? We've lost our way and forgotten the wholeness of our being.

Louise LeBrun, in her book Fully Alive: *Awakening Health, Humor, Compassion, and Truth*, writes:

> We are not encouraged to challenge the status quo but to embrace it; to run with the pack rather than to travel alone. Homogeneity and group-think are the expectation. Survival is in the collective, in that group-think and that group-speak. This perspective is destined to limit human expression since the process of embracing the status-quo leads to eating your own tail. Eventually you disappear.
>
> And we are disappearing. Our capacity for joy, for play, for delighting in our own existence is rapidly disappearing. We have become slaves to our own rules. Once again, we live in a time when the masses are controlled by a handful—whether in work systems, community systems, religious systems or your own home.[2]

How do we break free from the conditioning that holds us hostage to antiquated groupthink? How do we wake up to who we truly are? In a world full of crazy myths that keep us trapped in ludicrous belief systems, the way out is *in*. As long as we look outside of ourselves for what we ache for inside, we will never find what we're searching for. Because what we're searching for is the truth that exists only in our hearts. When we remember the pure potential that we once were, we remember that this is who we've always been. Within each and every one of us exists the gateway to peace—the essence of who we are. There is the saying, "Home is where the heart is." I'd like to revise it to read, "Home is the heart." In this remembrance, we have the power to create a beautiful new world, for ourselves and for all.

Albert Einstein once said, "A human being is a part of the whole called by us 'Universe,' a part limited in time and space. He experiences himself, his thoughts and feelings, as something separated from the rest, a kind of optical delusion of his consciousness. This delusion is a kind of prison for us, restricting us to our personal desires and to affection for a few persons nearest to us. Our task must be to free ourselves from this prison by widening our circle of compassion to embrace all living creatures and the whole of nature in its beauty."

Truth, unity, compassion, and love are how we find our way home.

As old systems unravel at unprecedented rates, we are clearly being shown the bankruptcy of our ways. Separation carries with it the germ of its own demise. As today's outdated paradigm crumbles, a new story is emerging. As we collectively rub the sleep from our eyes, we are realizing that we are not separate entities interacting in a world that is separate from us. We are interdependent. We are realizing that the loss of one species is a loss for the collective, that violence toward other living beings is violence toward all, that ecologies are wholly interconnected in beautiful relationships that symbiotically support one another.

A primal spiritual instinct is surfacing in the collective human psyche. We're questioning the separation-based belief systems that we've been taught are true, and we're embracing what we know in our hearts to be true. We're remembering our compassion as we give back to the planet and all of her creations. We're rebuilding community and rediscovering our relational existence. We're entering a co-creative partnership with the Earth as we transition into the adulthood of humanity. We're remembering the love in our hearts that is separate from none. We're awakening to the truth within and embarking on a path toward radical transformation.

Buckminster Fuller said, "You never change things by fighting the existing reality. To change something, build a new model that makes the existing model obsolete." The emergent new story is not about solving the problems of a broken world. It's about unleashing creative solutions that render old paradigms obsolete. It's about designing a new reality based on what lives in our hearts as we expand beyond the conditioned seduction of fear. The heart has a consciousness that demolishes all limits. When the head says "no," the heart says "Let's go!" This is the head-to-heart shift that will forever change our world.

As we move toward a new paradigm, we must realize that we don't need to *save* the planet; we need to *love* the planet. We don't need to save the animals; we need to love them. We don't need to save ourselves; we need to love our Selves. Saving implies superiority and perpetuates the Myth of Separation. The world does not need to be saved, but it is in desperate need of more love. To love is to feel. To feel is to heal. To heal is to be real, and to live the highest truth of our essential nature. Truth and love are intertwined. Love is the path toward wholeness, for ourselves and for all. As Gandhi once said, "Where there is love, there is life." It is love that will heal the world from the wound of separation and weave us back into the web of life.

Awareness of today's problems catalyzes their solutions. Abuse of power thrives in our silence but dissolves in our light. With the head in service to the heart, we bridge the gap between inspiration and action. By perceiving with our senses, feeling with our bodies, thinking with our minds, and acting from our hearts, we unleash the creative force from within to become an unstoppable force for paradigm-shifting transformation.

Margaret Mead once said, "Never doubt that a small group of thoughtful, committed citizens can change the world; indeed, it's the only thing that ever has." The new paradigm being birthed is emerging as a leaderless movement inspired by a collective awakening that no longer tolerates the absence of truth. It is being birthed by passionate people like you and me: integral players in a grassroots revolution of transformation fueled by passion, purpose, creativity, love … and action.

I hold an unwavering belief in the power of the human spirit. This is the force that compelled me to write this book. I know that we are all so much more than who we've been conditioned to be. It's time to lose the mindset that holds us hostage to smallness. It's time to embrace possibility and leave history behind. It's time to transform hope into faith, and faith into action. It's time for a revolution of consciousness that inspires each of us to live more, give more, be more, and love more. Considering the state of the planet today, we must settle for nothing less.

ONE

My Story
From Pain to Purpose

*"Those who live passionately teach us how to love.
Those who love passionately teach us how to live."*

– Paramahansa Yogananda

I'm frequently asked how I live so passionately in a world filled with pain. The simple answer is love: love for animals, love for the Earth, love for life.

There is a common misconception that love and pain cannot coexist. I challenge this mindset. You see, love and pain are intricately intertwined, opposite sides of the same coin. Authentic love touches the deepest pain of heartache and expands from the healing that follows.

I know this because I've been there. Grief, heartache, and pain have been steady companions in my life.

Bulimia was the addiction of choice to nourish a ten-year period of self-loathing. Alcohol became a habitual escape to dull the darkness of the world. My love, so pure—my humanity, so fragile. Despite my foibles, the seed of love remained faithful as my ever-present guide toward wholeness.

I've always had a profound connection to life. Perhaps it was the near-death experience that almost took me at birth. Blue and barely breathing, an umbilical cord wrapped around my neck with seconds to spare. Was this the defining moment that inspired me to revere life? Who knows?

What I do know is that I've always been different. Some label me empathic. I prefer "connected." I see life from a broader perspective. I feel life on a deeper level. The suffering of animals, the Earth, and humanity is my suffering. The joy of animals, the Earth, and humanity is my joy. I am not separate.

We are not separate. We are autonomous expressions of a greater whole in an interconnected world.

The cultural illusion of the outer world has always been clear to me. This has ensured my connection to the truth within. Life has been my passion. Love has been my fuel. Truth has been my driving force for action.

I feel. I care. I love. I act.

From a tender young age, I was known as the kid who cared. I became a voice for the voiceless early on. Injured birds, groundhogs, squirrels, skunks, rabbits, porcupines, geese, rats, ducks, turtles, mice, and stray cats and dogs were frequent house guests as I tenderly nursed them to health or found "forever" homes, often my own. Ongoing volunteering, activism, and charitable work have always been important staples in my life. I cleaned local parks and neighborhoods, returning home with bags of carelessly tossed garbage. I still do to this day. Against the wishes of my domineering, culturally conditioned father, I went vegetarian at the age of twelve, and in 1999 I adopted a vegan lifestyle to honor my innate love for *all* life.

Intense dedication to physical activity taught me the art of focused discipline. Swimming, water polo, golf, skiing, basketball, sailing, and triathlon were my chief sports of excellence. A driven work ethic and a dedicated focus led to exceptional success from an early age. Intuitively, I've always known that when I operate from a peak state of wellness, I'm at my best for all.

I enjoyed school and whizzed my way through, forging meaningful friendships along the way. But as I grew older, I found myself questioning systems of thought that just didn't feel right.

After three years of aimless university study, I dropped out. The "conform-to-a-capitalist/consumptive-culture" institutionalized mindset turned me off. This led to a startling realization: I needed to get out of town and go find myself. That's exactly what I did.

A backpack and a heart full of passion were my constant companions throughout Britain and Continental Europe, for a year of inner revelation and the most priceless education of all—life. Language, art, culture, history, and geography were peppered with friendships, loneliness, tears, laughter, fear, and courage—nothing likely to be found in an institutionalized classroom.

A year of Continental enlightenment was followed by a six-month stint of wanderlust in the Caribbean, crewing on sailboats and diving deeper into my soul—and the pristine turquoise waters of the Virgin Islands.

The heart spoke. I listened. Life was good.

Eventually I returned to "make something of my life," and I graduated from college with a diploma in communications and advertising. I made my mark in the world of graphic design. A perfect career for the creative maverick within.

Since then, I've done the corporate thing (slow death in a cubicle), studio gigs (a daily dose of deadline-infected angst), and I even gave the nonprofit route a whirl (close, but no cigar). I loved the work but despised the nine-to-five trap of working for someone else's vision. I realized that a paycheck was a sellout of the soul, so I started my own heart-powered design and communications business. I chose my clients carefully—clients whose missions aligned with mine, which was to raise awareness of issues that mattered, and to make a difference in the world. Together we spread the message of consciousness, compassion, and critical thought in a world so desperately in need.

My life has been good. I've traveled, I've studied, I've created, I've served. I've made a difference. I've faltered, screwed up, bumbled and fumbled along the way, but I've always managed to find my way back.

Despite what I thought was a mindful life, however, I still felt incomplete. A persistent darkness plagued my soul. I struggled with the pain of an anger that consumed me. I couldn't shake the rage-laced despair I felt toward the normalized violence imposed on everything I loved. I despised living in a world where animals were viewed with belief-infected entitlement: "ours" to abuse and destroy for food, clothing, entertainment, and experimentation. I felt a lingering fury from bearing witness to a collective mindset that treated the sacredness of nature as little more than a garbage dump, a sewer, or cheapened commodities for profit. I grieved the ongoing exploitation, destruction, violence, and abuse of everything beautiful in this world. In a collective population that didn't seem to care, I often felt isolated and alone in my passion for a better world.

The more I pursued the truth of what was hidden from view in our culture, the darker my world became. Sometimes the pain of the world was too much to bear because I took it on as my own. My love for life was tainted with judgment for those who were trapped in the ignorance of their indifference. I wanted to shout truth from the rooftops, but I knew few would listen. It hurt me.

Gloria Steinem once said, "The truth will set you free, but first it will piss you off." She was right. I was livid. I was outraged. My salve became my activism—a rage release for the injustices imposed on the marginalized in our world: animals, women, and the Earth. I coveted the fire of anger and used it as fuel for transformation. But it wasn't healthy, nor was it sustainable. It was merely a pressure release for my unhealed grief. It manifested in ugly ways: judgment, self-righteousness, blame, and shame. Despite my virtuous intentions, I had no idea that my unprocessed anger was perpetuating the very problem I was desperate to solve: separation. Because I loved so deeply, I believed I was living fully from my heart. But where I was lacking in love and compassion for humanity and myself, I was missing vital components of my wholeness.

It wasn't until the tragic death of my mother in 2010 that I was forced to face myself head on. One fleeting moment and life as I knew it came to a screeching halt. I was denied the chance to say goodbye. It was sudden. It was messy. It was complicated. It was not an ending I could have predicted. The utter frailty of life shattered my world.

My father was already eleven years pre-deceased—I was now an orphan. It was an impossible reality to grasp. My identity was forever altered. I was lost.

Compelled by a force beyond my reasoning mind, I signed up for an Ironman triathlon. The timing made no logical sense, but the impulse was clear; denial was not an option. Intense physical training became the much-needed diversion to prevent the agonizing grief, rage, and despair from overwhelming my soul. Ironman became the ideal mind/body distraction for igniting the perfect future storm.

Ironman is an all-consuming venture requiring immense physical, mental, and emotional bandwidth for months on end. The training protocol is arduous at the best of times—formidable with the added burden of grief.

My heart was encumbered with a profusion of heavy emotions. A higher purpose was needed to propel me forward. I transformed Ironman into a selfless endeavor by supporting a cause dear to my heart. Farm Sanctuary became my raison d'être. Located in upstate New York, Farm Sanctuary is a paradigm-altering organization that has made great strides in expanding consciousness for the forgotten beings in this world—the billions of animals commoditized for food. Under no circumstances would I let the animals down.

I swam, I biked, I ran. I finished.

The emotional burden of 140.6 miles of grief-drenched physical output played heavily on my body and soul. The post-race physical exhaustion was easy to comprehend, but the deep sense of emptiness confused me. I thought I would discover the "real me" through Ironman. Instead, I felt hopelessly lost.

An all-consuming meltdown followed, and I bottomed out emotionally, mentally, physically, and spiritually. I plummeted into the pit of despair, unable to function beyond the overwhelming grief that shrouded my heart. The dark night of the soul. My heart ached for ten more minutes of life so I could hold my mother close, look deeply into her eyes, and express what I had been denied: "Thank you … I love you … Goodbye."

Six weeks of tenacious depression brought me to my knees. I couldn't eat. I couldn't feel. I could barely get out of bed. I felt utterly alone—smothered by my anguish.

Eventually I reached a threshold where something had to change. That "something" was me.

The guilt of my emotional paralysis triggered a critical line of questioning. Where was my passion? Where was my courage? What now? I was jolted into the realization that life passes at lightning speed and that my next breath could be my last. Spiritual Awakening 101. I discovered that although I was living my life with integrity and purpose, my deepest core gifts were seriously under-utilized.

I slogged through the abyss, shook off the despair, and set out on a journey of self-discovery.

I had once believed the Universe to be a beautiful place, but now everything overwhelmed me. I couldn't stand the phone. I couldn't stand the radio. I couldn't stand the media. I despised the city. I needed to leave.

I withdrew into myself, searching for answers. Searching for more.

I removed myself from mainstream culture to take back my life. It started with a phone detox, which led to a media detox, which spawned a cross-country move, which culminated in the profound simplification of life. I unplugged with the most amazing results, and I recharged with greater fortitude than ever before.

I checked out to check in.

As I recharged, I began to reconnect. To what? To my joy, my strength, my courage, my passion, my purpose, my essence—my love.

As life simplified, I was liberated. There was no longer anything to prove. There was no longer anyone to please. I was hungry for expansion: to live more, give more, be more, and love more. I was no longer satisfied to play small. I became more outspoken with my caring, willing to stand up, speak out, and take action in ways I had not previously considered. I realized the seamless union between spirituality and activism. I plugged in to *all that matters in life*: truth, joy, passion, and love.

People began to ask, "How are you so peaceful?" or "What have you done?" or "You seem more grounded, happier, inspired, and connected." Conversations at dinner gatherings no longer included the headline news, because I didn't know what was going on. I'd lost all interest in the sensationalized minutia of global pain. By unplugging from status quo, my mind was quieter, my heart was freer, and I was so much happier. Conversations inevitably turned to the changes I'd made in my life.

As I continued on the path of self discovery, the most profound life lesson was yet to come.

Through intensive experiential studies of the mind, consciousness, yogic philosophy, and human essence, I realized on a deeply visceral level that there is only one absolute in life: death. When I made peace with this inevitable reality, it made room for the emergence of a heightened joie-de-vivre that revealed my soul's true purpose: live from the heart, lead from the heart, and inspire others to do the same. So obvious and natural that it was easy to overlook. My mother's death became the catalyst for a deeper connection to life.

Norman Cousins once said, "The tragedy of life is not death, but what we let die inside of us while we live." This speaks to a profound truth that many in today's culture have forgotten—myself included.

I inquired within and asked how I could live every day with intention, passion, presence, and purpose. The answers inspired me: "Live authentically, laugh often, move, extend your circle of compassion, take life less seriously, serve, live simply, create, embrace uncertainty, connect with nature, dance, live with gratitude, and unapologetically share your gifts with the world."

Out of death came new life. As I healed, a more vibrant, passionate version of my true Self emerged.

Have I freed myself from the anger that shrouded my earlier life? I wish I could say that I've fully released myself from the pain of a collapsing world, but that would be dishonest. I have, however, accepted the fact that because I love so deeply, I will grieve. Because I care so much, I will feel anger. Because I ache for a kinder world, I will feel frustration. But where I was once consumed by darkness, I now also see light. Within the depths of my pain is an expansive love that knows no limits. I no longer feel stuck, because I know my essence. The colors that now define my life are brighter, more vivid, and more alive. This is the place that I now choose to stand. Darkness no longer obscures my consciousness. Instead, it washes through me and ignites my soul.

In the wise words of Leo Tolstoy, "Everyone thinks of changing the world, but no one thinks of changing himself." This important statement indicates that we cannot heal the world by being just like it. We must first heal ourselves. We must stop conforming to a consumptive culture. We must embrace the unsullied child from deep within, the one that existed before parents, teachers, and culture taught us to become something that we're not. We must release our pain and reconnect to our essential nature.

When we are guided by our essential nature, we are transformed. Our hearts lead the way as our minds faithfully serve. Our pain becomes fuel for the action required to create a new world based on the foundation of truth, life, and love.

Love is the organizing force behind all that is beautiful, joyful, compassionate, peaceful, creative, free, and true in this world. Our world is merely a reflection of the levels of love or fear in the collective mindset. Authentic love banishes all fear, making extraordinary transformation not only possible, but inevitable. Love is the powerful force that runs through the heart of each and every one of us. Love is what expands consciousness. It is the essence of who we are.

As I connected to my own essential nature, I wondered how others connected to theirs.

This prompted a journey into the collective heart. I spoke with activists, athletes, authors, yogis, doctors, visionaries, and everyday paradigm busters to discover how they unplugged from status quo and plugged in to their own essential natures. Shared with transparent honesty, each story in this book is an inspirational expression of the human spirit with one common goal: unleashing the authentic Self for the creation of a better world. No gurus. No experts. Just fellow travelers on the journey toward wholeness.

Each of us carries within the seed of our own greatness and the potential for who we can become. The proliferation of this potential requires a single quantum shift—the shift from head to heart.

What's important to note is that this book was not written to convert you to a different way of thought. Instead, it was written to activate the unique voice of your own heart through the diversity of voices working for a better world. The intention of this book is to open your mind and heart to more expansive worldview that ignites the fullest expression of who you have always been meant to be.

There is a story by Swami Sri Yukteswar that likens the human mind to a little bird that has been caged for twenty years. If the cage door were to open, the bird would cower, fearful of the seeming threat that appears to beckon, that is, the vast open sky where it was designed by nature to fly. After a time, the bird may hop tentatively outside the cage, but she will hurry back in almost immediately, fearful of this experience of freedom for which habit made her unprepared. Only gradually, by longer and longer sorties, will the little bird stand at last outside her cage, rustle her wings, and fly away into the vast freedom of the sky.

Consider this book an invitation to liberate yourself from the confines of a lifetime of conditioning and to fly into the limitless freedom that awaits.

Author's Note

The stories that follow are preceded by short introductions that capture the essence of each interviewee through my essence. My intention is for the words to then reach directly into your essence. Each of these stories originated from conversations on my popular *Unplug* podcast, a project that I started as the concept for this book was developing.

One of my beta readers wrote to me, "I listen to your podcasts, but to me, there is a deeper effect reading your words." Through the editing process of this book, I've discovered that there is a marked difference between the written word and the spoken word. I've determined that this is because the written word leaves much more to the reader's imagination.

This book, like the podcast, was created to inspire a more expansive level of consciousness by igniting passion, compassion, presence, truth, critical thought, and purpose in the hearts and minds of a broader global audience.

The structure for each story is simple:

1) Introduction (written in my voice).

2) The story of each interviewee (captured in their voice).

For continuity, the questions I asked followed a similar theme, commencing with each interviewee's story of unplugging from status quo. This was followed by their subsequent path toward purpose. I also asked specific questions about remaining connected to passion, presence, and purpose in a world that doesn't make this easy. All of these stories have been distilled into inspiring narratives that clearly reveal the power of the heart.

Each conversation ends with a powerful question that inspires expansive thought. The question, "If you had a magic wand and could wave it over the planet, what kind of world would you create?" taps into the unlimited nature of the creative heart. My belief is that if we can imagine it, we can create it. After all, creativity emerges from the limitless expanse of our imagination.

Enjoy the inspiration that follows!

TWO

Ocean Robbins
The Radical Power of Love

"Until you are able to weep all of your tears, you won't be able to laugh all of your laughter."

– KAHLIL GIBRAN

Imagine being born to parents who had unplugged from the culture of consumption. Imagine being inspired by role models who had chosen a simpler life of meaning and service. Imagine a life where authentic expression was celebrated, selflessness was extolled, simplicity was cultivated, purpose was nurtured, and a deep love for life was your modus operandi. Imagine the potential for who you could become from very early on.

Ocean Robbins, son of John Robbins (author of the paradigm-shifting bestseller *Diet for a New America*), is a man who has offered his life to the world in a way that is not only leaving it a better place, but is also facilitating the transformation of thousands of lives along the way. His list of achievements is impressive.

At sixteen, Ocean cofounded Youth for Environmental Sanity (YES!), a nonprofit organization that connects, inspires, and collaborates with young change-makers to build thriving, just, and sustainable ways of life for all. The organization continues to thrive to this day.

As a captivating speaker, he's inspired hundreds of thousands of people to live more impassioned lives of positive action. He's a two-time author, an active board member in a myriad of well-known environmental organizations, and he's the recipient of many awards recognizing his devotion to service.

He is now the CEO of the Food Revolution Network, a powerful online-based education and advocacy-driven initiative with the aim of empowering individuals, building community, and transforming food systems to support a healthier planet. Ocean and his father work together as a dynamic duo that has mobilized over four hundred thousand people to engage in healthier, more sustainable, conscious, and humane food choices. The passion they exude for this project is palpable.

It's easy to place an accomplished man like Ocean on the pedestal of extraordinary. He's certainly deserving of such recognition. What we often fail to realize is that beneath most success is struggle. Extraordinary should never be defined by accomplishment alone. Instead, it would be more aptly defined by how gracefully we move through life's hard knocks. As the saying goes, "Success is a journey, not a destination."

Despite Ocean's exceptional upbringing, he's not been immune from hardship. He's the father of identical twins whose premature entrance into the world commenced with six precarious weeks in intensive care. Lifesaving measures were necessary to prevent their untimely deaths. The boys survived this harrowing ordeal, but not without repercussions. Both children were born autistic and live with its daily challenges. Under the loving care of Ocean and his wife Michele, however, they now have the potential to thrive. In Ocean's own words, "To this day the boys struggle with numerous developmental delays and special needs. They are also incredible reminders to me, on a daily basis, of the power of play, of the simple healing beauty of love, and of what matters most in life."

In the summer of 2014, I discovered that Ocean and his boys would embark on a car camping adventure that included a trip to British Columbia. Having previously connected with Ocean regarding this book, I invited the trio to sojourn with my partner and me should their plans include a trip to the Sunshine Coast. Much to my delight, they accepted the offer. Admittedly, I was somewhat guilty of celebrity awe. I was both excited and nervous. This was quickly overcome when the threesome arrived at our home, emanating happiness and beaming with smiles in their gear-stuffed Prius.

Hugs, laughter, and excited conversation ensued. The boys, still on a high from the previous night's Lady Gaga concert in Vancouver, eagerly provided a detailed report of the entire event, complete with their "take-no-prisoners" account of the opening acts that apparently went on for far too long. Their delivery was both engaging and entertaining. It was as though we'd known each other for years.

Their visit was brief, but we managed to pack a lot into those few days. Lake swimming, blackberry picking, sightseeing, meaningful conversations, collaborative home-cooked meals (including an impromptu blackberry pie), and numerous "Apples to Apples" board game experiences. Witnessing Ocean in action was truly remarkable. What I realized is that we all share the unique human experience that fuses joy with pain. No one is exempt from this dichotomy. Ocean has accomplished so much in his short life, but what struck me the most about this beautiful man was the depth of love that he has for his children. I witnessed firsthand the daily challenges of living with two teenage boys with special needs. It was exhausting. It requires immense patience, compassion, and a love that defies what we know from the limitations of our mundane humanity. The love that I witnessed—and felt—was the most beautiful love in existence. Love from the soul. Love without judgment. Love without condition. Love for no other reason than for love itself.

Ocean Robbins shines like a beacon in a world filled with darkness. When we finally parted ways, I found my eyes brimming with tears from a profound sense of gratitude for our connection. The life that Ocean has chosen as a devoted husband, superstar father, and transformational social change leader is proof that there is nothing greater than the radical power of love.

***

Ocean's Story

Unplugging: Path to Purpose

I'll start with a little intergenerational history. My grandfather started Baskin-Robbins ice cream company. My dad was groomed from early childhood to one day run the company. He had an ice-cream-cone-shaped swimming pool in the backyard and 31 flavors of ice cream in the freezer at all times. His father manufactured and sold more ice cream than any human being who has ever lived, and my dad probably ate more ice cream than any kid who has ever lived.

When my dad was a little older, he was offered the chance to join the family company. Remarkably, he said no. He walked away from fame and fortune and a path that was practically paved with gold (and ice cream) to follow what we jokingly refer to as his own rocky road.

He walked away because his uncle, Burt Baskin, was dying of heart disease. His father was also suffering from many of the typical health ailments that people who consume copious quantities of sugar, dairy, and animal products do.

Even though my dad knew that an ice cream cone wouldn't kill anybody, he also knew that the more ice cream that was consumed, the less healthy we'd be. He didn't want to dedicate his life to selling a product that would contribute to sickness in people. He wanted to contribute to health.

He not only walked away from the company, but also from all access to the family wealth. My parents moved to a little island off the coast of Canada where they built a one-room log cabin, grew most of their own food, lived very simply, practiced yoga and meditation for several hours a day, and named their kid Ocean. That's me.

I was born into an alternative lifestyle with parents who had chosen love and simple living over the materialistic fast track, the American dream of unlimited consumption.

They were both trying to reveal the deeper dream of unlimited compassion. I ended up coming of age in my teen years when my dad was becoming a bestselling author. He wrote a book called *Diet for a New America* that inspired millions of people to examine their food choices as an opportunity to better the world.

The media had a lot of fun with his story. They called him "the rebel without a cone." Millions of people were touched by my dad's work, writing letters that told how he had changed their lives. I was inspired. I wanted to reach out and make a difference for my own generation. At sixteen, I founded a nonprofit organization called Youth for Environmental Sanity, or YES! We organized a national tour where we spoke at schools about the environment, food choices, and how to make a difference in the world.

We reached more than six hundred thousand students. Eventually, I started focusing on transformational leadership gatherings for young change-makers in over sixty-five countries.

We organized weeklong events for people who wanted to change the world. We saw many activists who were burning out. There were many who were struggling—trying to change the world without realizing that their own inner conflicts were sabotaging their efforts. We wanted to help people create more integrity and congruency in their lives as they were working toward a better world. We helped them become more sustainable, grounded, and effective in their work. We helped establish consistency between their means and their ends, their values and their lifestyles.

I directed YES! for twenty years and eventually decided that I wanted to work on food issues with my father. Food is something that we all share. We all eat to live. What we eat literally becomes us. It is our most intimate communion with the web of life. When we turn our food consumption into a commodity and sell out to the lowest possible price with the highest short-term pleasure, our choices come back to haunt us. We get into real trouble when we have no regard for the web of life.

We are toxifying our bodies as we toxify the planet with this damaging food system. What I realized as I delved deeper into this issue was that our toxic food system is crippling our economy. It is bankrupting families and lives. It is causing millions of deaths. It is causing suffering to the majority of people in the United States today, and it's completely preventable.

We have the potential to radically alter our lives, our vitality, our energy levels, how well we sleep, how long we live, how well we live—all with changes in our diet. Of course, no healthy diet is a panacea for everything. There are many factors in optimal health, and eventually we're all going to die. No one gets out alive. But we might as well live as well as we can. We might as well be as happy, fulfilled, and healthy as we can. The nutritional science is very clear, and the majority of diseases in the United States today are caused by lifestyle.

A majority of the medical spending that's crippling our economy—that's 19 percent of US gross domestic product today—could be eliminated with changes in diet.

We can do so much better. We can ease the suffering of kids from diabetes. We can ease the suffering of elders from Alzheimer's. We can ease the suffering of people at every age from cancer and heart disease. These are real issues that affect real lives. I'm thrilled to now be working with my dad as CEO of the Food Revolution Network that we cofounded. We now have the opportunity to touch people's lives and spread truth. We don't have to be victims of a toxic food culture. We can become agents of change in our personal lives, in our families, in our communities, and on this planet. When we do, our whole world gets brighter.

So we are literally reweaving ourselves back into the web of life. We are reclaiming our food systems as a sacrament, as an active communion with life instead of an act of defilement of our bodies and our planet. The food revolution is emergent. It is something we can participate in on any scale, from taking one daily step to becoming an activist. We don't have to scream and shout with placards. We can practice it with our knives and forks every day.

Teachers for Life

Based on my personal and family history of achievement, when my wife and I decided to have kids, I imagined that they would be saving the world by the time they were out of diapers. I developed a bit of a superiority complex, a belief that somehow, some way we were better than others. Life was about getting to the top and being the best.

I believe that everyone has value and should be respected, but I realized that I wasn't fully living this myself.

When I was growing up, my dad told me that he loved me and that he appreciated all my accomplishments. He said that he would love me just as much if I were autistic. I was touched and thought it was very sweet, but it didn't really land on me until I had kids that were autistic.

I have identical twins who were born in 2001. They are my greatest teachers. They are sources of incredible love, beauty, and joy. They love life, but they also really struggle with things that come easily to most people.

They teach me about the sacredness of life and that everyone deserves love. Not for what we accomplish, not even for being a good person, but just because. My kids have forced me to look at the ways that I've made my own self-love and respect conditional. They've forced me to examine the ways that I've driven myself to do more and to accomplish more in order to prove that I'm okay.

I've realized that maybe we don't have to prove anything to anybody. When we actually know that we're okay, we're motivated by something deeper. We no longer have anything to prove, and we then have more to give.

I've come to realize that my greatest wholeness, my greatest integrity, and my greatest service are born out of a place of profound self-love. This includes the places that are brilliant and the places that are lost and confused, the places that know the way forward and the places that don't. When I hold all of that—what I know and what I don't know, my clarity and my confusion, my certainty and my uncertainty—I'm more real. My humanity and my wisdom are deeper. Accepting that we don't know everything is one of the keys to wisdom. Curiosity is one of the keys to learning. Learning is what leads us to more wisdom.

I've gained a lot of wisdom through my kids. I've learned that autism is more about overstimulation and overwhelm. Their nervous systems need a lot of kindness, respect, and special care. When I join my boys in *their* world and celebrate them for who they are, I discover they have gifts that I never could have imagined.

My son River had a time in his life when he liked to chew on things. He used to chew on Barbie dolls. One day he was chewing on a Barbie foot. I worried that he was absorbing toxic chemicals from the "made in China" plastic. But instead of trying to remove it from his mouth, I decided to join him. I sat across the room, picked up a Barbie, and started chewing on her foot.

River was ten years old and had never made eye contact with me. But in that moment, he looked right into my eyes and beamed at me. He then gestured for me to come closer. His Barbie had two feet and he invited me to chew the other foot of his Barbie.

I moved closer and started chewing on the other Barbie foot. We were now four inches apart, beaming into each other's eyes, falling in love together, chewing on Barbie feet. At that moment, I realized that when I try to control my kids and shape them into what I think they should be, we end up in power struggles. But when I join them in their world and meet them where they're at, we find connection. From that connection, we're able to go places together and expand our lives. This is real love.

Living From Purpose

There are more than seven billion parts to play in the healing of our world. This accounts for each person on the planet. Our pains and struggles, and our gifts and blessings are what prepare us for what is solely ours to express.

I know a lot of people who feel like they could give so much if they weren't burdened with emotional pain, if they hadn't been abused in their childhood, if they didn't struggle with money, if they didn't have kids with special needs, if they didn't have some injury, or if they had someone who loved them unconditionally. There are so many excuses and reasons why we struggle in life and why we feel that life is unfair.

Here's the thing. Every struggle and pain we've ever known is part of us now. I never would have guessed that having autistic children would be my greatest teacher; that it would make me more human, more humble, or make me a better human being. I never would have guessed that it would give me more love or that it would deepen my love for myself and for humanity. I never would have guessed that it would be fundamental in my life's purpose.

I wouldn't have wished it on myself or anyone else, but here I am. I'm grateful for that. I have a friend who's helping people with eating disorders. Had she not been through the struggles of eating disorders in her own life, she wouldn't understand what her clients are dealing with, and she wouldn't have unlocked the potential that she now has to heal others.

We never know what our pains will be or how they will shape us. But when we feel lost or alone in the dark night of the soul, we must ask ourselves, "What can I do with this pain to be of service to others? How can I use what has happened to me on behalf of what I love?"

When we're in the presence of pain, our own or someone else's, we have a simple choice. Do we shrink away or do we expand? If we shrink away from every source of pain, every place that hurts, we're going to get smaller and smaller. If we want to expand, we say, "My heart is big enough to hold this. I may not be able to fix it. I may not be able to solve it, but at least I can love through it." Then our heart gets bigger, our life gets bigger, our world gets bigger, and we have the capacity to make a lasting contribution.

I think that living a life of purpose means expressing who we authentically are on behalf of what we love. This is the hero's and heroine's journey of our times. In a world beset by enormous suffering and pain, the question isn't how to avoid suffering, the question is how do we create less suffering and more love?

Each of us has our own answer to this question. We're going to stumble and fall. We're going to get hurt and we're going to hurt others. But hopefully we can learn along the way and become more true to what lives in our hearts.

Reconnecting

I don't think that the pain of the world and the pain of my own life are separate. It's important to remember that sometimes things hurt because they're connected to collective pain. Sometimes I think about the suffering of kids or various people in the world. I realize that part of the reason this hurts so much is because I know what it feels like in my own life.

I believe that pain can be the doorway for reconnection. If part of what we suffer from today is the illusion of isolation and disconnection, then reconnection is actually sacred and beautiful. The ability to feel pain may be a call to change something. If my toe is hurting, for instance, it might be time to take the chair off. We rarely make big changes if we aren't feeling big frustration or pain first. As creatures of habit, we tend to stick with what works—until it doesn't work anymore.

If it really doesn't work, then this is often what inspires us to change in bigger ways. Frustration can be a wonderful catalyst. For me, when I feel frustrated, I often think, "Oh, this is exciting." If I'm not content with something, then it means that something better is possible. I like to focus on what can be instead of complaining about what isn't right. There's the old saying that is so true—it's always better to light a candle than to curse the darkness.

If You Had a Magic Wand …

More love and less pain. More connection and less isolation. That about sums it up for me.

To connect with Ocean and his work please visit oceanrobbins.com or foodrevolution.org.

THREE

Kathy Stevens
All You Need Is Love

"I have found that if you love life, life will love you back."

– ARTHUR RUBINSTEIN

As I pondered the words for this introduction, the old Beatles song "All You Need is Love" looped through my mind. This comes as no surprise, since thoughts of Kathy Stevens are enough to blow any heart chakra wide open.

Kathy Stevens is a woman who epitomizes love.

I want to make it clear that when I refer to love, it's not the fickle, lust-drenched "love" of Hollywood fame. Rather, I reference the love that connects us all—big Aloha love. In Hawaii, the spirit of Aloha means unity. Despite perceived differences that separate us from one another, big Aloha love knows no separation. Race, gender, age, class, or species, we're all united in big Aloha love.

Before family systems, belief structures, and cultural conditioning separated us from one another, big Aloha love was all we knew. Collectively, we've been duped into a cultural paradigm that has us believing that we are separate. As we know from the current state of the world, this notion has not served us well. Because big Aloha love emanates from our core, however, it is omnipresent. It is the eternal umbilical cord that connects us to life, joy, compassion, unity, and meaning. It is the essence of who we are. Without big Aloha love, we're empty, soulless shells.

The leaders of the emerging new paradigm are those who live with their minds in service to their hearts. These are the cultural renegades who reject the captivity of status quo in favor of the transformative power of big Aloha love.

Kathy Stevens is a two-time author and founder of the Catskill Animal Sanctuary in Saugerties, New York. She's also a big Aloha trailblazing renegade extraordinaire.

I was privileged to hear Kathy speak at the Toronto Vegetarian Food Fest a few years back. She staggered me with her passion, compassion, and her fearless expression of big Aloha love for all beings. I knew I was in the presence of someone who was making the world a better place.

There's more to this story, however. While in Toronto, Kathy extended her stay to support the Toronto Save movement in their efforts to raise awareness for the forgotten beings on this planet. The Toronto Save movement is comprised of many dedicated grassroots activists who bear witness and expose truth outside of Toronto's chicken, pig, and cow slaughterhouses. Their weekly peace vigils are based on a foundation of love rather than the shame-based, divisive activism so familiar in today's world. Their methods are working.

Kathy's time in Toronto left a lasting impression on many. Her effect on the members of the Save group, as well as the slaughterhouse workers, was profound. In Kathy's world, there is no separation. While at the vigil, she lovingly approached a group of locked-out slaughterhouse workers and bridged all illusory divides. She sat with the men and affectionately shared stories of the animals at her sanctuary. She gave them copies of her books. She pretended to be a cow and placed her head on the shoulder of the slaughterhouse owner, smiling and gently nudging him as a cow would. She offered an open invitation for them to visit the sanctuary and partake of cow kisses and porcine belly rubs. She laughed with all of the men and connected in ways that unified. There was no judgment, only big Aloha love.

To Kathy, we really are all one. How we label ourselves is irrelevant. Be it activist, slaughterhouse worker, chicken, pig, or cow—a soul is a soul, is a soul.

One would think that the chasm between animal activist and slaughterhouse worker would be vast. On a superficial level this may be the case. But beneath it all, we are equal in our humanity. We are all doing the best that we can. Let's face it, the only reason the soul-annihilating vocation of slaughterhouse worker exists at all is because of the collective addiction to the tortured flesh of innocent sentient beings. But it doesn't have to be this way. Not for the animals or for the people, who often choose this hideous work out of desperation. No consumer demand equals freedom for all.

Kathy's presence made an impact. The slaughterhouse workers spoke of her kindness for many weeks afterwards. I would surmise that her unifying presence left a permanent mark on their hearts. Kathy also raised the bar for activism. Her big Aloha love leadership is a reminder that deep down, we're all the same. Across all illusory species, gender, and race barriers, we all need kindness and compassion. We all need to be seen. We all need to be loved. End of story.

I am honored to invite you into the beautiful world of Kathy Stevens.

***

Kathy's Story

Unplugging: Path to Purpose

I grew up in Virginia on a horse farm where my dad bred and raised thoroughbreds for the track. We also had a couple of cows, a donkey named Linda, and a few goats that I used to sneak into the house. My childhood was a rare and precious gift.

I've always had a deep connection with animals, as well as a passion for teaching and learning. For about twelve years, I was a high school

English teacher. This was my path: improving the world by empowering young people to become more articulate speakers, more effective writers, and more critical thinkers. Most importantly, I encouraged them to be braver and kinder people. That was my real purpose.

In 2000, I was asked to be the principal of a new high school in Boston. Much to my own shock, I turned down the opportunity. While it was the next logical step in my career, I couldn't make the leap. Part of me was saying, "What are you doing? You just turned down the opportunity of a lifetime!" The other part of me realized that it was not the right kind of school. It was a media and technology school, not a social justice school, or a school for the humanities. Either of which would have been a better fit. I graciously said no, simultaneously realizing I had no idea what I wanted to do for the next thirty years of my life.

I took lots of long walks with my wonderful dog. I wrote. I talked with my friends. I had never taken time off as an adult—even summer vacations were used for teaching teachers!

What came up for me over the next few months was clarity about my two passions. I loved animals and I loved teaching. I started brainstorming about how to combine these two passions, and what eventually came to me was the idea of a teaching sanctuary. This felt so right to me.

While I had no idea how it would happen, I knew in my bones that it would happen. From the very moment that I had the idea, I never questioned it, despite the fact that everyone in my life thought I was nuts! After many months of research, travel, and internships at successful farm sanctuaries, Catskill Animal Sanctuary was born. That was in 2001. Since then, Catskill Animal Sanctuary has saved more than 3,500 animals through direct emergency rescue, and exponentially more through our signature programs that encourage people to explore the vegan path.

Since that time I've also written two books on the work of the sanctuary, I have a blog on The Huffington Post, and I speak in the US and Canada on issues related to farmed animals and the impact of animal agriculture. It has proven to be an amazing, life-altering choice.

Our Changing World

I think America is the worst model in taking us the farthest distance possible from the place where we are connected to all life. There's an interesting struggle between darkness and light happening in the world today. On one side we've got huge corporations, with their powerful lobbyists and governmental friends, driven by greed at the expense of our planet.

For these people, the air doesn't matter. The water doesn't matter. The soil doesn't matter. People's health doesn't matter. Animals don't matter. As long as stock prices are high, that's all that matters. There are so many destructive practices that profit a few and cause horrifying consequences for the rest of us—whether it's the Earth, animals, or people. We're all affected by this selfish blindness. That's the dark side.

On the other side, however, there's a growing awareness of the destructiveness of corporate greed, and a hunger to learn the truth about our food system and its inevitable impact.

For instance, there are more people practicing yoga now than ever. Yogis aren't just weird hippies anymore. Yoga studios are popping up all over the place. There are probably fifty studios in the relatively small region where I live. Similarly—maybe because they now understand that a meat-and-dairy-based diet is killing them, or at least making them fat—people are making more compassionate food choices. Whether it comes from a health perspective, from fear about the reality of global warming, or from the growing awareness of what we're doing to animals, veganism is growing at an exponential rate. People are waking up and it's causing rapid change.

I believe that for the world to be a different place, we must stay true to our inherent compassion. We must be compassionate toward whomever we encounter. It doesn't take much to offer a smile or a gentle touch on the shoulder.

Unity and Non-Separation

I grew up in a racist family and community, always bumping up against my strong-willed father and the prevailing culture. This caused me a great deal of pain and confusion. I was considered the "odd" one— the one who didn't see color as a basis for judgment. I feel lucky that I've always seen and felt the essence of a person right away—whether the person is man, woman, black, white, religious, atheist, gay, straight, old, young, wealthy, or poor has always been immaterial to me. *Who*, not *what*, a person is has always been more important.

The same is true for animals. I've always felt their purity, their innocence, their desire to love and be loved. No matter our species, we all share the same desire to move toward joy and away from suffering. This is one of the many truths that unite us in life.

I don't care if you are gay. I don't care if you are Catholic. I don't care if you are skinny. I don't care if you have curly brown hair. Similarly, I don't care if you are a chicken, pig, dog, or cow. I see beings for who they are and embrace their essence. I've always been this way, even more so now that I'm living among so many beautiful animals. They are incredible teachers.

The differences between pigs, dogs, elephants, fish, and humans are about as meaningful as the differences between old and young, black and white, secular and religious. They are completely superficial, and have very little to do with what's inside.

I see what unites, rather than what divides. In our essence, we are all the same.

Bridging the Divide

When I was in Toronto, I was honored to participate in a couple of peace vigils with the Toronto Save movement. There was a group of locked-out workers at the slaughterhouse. I knew that this would be a great opportunity for connection. After all, they're just people doing a job they hate in order to eat. They probably don't have a large skill set, so they take work that nobody else wants. I mean, who would consciously choose to slaughter for a living? Consumers want the meat, but they don't want to have to do the killing themselves. I have no doubt that the people who actually take these jobs would choose to do something else if they had the skills, the opportunity, the education, the motivation, the confidence or … fill in the blank.

My take on this is as follows: how dare I, who have been vegan for less than half my life, judge these people because they're not where I am today?

I have a hard time with righteous vegans who are angry and judgmental with anyone who isn't where they are. We were all brought up to support the meat-eating machine, and we're left to discover the truth for ourselves. Society certainly doesn't offer it to us. It's a big effort to bypass the conditioning, the brainwashing, and the pervasive messaging that tells us to eat meat and dairy. It's so counterproductive for vegans to be angry or judgmental.

When I sat down with those slaughterhouse workers, I saw alienated people shut out of a job. Why wouldn't I have a conversation with them? What a wonderful opportunity that was.

I gave all of the workers copies of my book. A couple of them called me later to thank me. One guy named Nick told me that he was vegetarian. He said to me, "I have three kids and no other job pays the bills." This is so tragic.

Reconnection

I have always been innately joyful. I almost never feel despair. I realize that I'm really lucky in this way. In the moments when I do feel despair, after I've seen a particularly difficult video for instance, I'm able to quickly move back to a place of joy. I think it's partly because I can't function in an unhappy state. I don't like how "unhappy" feels in my body. I'm not as effective in the world when I'm unhappy. I'm certainly not serving the animals or humanity the best I can when I'm not happy.

People ask me all the time, "Why are you not angry with all of the suffering imposed on animals?" I have a hard time answering that question
because I don't really have an answer. I'm just not an angry person. I'm
grateful that I don't hold anger, or despair, or sadness. I do feel these difficult emotions, of course, but I don't fight them when they come up. Perhaps because of this, negative emotions move through me very quickly.
Once that happens, I return to my natural state: feeling good about life
and positive about why I'm here.

The key for me to remain connected to the pure love inside is to never
hold back from what I'm feeling in every moment. If I suppressed it, I
think I'd be a mess. So many people do this. They hold it all in, run away
from it, or numb it with pharmaceuticals or alcohol. Then they wonder
why they're never truly happy.

I can't imagine being like that. That would be horrible.

A Heart-Centered Life: Recharging

I feel love for every living thing, whether it's a human, an animal, a
flower, a tree, or a river. I talk to my "friends" in the natural world. I do
things that some people might find a little odd; like when I walk in the
woods each morning with my dog Chumbley, I spread out my arms, look
up to the sky, and shout, "Good morning, beautiful world!" Living from
my heart means simple things like lying in the straw with the pigs and
quietly appreciating the essence of who they are.

It means thanking the world for the beautiful sunset on any given
day. It means appreciating the beauty of life—all life—animals, nature,
humanity, all of it.

So many people care more about their "stuff" than they do about living. They're really missing out. Life is so beautiful, and doesn't have to be
complicated.

Hope for a Better World

Everything gives me hope! Children, spring, flowers … the fact that the world hasn't sneezed us off like a bad idea. I feel like we have a very kind, benevolent planet that allows us to continually screw up. There was a lot of doom and gloom about how the world would collapse in 2012, but it didn't. We keep poisoning and disrespecting her and she continues to tolerate the abuse.

Yes, there is despair and sadness in the world, but we need to see the hope and the beauty and make decisions that will create more hope and beauty. For instance, I feel incredible hope whenever someone reads my books and says to me, "I get it. I'm going vegan."

There are also the thousands of people every season who visit the sanctuary, come to my talks, or read my writing. I get many messages that say, "Thank you. I understand. I get it. I'm not eating animals anymore." This happens all the time and it really inspires me.

I love the mornings. Sunrise gives me hope. The world is a pretty amazing place.

Here's my bottom line: If you are a human being, you are the most gifted being alive. If you are a white, Western, middle-class person who has been raised with love and who has had the opportunity to get an education, there is *nothing* to complain about! You could have been a rock. You could have been algae. You could have been a child born to a drug-addicted single parent, or an impoverished child in a war-torn part of the world. You could have been a pig on a slaughter truck.

You have been blessed with the most precious gift there is—a human body. Be grateful for it. Live well. Be conscious and live compassionately, with purpose, passion, and kindness for *all* beings.

If You Had a Magic Wand …

It's pretty simple. I'd create a world where all beings, no matter their species, their geography, no matter what—where all species lived in harmony and experienced joyful lives. That's my magic wand world. It's that simple.

For more information about Kathy and Catskill Animal Sanctuary, visit casanctuary.org.

FOUR

Dr. Andra Brosh
The Alchemy of Life: from Adversity to Gold

"Opportunities to find deeper powers within ourselves come when life seems most challenging."

– Joseph Campbell

Without mincing words, I'll tell it like it is. Andra Brosh changed my life.

It was sparked by an inspired thought that led me to a five-day writing retreat in February 2013. The gestation process had already begun, but the birth of my book needed help. Was I on the right path? How do I make it the best that it can be? How do I maximize reach for my message? This inquiring mind needed to know, and what better way to learn than from other nascent writers?

We were four strangers united on a collective journey of self-discovery and creative expression. The setting was inspiring: a lovely home overlooking the ocean in beautiful Carmel, California. Linda Sivertsen, aka Book Mama, created the sacred container to hold our dreams so they could be safely birthed into the world.

The tribal bond was immediate. We shared our hopes and fears, laughter and tears. The communal enthusiasm was palpable. Four passionate women longing to unleash the writer from within.

Andra stood out. Her essence shone brightly through the warmth of her smile and the inspired wisdom of every spoken word. I felt an instant connection, an inner knowing that this would become a lasting friendship. Little did I know the profound impact she would have on my life.

Andra's path to such deep wisdom wasn't an easy one. For twenty years she lived the dream life. A beautiful home complete with loving husband, two kids, a dog, and everything that makes for a "happily-ever-after" existence.

Life is notorious for throwing curveballs into the zone of comfort, however. Andra's life was turned upside down by two unforeseen events: a cancer diagnosis and a divorce. In one fell swoop her reality was forever altered. Not only was her life in jeopardy, but her entire familial paradigm was demolished.

The wisdom journey is rarely mundane. It is filled with pain, grief, and a deep commitment to healing work that promotes wholeness. There are few who choose to walk this tempestuous path. Those who do are often guided by a higher sense of calling. Andra is no exception to this universal truth.

Her chosen vocation as a clinical psychologist is one she has embraced with deep spiritual wisdom and a profound passion to make a difference in the lives of others. Her extensive training as a clinician has given her the respected title of "doctor," but what makes her truly exceptional is how she uncovered a deeper sense of purpose through her pain. Her capacity for compassion far exceeds the norm, because she's been there. As the saying goes, life is often the greatest teacher.

Andra is also a gifted writer who aspires to reach the masses with her story of healing and self-discovery. It's this shared vision that united us for that pivotal week in Carmel.

Andra is a keen listener whose heart is as attentive as her ears. During our first group brainstorming session, she honed in on my words and excitedly ran with them. In that moment, everything changed for me. My book took on a new direction, and the seed was planted for a more expansive life path. As the week progressed, the seed took root and I knew that my life would never be the same.

All of our answers really do lie within, but sometimes it's difficult to discern what should be so obvious. With a nudge from an open heart and an attentive ear, however, we can be guided toward a more expansive calling. Andra saw possibility where I didn't. She revealed a path that was routine for me, yet exceptional for others. This book, my podcast, my entire life's message—all were revealed through the keen listening skills of Dr. Andra Brosh.

I am eternally grateful for my fortuitous encounter with this remarkable woman. In so many ways, she exemplifies the best of the human spirit: compassionate, loving, authentic, resilient, and wise.

***

Andra's Story

Unplugging: Path to Purpose

I was married at a relatively young age and had two children by the time I was twenty-seven. As a stay-at-home mom, my time was pretty well occupied by my kids. When they were old enough to go to elementary school, I had more free time on my hands. That was when I began to notice how lost I felt.

So I began to search. I wanted to do something that helped people. I always knew that I had a capacity for healing, but I'd never honored it. I was confused about this and couldn't figure out which way to turn.

In my quest for answers, I went to my therapist for help. She asked me a question that changed my life. She asked if I had ever thought about becoming a psychologist. My answer was yes, absolutely. I'd considered it in college. I just never felt like I could—or that I was allowed. I didn't give myself permission to go in that direction.

I went back to school in my early thirties and fell in love with it. I immersed myself in my studies, so much so that it became my life. I'd found my passion. I'd found my calling—the thing that I could offer this world and really be effective at doing. I loved working with people.

Around the age of forty, life threw me some curveballs. I was diagnosed with breast cancer. It was so unexpected. I'd always been such a healthy person, but there was a part of me that had always feared getting sick. It makes me wonder if I manifested it. At the same time, I also know that I have no control over these things.

I devotedly put one foot in front of the other in determination to heal. I was very fortunate to overcome it. It's been over five years now. It was a really rough road, but I learned so much from that experience. I believe that the bulk of my wisdom comes from facing death and having dealt with something so unexpected that it shattered my entire worldview.

We often live with ideals and perspectives that protect us from facing the reality of death. Cancer was really confrontational for me. It was a clash of fantasy and reality, but in the end, it made me feel more grounded. It forced me into my body in ways that I have never been in my body. It made me value my body in ways that I've never valued it. It also gave me great appreciation for my health.

The main thing that I learned from cancer is that there's no point in being afraid. Worry and fear are such a waste of time and energy. As a psychologist, I understand why they happen, but they cause so much unnecessary harm.

I also learned to live in the moment with a deep sense of trust. I realized a capacity for inner strength that was surprising. This was all very profound for me.

It wasn't long afterward that I had another earth-shattering experience, when my husband of twenty years announced that he wanted a divorce. It was surreal. I'd had dreams of growing old together. When we married and shared our vows, it was forever no matter what. I am a very committed person. I come from a divorced household, so I had vowed to never get divorced myself. But like the cancer, I had no control over the situation. He made the decision. I tried to fight for the marriage, but ultimately I had to surrender to what life was bringing me. I knew that I had to learn from this. So I juiced both of these experiences for all of the good I could get out of them. Even though they were both very painful, in the end I felt like I had spun gold.

I turned these difficult situations into something really profound. I needed to discover the greater meaning so that I could become a better person. That's what I ended up doing with both of these experiences. I now apply this to my work. Much of what I now do is help people figure out how to become better and stronger for the darker moments in life. Nobody lives a peaches-and-cream life. We're all going to have curveballs thrown at us. Why not learn the tools and skills to manage them? That way, when the storm hits, we can stay solid and grounded while gracefully riding out the waves. That's my general philosophy of life.

I think that the moral of my story is found in how grounded I feel. I have never felt wiser and more authentic than I do now. I really believe it's because I had these two major hardships that completely altered my life. Having personal experience with enormous pain, I'm passionate about helping other people move through their own challenges so they can transcend their devastated world. I want to share my experiences in ways that really benefit the world.

Shortly after being diagnosed with breast cancer, I was on a plane seated next to a guy who wanted to chat. I was still wearing my hospital bracelet, and he started asking questions. I told him about my breast cancer. When we got off the plane, he looked at me and said, "Share that story. Don't keep it inside, because there are too many people who need to hear it. It will help so many others." His words stayed with me. I never forgot him and I'm honoring his advice.

In my own life, it was hearing the stories of others that saved me. I would read *Chicken Soup for the Soul* types of books because I wanted to know what other people were thinking and feeling through their own healing journeys. I think there's so much power in story. It's fundamental for healing. When we share our stories, we connect with one another in ways that show that we're not alone in our struggles. This is really powerful because it shows that no matter who we are or what our story is, we all matter.

Reconnecting and Spirituality

My spirituality comes from multiple places. I've experimented with many things. Some things worked and some things didn't. I tried to expand my worldview enough so that I could eventually narrow it down to what feeds my soul so that I feel connected.

Some of it is faith-based. Not necessarily religion-based, but faith-based. I'm a big follower of Buddhism and Sufism. I also know that I need to be in certain environments to nourish myself. For me, that means connecting with the elements. There's a spa in L.A. that I like to go to that has a Himalayan salt room. Lying quietly among the pieces of salt and rock is very grounding for me. There's also nothing more grounding than being in nature.

Through the traumas that I went through, I learned the necessity of grounding myself to return to my center. I was able to find what works for me. I discovered how to connect with that internal sense of presence that no one can ever take away. But I have to nourish it so that it isn't depleted by everyday life. It's a daily practice, which I honor by journaling.

I'm also an introvert, and this helps me to understand more of my core needs. This is one of the things I help people discover about themselves. Are you an introvert? Are you an extrovert? These are really important things to know about ourselves. For instance, as an introvert, I know that I need solitude. I need to be alone. I can only handle social situations for small periods of time before I feel drained. I used to ignore that. I used to criticize myself. What's wrong with me? Why can't I be friendlier? Why don't I want to go to more parties? Why am I such a loner? Why don't I have more friends?

Now I've learned to love that about myself, because it's who I am. I have the capacity to be social and friendly, I just have to manage it in a way that doesn't deplete me. I don't have the bandwidth that someone who is gregarious or outgoing does. And that's okay, because I'm okay.

Self-compassion is a huge component of my spirituality. I now practice a lot of self-love. I used to make fun of people who talked about self-love and all of that hokey-dokey stuff. But I changed my tune when I started practicing it myself. It's had an incredibly transformative effect on my life.

I feel the most connected to myself when I'm connected to other people in small group settings or one-on-one—when the energy is open and intimate. I feel inspired by the spark that makes me want to give more. I feel confident. I feel content, peaceful, and joyful. I feel so good—like I need nothing else. It's self-containing, not at all about material things.

Shopping would not give me the same feeling. Working out doesn't do it. It's so much deeper than that. I really do feel a oneness when I'm connected to others. This is actually very recent for me, and it's something I'm very excited about. I feel like I'm at a place in my life where I feel such an incredible love for everyone. It's amazing—especially because of my introverted nature.

I actually feel very loved by the world, which is so different than the love from a parent or a partner, for instance. It's a universal love. It's hard to describe, but it's something we all have within us. It was a pivotal moment for me when I realized this.

It emerged from the chronic disappointment that I felt from being let down by the people in my life. I finally got fed up and decided to step back and let the universe support me. I realized that the universe had had my back all along and that I didn't necessarily need to rely on any one person. It's nice to know that there are people out there who love me, but it's liberating to trust that I'm always okay when I'm connected to my essence. That's where I would like to stay all the time, but it's not easy. It's an ongoing practice, but it's worth it. I look at people differently and feel more love for everyone, because it's now generated from within, from that place of unchanging love inside.

Hope for a Better World

As hard as this world is and as ugly as it can be, I really believe in the human spirit. I think that's why I do what I do. I see the light in people. I just know that people are perfect in their imperfection.

If our ideals about the world come from an acceptance of shared imperfection, I feel more hopeful. When we try to make things perfect or we try to rectify things that don't need to be rectified, that's when I start to waver in my sense of hope.

I believe in the greater good. I believe that there are millions of people doing selfless work like I'm doing. This is bound to have a big impact.

Another thing that gives me hope is accepting the truth about the short amount of time we have to live on this Earth. We're not here forever. There's a lot of uncertainty around our expiration date, and the unknown is really frightening for many people. But death is the one certainty that we all share. For me, there's something about the unknown and not having all the answers that is very liberating. I can embrace the reality that my world is going to come to an end sooner or later and be okay with that. I know that may sound dark, but if we can embrace that fact and live from that space, then we can live more meaningful lives right now. We stop wasting time. That's when we really come alive.

Ultimately what gives me hope is the awakened human spirit. I really believe in people. I know that there's a greater good out there, and it's emerging. You can tell. People are sick and tired, and they're waking up en masse to create really exciting solutions for today's global problems.

If You Had a Magic Wand …

I would create a world where we all felt that sense of universal connection, where we all had a deep compassion and understanding for each other that eliminated the separation responsible for all of the angst and despair in the world. I envision one big circle around the planet with everyone holding hands.

I don't think we're very far off from that world.

For more information about Andra's work, visit drandrabrosh.com.

FIVE

Julie Piatt
Inspiring an Authentic Way to Learn

"Educating the mind without educating the heart is no education at all."

– Aristotle

The past several decades have seen rapid transformation in many areas of modern life. From the internet to social media to crowdfunding, nearly every sector in the Western world uses new technologies to innovate, create, connect, and communicate in ways that were previously unimaginable. The merits and drawbacks are arguable, but the accelerated momentum is undeniable.

There is one sector, however, that remains virtually unchanged.

Established in the mid-nineteenth century, the factory model of education prevails to this day. In 1902, John D. Rockefeller created the General Education Board, which was responsible for funding the American public school system. Mr. Rockefeller made his agenda very clear when he declared, "I want a nation of workers, not thinkers."

The General Education Board was the catalyst for the creation of the American public school system—a soul-suppressing model that has been used around the globe for more than a century.

Modern day education has its merits, but in many ways, the negatives outweigh the positives. Learning does indeed occur in the classroom, but students are not encouraged to challenge what they're taught, nor are they encouraged to actively question the world around them. As a result, conformity, compliance, and competition supplant creativity, curiosity, and collaboration. It is a stark reminder of an antiquated model designed to perpetuate the docile paradigm of separation.

With its rigid bell schedules and age-based grade levels, the factory model of education was designed to produce assembly line workers for repetitive tasks without the need for problem solving, analysis, creativity, intuition, or critical thought. By monotonously teaching the same curriculum at the same pace year after year, compliant thought is ensured.

In his 2008 *Deschooling Ourselves* workshop video, author Charles Eisenstein says, "School is really our first experience of an authority outside of the family. Our relation to this authority teaches us to relate the same way to an internalized authority (our inner critic). Eventually, we no longer need externalized controls, rewards, incentives, punishments, and threats. When this happens, we're considered educated and mature. We then get a document to certify that we've learned the lessons of school and have internalized the programming of self-control that ensures our cultural compliance. That certificate of compliance is called a diploma or degree. And if you want to prove your exceptional submissiveness and compliance, you can get a graduate degree or a Ph.D."

In response to the greater availability of information in today's world, many educators feel obligated to instill more rote facts, procedures, logic, strategies, and beliefs into the minds of their students. Passive memorization, under the guise of learning, is required for outdated grading procedures that sacrifice critical thought for compliance.

The Dalai Lama recently said "Education is in crisis the world over. There is unprecedented literacy, yet this universal education does not seem to have fostered goodness, but only mental restlessness and discontent instead."[3]

With few opportunities for engaging conversations and creative problem-solving, students are unable to make important connections that lead them to self-discovery, goodness, and truth.

Critical thought is one of the greatest assets in a conscious, awakening mind. In a cultural paradigm that promotes sameness, critical thought challenges the status quo and activates intuition, creativity, authenticity, compassion, creativity, and truth.

It is in our biological nature to think, yet much of our thinking is externally sourced. The blind acceptance of the status quo ensures mindless choices, behaviors, and actions that sustain the consumptive patterns responsible for alarming planetary destruction. A mental realm devoid of critical thought is judgmental, uninformed, biased, and outright distorted.

In his 2013 book, *Wild Mind*, psychologist and author, Bill Plotkin writes, "Our mainstream educational and religious institutions have suppressed our human potential and magnificence, or at least failed to evoke and foster our brilliance and virtuosity, our capacity to truly mature and to help make the world a better place."[4]

When we suppress our brilliance, we suppress critical thought. When we suppress critical thought, we suppress wisdom. When we suppress wisdom, we deaden the soul. When we run on knowledge alone, we destroy the earth. Author Thomas Berry states, "Most of the destruction of the planet is being accomplished by people with PhDs."

What is critical thought? The basic definition implies the ability to make one's own decisions, along with the willingness to continually challenge one's own thinking. It also implies the non-acceptance of beliefs, opinions, facts, and statements as valid without first considering a more expansive worldview directed by internal truth. Critical thought is self-directed, self-monitored, and self-corrective. It inspires, enlightens, and empowers. Critical thinking provides us with the mental tools to overcome our egocentrism and return to our internal truth.

Critical thinking unites head with heart.

The cultivation of critical thought inspires compassion. Compassion elevates consciousness. Compassion in action transforms the world.

Enter "unschooling," an innovative educational philosophy that eliminates the institutionalized, "one-size-fits-all" approach of the factory model of education. Peter Gray, psychology professor at Boston College and author of *Free to Learn*, states, "Children come into this world burning to learn, equipped with the curiosity, playfulness, and sociability to direct their own education. Yet we have squelched such instincts in a school model originally developed to indoctrinate, not to promote intellectual growth."[5]

Unschooling accommodates a child's natural passion for learning by nurturing curiosity, creativity, and critical thought. In a world where self-confidence has reached an all-time low, unschooling fosters self-expression, self-esteem, and empowered learning through self-initiated activities and natural life experiences. Unschooling feeds the soul.

"I find that almost everywhere I go, I meet a mother, parent, or a family who has a child that is not plugging into the system and they don't know what to do. I really feel that we are the ones we've been waiting for, and the answers lie within us. I have great trust and faith in mothers, fathers, and families to be able to come up with a new system that fits everybody, preserves self-esteem, and embraces the diversity of every child." These are the sage words of Julie Piatt, mother and passionate crusader for the unschooling movement.

Julie is a multi-passionate woman whose journey through life has been anything but traditional. Her spiritual approach to living offers a more expansive lens through which to see the world. It's this openhearted lens that has inspired the exploration of "out of the box" solutions to challenging life situations.

Julie and her husband Rich Roll are coauthors of *The Plantpower Way*. She's a singer-songwriter, plant-based chef, healer, and mother of four children. Julie is also an impassioned wellness advocate who believes firmly in the body's innate ability to heal itself. By embracing a plant-based diet and devoting herself to a deep spiritual practice, Julie healed herself from what was deemed an incurable ailment. It was this same commitment to truth that motivated Julie to explore progressive-minded solutions for a daughter who could not be contained within a cultural system of institutionalized thought. Unschooling proved to be the perfect solution.

Despite ongoing judgment from the status quo mindset, Julie intrepidly presses on. As a result, her children are thriving, her familial relationships are stronger, and her zeal for the creation of a new paradigm of education is contagious. Unschooling works. The proof is in the kids: creative, curious, and compassionate critical thinkers with self-esteem intact.

In a world that is begging for more creativity, critical thought, and authentic expression, unschooling delivers. Julie Piatt proves this. With faith, trust, and love in her heart, she's become an inspiring catalyst for the radical change this planet so desperately needs.

***

Julie's Story

Unplugging: Path to Purpose

I was born with the burning desire to know what happens when we die. This powerful question has been the driver of my life.

There were five kids in our family, which meant that there was usually a lot of commotion. My experience as the youngest child was often observational. I would just sit back and watch the chaos unfold. I was eager to grow up so that I could be more independent from my family.

I've always loved animals and nature. I spent a lot of my formative years hiking in the mountains of Alaska. Most of my time outside was unsupervised. I'd sometimes go into the wilderness for up to twenty hours with a few friends. We'd forget to bring water, so we'd drink out of streams. Now that I'm a mother, I look back on that time and wonder how I got away with it. Somehow, I always managed.

Most of my play happened in the forest. It wasn't with plastic toys. I created imaginary worlds in beautiful natural settings. I had a lot of freedom as a child that nurtured my creative expression. This freedom also helped me to discover my authentic voice. I feel that this time in nature was key to my personal evolution. Now that I'm a mom, I trust and honor my children in the same way.

My life began to really change when I discovered yoga. With yoga, I naturally gravitated toward things that were nourishing and in alignment with my spirit. Anything that was out of balance just dropped away from my life. My father was a hunter and fisherman, so I grew up eating moose tacos, caribou stew, reindeer sausages, and an extraordinary amount of salmon. We didn't eat many fresh vegetables, because for about nine months of the year there just *weren't* many in Alaska. When I delved deeper into yoga, I began eating a lot cleaner and eventually switched to a vegetarian diet.

Fast forward a few years. I was in my forties and had been doing yoga for quite a while. The healthy, mindful yogic lifestyle had become a significant part of my identity. One day, though, I got quite a surprise.

Rich and I had been married a couple of years, and we were planning to have a romantic anniversary evening in our teepee to celebrate. At that time we were living in a teepee and an Airstream while our house was being built. I packed my bag to bring down to the teepee, and as I passed by the mirror, I noticed a huge mass on my neck. It was the size of a golf ball. I thought to myself, "Wow. Is that my Adam's apple?" I was surprised because it came on so suddenly.

I was really stunned, but I decided not to tell Rich that night. The next morning, however, I told him. I could tell by the look on his face that he was very concerned.

I'm not one to frequent doctors, but this time I agreed to have it checked out. I went to see a specialist and was diagnosed with a cyst that required surgical removal. I went for an MRI which revealed that I had a thyroglossal duct cyst. It was infected and fused between two bones. It's a rare condition that's usually only seen in kids between the ages of eight and twelve. I was in my forties. I was told by three different surgeons that there was no possible way it would heal on its own.

The doctors explained to me that surgery was the only option. I wasn't keen on this, because I'd experienced a botched tonsillectomy that ruined my taste buds for almost a year. In the wake of that trauma, I could barely eat. I lost about twenty pounds, which was significant because I'm already so thin. I was also in massive pain that couldn't even be relieved with morphine.

When the doctors said they had to surgically remove the cyst, I was determined to treat it holistically. I told them that I was a healer and into natural methods. They were patronizing with their response, but they said there was time to experiment. They were certain I'd be back in a few months for the surgery.

From my perspective, I felt that I'd been given a gift. I was inspired to explore the healing properties of food. In hindsight, now that I'm a vegan chef who speaks about food as medicine, I realize that this was a foundational point in my evolutionary journey.

Much to Rich's horror, and against the wishes of everybody around me, I decided to heal the cyst myself. I contacted an Ayurvedic doctor, and with his guidance I embarked on a journey of healing. We shared a love of the *Bhagavad Gita*, spirituality, and a deeper knowing that there are greater forces at play. With this beautiful spiritual base, he never doubted that my body would heal itself.

The beauty of Ayurveda, which is the Indian science of natural medicine, is that it restores the body to perfect balance so that it can heal itself. Ayurveda recognizes the divine perfection of the body. I often say to people that if you doubt the existence of a God, just witness the involuntary actions inside the human body. Breath, heartbeat, and digestion—all day long, without a single thought. The human body is miraculous.

Ayurveda inspired in me a divine relationship with food. I was already eating better than many people, but there were still changes to make to heal the cyst. When I chose the Ayurvedic path, I changed my entire diet. I ate predominantly dark leafy greens, sweet, green fruits, and a lot of lentils and rice. I also began a mindful way of living to keep stress at bay.

I would rise at an early hour for prayers and meditation, and then

I'd practice yoga before my day began. My day would wind down at six in the evening. One of the prescriptions of this path was to be in bed before I was tired. I had to shift a lot of things with my lifestyle, but the biggest shift was moving into faith. I had a lot of judgment from people who thought I was insane, but I was resolved in my commitment to heal myself.

As I continued along this path, with meditation and a deeper connection to food and herbs, I began receiving musical inspiration through my meditations. I had no musical training, but the experience inspired me to become a musician. Over the next seven years, my boys and I became musicians together. I received profound healing from this. I'd wanted to be a singer since I was six years old, but somehow I had avoided it. I'd done many creative things in my life, but had neglected the one thing that called to me since childhood. The cyst was my soul's way of getting my attention. By sitting in quiet meditation, I was able to hear my soul speak to me in profound ways. The messages came in the form of songs, which are now two albums, *Mother of Mine* and *Jai Home*. I recorded this music with my sons, Tyler and Trapper, over the next eight years. Creating music with my boys is one of the greatest joys in my life and the most beautiful gift that God has given me.

It took about four months before I noticed a change in the cyst. Within six months, the change was significant. This increased my resolve to keep working on it. I continued with yoga, asana, meditation, singing, and a plant-based lifestyle. I believe that this whole life connection, including releasing the singer/musician from within, helped me heal without the need for surgery.

An Authentic Model for Education: Unschooling

I never dreamt of being an unschooling mom. The catalyst was my daughter Mathis. She literally did not fit into any system.

In her early years, there were signs of what some might call mild autism. She was extremely sensitive to people, places, rooms, and sounds.

She had a lot of energy running through her body that was difficult to process. This continued from the time she was a baby until she was seven years old.

I spent a lot of time doing healing work with her. She found my energy to be very calming. She needed to be physically close to me 24/7. Despite many attempts to settle her in her own space, she refused to sleep without me for eight years.

This puzzled me. I couldn't figure her out. I was an experienced mother by the time I gave birth to Mathis and had raised two sons with no issues. Like many children, they'd have their baths, read books, go to bed by 7:30, and sleep until the early morning hours. But when Mathis arrived, she was on a totally different trajectory. I had to throw out my entire parenting toolbox and start over. Nothing that worked for the boys worked for Mathis.

At the same time that I was experiencing all of these issues with Mathis, Rich was going through his own transformation. He was transitioning from lawyer to vegan endurance athlete. It was a really challenging time for us. There were many times when we questioned our sanity and felt as if we were traversing a razor's edge.

I reached out for the support of a spiritual healer, who prescribed flower essences as a treatment for Mathis' parasympathetic nervous system. I also began saying yes to her as often as I could. I wanted to create a positive experience for her, because saying no carved a groove of negativity that made her feel like the world was against her. I explained to Rich and the boys that her sensitivity was a quality that should be nurtured. We needed to recognize and celebrate her unique approach to life. By doing this we would all be much happier. It worked. This helped us realize that Mathis was not just being unreasonable or difficult. For example, if we went out to eat at a restaurant and she didn't like where the host was seating us, we accepted that she was picking up on something, some energy in that area of the room. We decided to trust her instead of resist her. Moving tables is an easy thing to say "yes" to.

Mathis, more than any human being, has transformed me. She's very free, determined, loving, loyal, and larger than life. She's called me to task more than anyone else in my lifetime. From birth to around age eight, she demonstrated psychic awareness, where she knew things about people that they often didn't know themselves. It came very naturally to her.

Over the years, I enrolled her in a couple of newer schools for short periods of time. There were a few forward-thinking local schools attempting to create something different, but they ended up being only slightly better than the status quo. They weren't the right fit for Mathis. No school system seems to understand that we come from a divine source, and this is what Mathis needed.

We live in a society where so much of our focus is on external fantasy created by pop culture. Most families have two parents working while the kids go to school. Everyone is often tired by the end of the day. The TV goes on and the family zones out. In that environment, kids mimic bad behavior. As a result, judgment and comparison begin at a young age.

The reason my kids know who they are is because we live a spiritually focused life. My kids have understood from a very young age that we are all divine. I don't believe that children need to be taught how to live; instead, they need to be exposed to many things and guided along the way. In my experience, most kids are light years ahead of the adults who are teaching them.

The day I decided to homeschool was liberating for everyone in our family. I didn't have to drag Mathis out of bed, shove her into clothes she didn't want to wear, feed her when she wasn't ready to eat, and drive her to a place she didn't want to be. I decided to do it my way. At first it was homeschool because I was trying to appease Rich and his Stanford mindset. He was freaking out about the idea of Mathis not being in school. But homeschool was still too structured for Mathis. Homeschooling eventually morphed into unschooling.

My boys were older and had gone to private school in their younger years. Finances eventually mandated that they go to public middle school. By that time, they had little interest in school, but they decided to give high school a try. After one year, they asked to be homeschooled. They had little in common with their peers. I was shocked to discover that they'd never told anyone about their music. As an artist, I was horrified that they didn't feel safe enough to reveal their art. I believe that young people are supposed to share and create together in a safe, free world. Sadly, their high school experience proved otherwise.

According to my boys, the road to acceptance is very narrow. If you don't fit in, you face isolation. It was safer to get by without being noticed. Socialization is often the misperceived pitfall of unschooling, but I argue that the socialization found in status quo schools doesn't benefit children. Allowing kids to be self-directed critical thinkers is of much greater value for everyone. I give my kids a lot of freedom. I allow them to self-regulate and offer support when they ask for it.

My boys don't drink or do drugs. They're creatively connected through writing music, singing, yoga, and cooking. There's nothing in high school that nurtures those experiences. Luckily, we found a hybrid program where they could do their school work from home and check in monthly with a teacher without having to go to classes. They both thrived as straight A students in this program. They also had a lot more time to create music and do the things they enjoyed. We traveled a lot during those years, including a three-month experience living in yurts on Kauai.

Most kids in today's culture are completely disconnected. They're on a fast track to get good grades for college. They've become stressed out "test-takers," memorizing information for the sole purpose of exams. There's no experiential learning. This approach shuts down creativity, intuition, originality, and individuality. Pretty soon they don't even know whose life they're living.

Our entire culture is based on the thinking mind, but true wisdom resides in the heart. We're better off feeling our way through life rather than thinking our way through. We've disconnected from our intuition. If something doesn't feel right, it isn't. We've lost this simple wisdom.

As a mother, my role in life is to stand for my children. If I won't do it, then who will? I'm here to protect and offer them guidance and experiences that foster intuition and healthy self-esteem.

In the early years of unschooling I had no money, so I used free resources and connections: friends, free online programs, and meetings with other homeschool groups to figure things out. We spent time in nature and did a lot of painting. We learned about plant-based food, meditation, and spirituality. We also took many field trips to museums, beaches, mountains, and historical places.

When Mathis was around four years old, I tried to teach her how to read using flashcards. She hated this method so much that she would collapse, crying, on the floor. There was so much resistance that I decided to just let her be. I figured she would read in her own time. She was very smart and self-initiating. Everyone in my world freaked out at this approach. My mother would call me regularly to tell me how many books my niece, who is younger than Mathis, was reading. The comparison was meant to instigate competition and get Mathis up to speed. This is the exact distorted motivation used in the standardized educational system. But I refused to fall prey to this antiquated method of thought. At seven years old, she taught herself how to read. Now she reads books all the time.

Children learn many things on their own without interference from adults. Chances are they know a better way to do things than most adults do. They already know how to be loving, humane, conscious, creative, and engaged. What my experience has shown is that the single act of treating children with respect, with an equal right to be heard, consulted, and even considered—this is the most powerful act of love. This empowering energy creates a bond with the child that lasts throughout time. They also have a greater chance of experiencing healthy self-esteem.

When Mathis was eight years old, she became very interested in fashion design. I'd been a fashion designer with my own collection, and she loved going through my college portfolio. We hired a mentor to teach her for a few hours a week. She would stay up late drawing new designs and sewing in her room. She had her own blog and fashion line for a year and a half. She's always been a natural leader and entrepreneur. She's smart, determined, and has amazing focus. She knows what she wants and she goes for it.

Recently, she dropped fashion and is now playing in a coed hockey league. I'm sure that it will be something different next year.

Unschooling hasn't always been easy. There was a time when we were struggling financially and I had few allies in my alternative parenting ways. Over time, I was able to experience more support than I had in eighteen years of motherhood when I homeschooled with two other families. We were able to live more like a close-knit tribe with three mothers caring for seven children.

I've learned so much through this experience. Mathis has helped me understand that children come into the world with all they need to realize themselves. I believe that the number one issue plaguing humanity is the cultural violation to self-esteem that causes people to lose themselves.

I strongly believe that if we left our kids alone so that they could just be themselves, they'd find their passion, their sense of self, and they'd be amazing citizens of the planet. I don't care if my children can spew out historical facts; I just want them to claim their authentic voice. That's all. The whole world is looking externally for answers. I want my kids to be connected to who they are inside.

This way of living has inspired a lot of chaos, independence, critical thought, amazing creativity, and a level of intimate connection with my children that I never imagined possible. Unschooling has been a most wonderful way to experience life with my children.

If You Had a Magic Wand …

I would create a world of beauty and creativity, with magical smells, tastes, feelings, and sensations—a magical, sensual, creative world.

Discover more about Julie, her music, and her heart at srimati.com.

SIX

Peter Russell
From Science to Spirituality

"We should take care not to make the intellect our god; it has, of course,
powerful muscles, but no personality."

– ALBERT EINSTEIN

Upon emergence from the amorphous cocoon of grief that followed the untimely death of my mother, I was eager to fly. My heart was open and I was hungry for more … of me. The year was 2012, a powerful year for healing and self-discovery.

Although predicted by many, the world did not end in catastrophe. In my own life, however, the world as I knew it would never be the same. The year 2012 was when I unplugged from a reality that no longer fit and set sail on the infinite journey within. I was ripe for transformation.

Transformation is a life-altering process involving radical change that inspires a greater state of being. By transcending the circumstances in our lives, we can actualize the potential that emerges from it all.

The truth is, the path toward wholeness is always available. When the heart opens, guidance arrives with remarkable clarity. It may not always make sense, but when trust is affirmed, we are invariably shown the way. As Caroline Myss says, "The soul always knows what to do to heal itself. The challenge is to silence the mind."

Ah yes, the human mind, a limitless reservoir of endless possibility, too often silenced by the impervious obstacle of fear. Ideas that seem far-fetched are often discarded. As rational thought descends to ensure our "safety," we excuse ourselves from anything that may propel us from the zone of comfort. And so we remain, steadfast in our pain, hostage to smallness.

But what if those wild, "out there" ideas that confuse the intellect and instigate fear are the voice of the heart—the soul—pleading for freedom?

The intellect, as brilliant as it is, was never suited for leadership. The heart, on the other hand, knows all. When we live our lives with the mind in service to the heart, we expand beyond the realm of fear and life becomes clearer. What were once mere coincidences become guideposts on the path toward wholeness.

I believe that there are no accidents in the Universe. In my life, I've always been blessed to meet exactly who I needed at the time I needed them most. Sometimes I find them in unlikely places. Such was the case in 2012. My voracious appetite for expansion freed my soul to lead me to one such unlikely place: the Monroe Institute.

At first glance, the Monroe Institute website baffled me. Campus programs about remote viewing, astral travel, and lucid dreaming spawned judgments in my mind of new age hocus-pocus. But the excitement in my body could not be denied. I squelched my judgments and signed up for the inaugural Gateway Voyage with an open heart and no expectations.

What followed blew my mind. There are no words to articulate the experience; it is so personal. Suffice it to say, I was hungry for more. The Monroe Institute's tagline, "explore consciousness, transform your life," did just that. I followed the Gateway Voyage with three subsequent programs. The final program, Exploration Essence, still guides me to this day.

Exploration Essence was the brainchild of Karen Malik and Peter Russell. Peter is a well-known author and filmmaker in the field of consciousness and also a practicing Buddhist. The aim of the program was to facilitate the opening and experiencing of our essential nature—the source of who we truly are. The five-day program was multifaceted in its approach. Within the group exploration, we examined the personality and psychological overlay that inevitably forms our humanity. This is often what separates us from our true nature.

In the Far East, they say that the innermost channel of the heart is the non-dual channel—our essential nature—our spirit. Non-duality is the philosophical, spiritual, and scientific understanding of non-separation. It is our fundamental oneness with all living beings. When our hearts are connected, the veil of separation dissolves and we are unified, regardless of race, gender, age, or species. At our core, this is who we are.

My soul yearned for this program. Having read Peter's books, *From Science to God* and *Waking Up in Time*, I was excited about the opportunity to learn from a man with such profuse wisdom.

Peter Russell is highly regarded in the consciousness movement. He began his life as a rather unlikely spiritual pioneer, studying mathematics, computer science, and theoretical physics at Cambridge University. Over time, he became increasingly fascinated with the human mind and shifted his course of study to experimental psychology. This eventually led him to India, where he studied meditation and Eastern philosophy with the likes of Maharishi Mahesh Yogi—yes, *the* Maharishi of Beatles fame.

His deep-dive into the world of spirituality inspired extensive exploration of consciousness from the world's various spiritual traditions. His mission is to refine this wisdom so that its teachings can be expressed in uncomplicated ways that captivate and inspire. I can tell you from personal experience, he's mastered his mission.

In life, there are many steps on the path toward wholeness. There are baby steps, sidesteps, and "fall-flat-on-your-ass" steps. There are also quantum leaps that bypass the minutia of all steps. My time with Peter Russell fell into this final category. For that, I am eternally grateful.

I end my story with this: Never doubt a far-fetched idea that leads to an unlikely place. The soul always knows what is required for expansion and may be facilitating a connection to someone who can lead the way home.

Indeed, there are no accidents in the Universe.

Peter's Story

Unplugging: Path to Purpose

As a teenager, I was fascinated by science and mathematics. I really loved these subjects at school and thought I would grow up to be a scientist. I would spend hours working out equations, solving them, and drawing out graphs. This was all back in the '60s when computers were still in the early phases.

The computers at that time ran on vacuum tubes. The transistor wasn't around yet. I was actually building my own computers out of bits of wire in my dad's garage. Before I went to university, I had an interesting job in computing, so I thought that perhaps this was the right path for me.

I ended up going to Cambridge, where I studied mathematics and theoretical physics for three years. I thought this would be my path. But as time progressed, I became more fascinated with the mind and consciousness. It eventually dawned on me that physics and mathematics were not going to teach me about consciousness.

I got to a point where I could solve Schrödinger's equation for the hydrogen atom. This is meaningless to the non-physicist, but it's fascinating from a scientific point of view. It means from a pure mathematics perspective, you can start deducing that hydrogen should not exist with the chemical properties it has. That's a great intellectual achievement. Schrödinger's equation for helium is too complex because there are four particles, but for two particles, it's doable.

What struck me was that according to current models, the universe began with hydrogen. In other words, hydrogen was the first element to be created. Then out of hydrogen came helium and all the other elements. From that came molecules, and from that came life. From life, ultimately, came human beings; and here I was, a human being studying hydrogen. It occurred to me that hydrogen had evolved into a system that could actually do the mathematics of itself.

How could that happen? I realized nothing in physics was going to tell me. I couldn't even work out the equation for helium. How on earth could I understand how hydrogen got to the stage of understanding itself? I realized that we humans were like the universe's way of studying itself. I became more and more fascinated by this—that there was consciousness in the universe and how nothing in science predicted that any of us should ever be conscious.

We may be able to understand how stars evolved, how life came into being, and how life evolved, but none of these discoveries indicate anything about consciousness. Yet consciousness is the one thing we cannot deny. The fact that we are conscious, experiencing beings is the absolute truth. We can doubt almost everything else.

I became increasingly fascinated by the existence of consciousness in the cosmos, and I became less enthusiastic about mathematics. So I moved into the study of experimental psychology, thinking that an understanding of the brain would help me understand consciousness.

I learned a lot about the brain: how it functions, perception, memory, how it works with the body, how the neurons work with biochemistry, all of that. But nobody was really interested in consciousness. So I began dabbling in Eastern philosophy, realizing that these were the people who explored consciousness.

The study of consciousness doesn't involve strapping EEGs on people's heads and examining the resulting electrical activity. That's just a study of the physical world. The way to study consciousness is to actually observe it, to dive in and watch one's own experience. I was fascinated by what was going on in the East.

What kept showing up in my exploration was meditation. I experimented with different meditation practices, and eventually I came across transcendental meditation. This was at about the same time the Beatles were involved in it. I was so fascinated by it that I went to India to be with the Maharishi.

I was actually invited to be with the Beatles while they were there, which would have been quite an experience. But I'm glad I didn't go then, because it turned out to be more of a party. When I arrived after they'd left, it was a more serious place. We went deep into the understanding of consciousness and Indian philosophy. It was absolutely fascinating and became a turning point in my life. There wasn't any major "aha" moment; it was more like a gradual dawning that happened during my time in India, where I realized that there was something to spirituality.

As a teenager, I'd rejected religion. When I was about thirteen, I went through the process of confirmation in church. I had thought that the Nicene Creed was something to be chanted on Sundays. But it turned out that, no, we're actually meant to believe it. It started off with, "I believe in one God, the Father Almighty, Maker of heaven and earth, and of all things visible and invisible." I thought to myself, I can't believe this stuff. So I rejected religion.

In India, I began to see that spirituality and religion were very different things. The way I saw it, religion was like the dead embers of spiritual teaching. There had been many spiritual teachers who explored human consciousness, and their discoveries were life-altering. They wanted to share their knowledge with other people. But as this knowledge was shared through many generations, it inevitably got lost in translation. All that remained were the misunderstandings and misinterpretations of the words.

I got really interested in learning about the essential wisdom that came out of the original studies of consciousness. At the same time, I began to see that so many of the problems in the world have to do with human consciousness, either because of human attitudes, decisions, values, or what we think is important. Because we're so caught up in our beliefs about what should happen based on our needs for security and control, we never actually deal with the problems.

It seemed to me that almost everything comes back to human consciousness in one way or another, and yet it's the one thing we never look at. We always look at how to solve problems "out there" rather than wondering why we created them in the first place.

That was my motivation to pursue this calling. I came back from India eager to explore the essence of spirituality and share it as widely as possible. This has been my life's work. I've gone through many phases since then, but the underlying motivation remains unchanged. My work is all about the exploration of consciousness so that I can distill the essential spiritual teachings and disseminate these teachings in contemporary terms.

Accelerated Consciousness

Evolution has been accelerating from day one, from the moment the universe was born. Life is continuously speeding up. We can see this with how busy our lives have become. We often feel the need for new software, cell phones, or whatever it is, every six months, because things are continually moving faster.

It's not just a twenty-first century phenomenon. It's something that has been happening throughout the history of evolution and it's going to continue. It's going to be even faster in the future. There's no stopping it. I see a future where things happen faster and faster in all areas of life. We can see it most distinctly in science and technology. This fascinates me.

How many of us could have imagined the internet twenty years ago? The internet existed in the early '80s, but the World Wide Web began only twenty years ago. Nobody could have predicted that it would be about gaming, online shopping, videos, and listening to music from the cloud. Nobody saw any of this coming.

Here we are twenty years later and we simply take it for granted. Given how things are accelerating, I don't think any of us have any idea where we'll be in another ten years. We simply can't see that far into the future. So we're moving faster and faster into a world which is going to look fantastical compared to the world today. That's how the whole scientific, technological acceleration is playing out.

On the flip side, we're experiencing the repercussions of our technological acceleration with dramatic effects on the environment. There's also the accelerated explosive growth of the human population due to medical advancements. The most concerning acceleration is that of consumption of energy—particularly fossil fuels. This is accelerating the rate of carbon dioxide being discharged into the atmosphere, which in turn is accelerating the rate at which the planet is warming. We're seeing the dramatic side effects of this all around the globe.

You can say that almost every problem we're facing in the environment today is due, in one way or another, to the acceleration of technology. On its own, the planet could cope with and absorb a moderate production of CO_2. But we're now producing CO_2 and other waste products thousands of times faster than the planet can absorb.

So the technological acceleration is also behind the crisis we're facing. I think a lot of people are aware of the acceleration of technology and are excited about where it's taking us, but they're blind to the fact that we are also accelerating into catastrophe because of it.

There's a third acceleration happening, and that is the acceleration in consciousness. Many of us are waking up to who we really are.

The acceleration of consciousness started taking off in the '60s. Yoga used to be weird, but by the '80s it was completely acceptable. In fact, in the '70s I was teaching meditation in corporations, but the corporations didn't want anybody to know about it because they feared what the press would do to them.

But now it's grown so much that companies like Google, Yahoo!, and PayPal proudly speak about their on-site meditation classes for employees. There are now over thirteen million people in the US practicing yoga. These days, most cities and even small towns have bookstores devoted to spiritual development. This rapid acceleration in consciousness really fascinates me.

I think one of the reasons we are in this crisis, aside from all of this acceleration, is human consciousness. We've been stuck in a shortsighted, materialistic, self-centered mode of seeing the world for so long. Spiritual growth is about freeing ourselves from that self-centeredness and functioning in alignment with the whole—where we remember that we're not separate from the world. That is the shift in consciousness that we need to solve our problems in today's world.

So we have these three accelerating trends coming together: the acceleration in science and technology, the acceleration toward catastrophe because of the unbridled use of technology, and the awakening of consciousness that can free us from it all.

It's all quite exciting and fascinating. We have never been in this situation on the planet before. We've never had such powerful technology. We've never been in such a state of crisis, and we've never had the potential for so much awakening. What would the world look like if we had people making decisions who were awake, free from fear, and had love and wisdom in their hearts?

I have no idea how it's going to play out, but we are moving into the most uncertain, fascinating, and challenging times ever to have existed.

Recharging and Reconnecting

I hear many people saying things like, "Everything is going to be okay. I have faith that it's all going to turn out fine." This is a dangerous form of denial that pushes down our underlying despair. We need to allow our despair in. Many psychological teachings tell us that when we repress our feelings, they don't go away. They only control us more. In fact, it was Carl Jung who said, "What you resist persists," meaning that what we suppress in our consciousness controls us. That's why so many psychological models encourage people to get in touch with shadow feelings such as despair or fear. Experiencing these feelings more fully is the only way to gain freedom from them. It doesn't mean that they go away, but by allowing them into our consciousness, they're no longer in charge.

Whatever I'm experiencing, whether it's despair, grief, or something else, I bring myself back to my essence. That way, I'm more aware of what's really happening. My meditation practice is what brings me back.

It reminds me that I am not my thoughts or my feelings. Instead, I'm the observer of it all.

It's easy to get caught up in the stories, but when I'm the observer of my stories, I'm in my essence. When I return to my essence, there is no sense of right or wrong. There's only a sense of peaceful being-ness that comes from observing.

The thinking mind is what traps us in our stories. It always wants control of the outcome. It creates the different moods, emotions, fears, and hopes that make life painful. When we return to our essence, we unplug from the stories. Our essence is always at peace. It gives us that sense of lightness, joy, and life. We know that, no matter what, we're okay when we're connected to essence. That doesn't necessarily mean that everything is okay in the world, because there are lots of things we need to do to help this world along, to help other people, and to help ourselves. It also doesn't necessarily mean that the *situation* is okay. But there's a deep sense of okayness in our being that changes things. When we can function from that sense of okayness and peace, then we're in a better position to understand what needs to be done in the world and in our own lives.

My meditation practice happens moment by moment. I like to sit each morning with my tea and meditate so that I reconnect with the sense of being-ness that I've mentioned. But I don't do it in a formal setting. For me, meditation is continuous. Whenever I feel off-center, I can return to my essence in a moment. I have what I call "micro meditations" where I pause and stop whenever I notice myself caught up in a story or thought system. When I realize that I've lost touch with myself, I bring myself back to center in that moment of conscious awareness.

I also love to take long periods of silence, usually up to ten days on retreat. It often takes a few days to settle down from the fatigue that emerges. Most people I know have similar experiences. We often think we're fine because we don't feel tired. But when we stop, we realize how tired we actually are because of the busy world we live in. I'm no exception. After a few days, there's such clarity. On the other side, my mind is so much clearer and I realize how dull my normal day-to-day consciousness is in comparison.

I would say that almost everything I've learned about the way consciousness functions comes from sitting in silent retreats and watching the mind. It's my personal fascination.

Hope for a Better World

People have many different ideas about where we went wrong. I don't think we ever went wrong. I think that this is what needs to happen. Crisis is inevitable in order for us to realize that something significant must change in our consciousness.

I have great hope for what people can become and how they can change. I'm also excited about the rate at which consciousness is awakening. We're a long way from a world where everybody is fully awake. We may never get to that stage, but the fact that things are moving in that direction gives me hope.

I look at the changes that have happened in our culture over the last forty years—our attitude is so different now. I look at the kids today and see how so many of them are caught up in the material world. But there are also many kids who are aware, wise, and caring in ways that many of us weren't forty years ago.

It gives me incredible hope to see the way things are changing. Not because I'm forty years older, wiser, and more awake. Our whole culture is forty years older, wiser, and more awake. We're moving together in this. Everything is accelerating and we don't even notice because we're too focused on what's going wrong.

When I first became interested in consciousness and awakening, I was reading Indian philosophy and it seemed to be a lot of work. If we were dedicated to meditation, to all the practices, and read all the texts, then maybe enlightenment would arrive in this lifetime. What gives me the greatest hope is how we now have a clearer understanding of what awakening of consciousness means. As it gets clearer, it also gets simpler.

This fascinates me.

Over the years, the world has become smaller. We're experiencing an incredible global phenomenon that has never happened in human history. We've never had the global technologies of communication, telephone, television, radio, and internet that we do now. When there was a spiritual teacher in the past, that teacher influenced the local community and it may have spread somewhat from there.

Today, there isn't one single spiritual teacher. There are thousands. We could say there are millions, because we're all teachers for one another. We are all learning from each other, whether it's the way we share things in our family, in our workplace, with our writing, or whatever we do that is unique for us. We're all sharing and learning from each other all the time.

Whenever there is mutual learning, acceleration is fueled. It's positive feedback. As we learn from each other, the process of awakening accelerates. It's no longer about achieving an incredible state of higher consciousness where everything changes. It's more about recognizing how to step out of an ego-centered mode of consciousness and returning to a state of inner freedom—or self-liberation. This means that we're liberated from the machinations and concerns of the ego mind so we can return to our true selves.

We no longer have to go to India or Tibet to find spiritual teachers. I think there are very wise, awakened, fully liberated teachers among us, and they're showing up more than ever. It's like we're collectively honing in on that essential spiritual wisdom.

I was giving a talk a while back and at the end of the talk, somebody stood up and asked me, "What is it you're saying that is different from what everybody else is saying?" My response was, "Nothing, because if I'm saying anything different, I'm out of alignment."

So when we're all saying the same thing and we're all pointing to the same thing, it gets simpler and easier. This is a wonderful thing for facilitating great transformation.

If You Had a Magic Wand …

I would create a world in which our thinking is no longer dominated by the needs of a separate self driven by worry and fear.

The separate self, or the ego, is useful if there's a physical need or danger that needs to be addressed. That's when we need to move into a mode of consciousness that looks after our individual organism.

In our culture, we hardly ever need to be in that mode—sometimes, but not often. Yet we're in that mode most of the time, worrying about our safety, our needs, what others think of us, and so on. That's the mentality of the separate self. That's what drives our culture into calamity and causes so many of the problems we're facing socially, environmentally, and politically.

So I would like to see a world where we were no longer controlled by that way of thinking. When we're not controlled by that way of thinking, we let go of fear and we return to love, wisdom, caring, and respect. I would like to see a world where we are all in touch with our own essence. We would intrinsically be at peace with ourselves. We would still be doers in the world, but we'd do what was needed to make the world function in alignment with truth. We would be called to action by the needs of the situation rather than by the needs of our separate self. Our actions would then be from a context of love and caring rather than fear and concern.

To learn more about Peter's work, visit his website at peterrussell.com.

SEVEN

Jenny Brown

Remembering the Forgotten Ones

"How wonderful it is that nobody need wait a single moment before start-ing to improve the world."

– ANNE FRANK

"I had no idea that showing leg would draw this much attention. If I could chop off another body part for the animals, I would."

This was my introduction to Jenny Brown, cofounder of the Wood-stock Farm Animal Sanctuary in Upstate New York. I was in love.

You may be wondering, who is this woman who lops off body parts for the animals? Let me assure you, it's not what you may be thinking. Jenny's story is not one of self-mutilation, but one of awakening.

Raised in Kentucky by her Southern Baptist mother, Jenny grew up with the typical childhood zest for life. Like most kids, she loved to move. Running, swimming, dancing, and gymnastics were the childhood ac-tivities that filled her soul. Life took an unexpected turn, however, when at the tender age of ten she was diagnosed with bone cancer in her leg. Despite aggressive chemotherapy, the cancer refused to leave. The only medical option was amputation.

Devastated by the loss of her leg and weakened by chemotherapy, Jenny became increasingly frustrated with her condition: sick, bald, and unable to do the things that normal kids do. Her loneliness inspired the adoption of a kitten named Boogie. For eighteen years, Boogie would be Jenny's steady companion—and one of her greatest teachers. The depth of their relationship provoked an awareness that altered Jenny's world—

the awareness that animals are intelligent and loving beings with personalities as unique as the rest of us. Her life would never be the same.

Jenny Brown's life exemplifies the powerful combination of passion
and compassion. Her sassy, no BS fire fuels the infinite depths of so-
licitude for the forgotten beings in our world. When I read her book,
The Lucky Ones: My Passionate Fight for Farm Animals, I knew we had
to meet.

The Toronto Veg Food Fest is an annual celebration of love, compassion, and joy. It's also a hub for inspiring speakers in the plant-based
movement. Jenny would be speaking at the 2013 event, and I planned to
be there.

I'll be the first to admit that I am not a morning person. My childhood years of 5 a.m. swim practices left a scar that remains to this day.
It takes a Herculean effort to rouse me from sleep before nature intends.
When there is reason to haul my butt out of bed at an unpleasant hour,
however, I'm "up and at 'em" with relative ease. Jenny Brown gave me
reason to rise.

It was five-solid-hour drive from Ottawa, my then-hometown, to Toronto. Jenny's talk was scheduled for noon. Basic math indicated an early
start to the day. There were cats to feed and chores to complete before departure could be considered. The alarm would be set for ... you guessed
it, 5 a.m. Groan.

After tackling torrential rain, construction work, traffic, and big city
parking, my partner and I arrived at Jenny's talk with moments to spare.

As we settled into our seats, Jenny made her way to the podium. She
approached center stage, paused, and rolled up her right pant leg to reveal a partial prosthetic leg. She proceeded to tell the audience how only
two years into the creation of the sanctuary, the story of her leg hit the
New York Times. But the story wasn't just about her leg. It was also about
Albie's leg. Albie is a sanctuary resident who lost part of his leg due to an
injury suffered at a Brooklyn slaughterhouse. Albie is a goat. In a world
that nullifies the worth of animals, Albie was considered an unusual

candidate for a prosthesis. The sanctuary/amputee thread uniting Jenny and Albie prompted the *Times* to write a heartwarming article that led to a flood of donations, worldwide media attention, and calls from eager literary agents.

She concluded her story with the comment that begins this written introduction: "I had no idea that showing leg would draw this much attention. If I could chop off another body part for the animals, I would."

Jenny's Veg Fest talk enlightened, entertained, and warmed the heart. I was inspired.

A book signing followed her talk. I stood in the wings, patiently waiting for the crowd to clear. When the opportune moment arrived, I pounced. I could barely contain myself. I enthusiastically explained my mission and invited her to join this project of passion, purpose, and compassion. Even though we'd just met, I felt like we'd known each other for years—soul sisters.

Since that pivotal day, we've become wonderful friends. I've delighted in visiting the sanctuary and spending intimate time with Jenny and her husband, Doug Abel, the sanctuary's cofounder. I've also had the pleasure of a volunteer afternoon helping out with the cows and goats. And yes, Albie was right there with me.

Jenny's love for animals and her passion for creating positive change are extraordinary. There are no limits to the depths of her compassion. Just as Boogie was the catalyst for altering Jenny's perception of animals, Jenny is now a catalyst for global change, altering the way the world perceives farm animals—the forgotten ones ... and the lucky ones.

***

Jenny's Story

Unplugging: Path to Purpose

I always considered myself an animal lover. I think we all do when we're young. My mother and I lived with my grandparents and I wasn't allowed to have animals, but I always wanted a dog, a cat, a bunny, or a furry somebody when I was growing up.

When I got the news that I had cancer at ten years of age, I played up the cancer card with my mother. I figured that because I had cancer, I was now entitled to an animal companion. That's when Boogie entered my life.

When I wasn't in the hospital, I spent a lot of time at home. I was too sick to go to school, so I was quite lonely. My sister and friends would be at school, and my mother would be sleeping during the day after working the nursing night shift. My constant companion was Boogie. She lived with me for eighteen very formative years. It was my relationship with Boogie that catalyzed a greater appreciation for animals. Prior to that I never questioned the indoctrination that separated me from animals—that separates all of us from animals. Collectively, we just don't make the connections. A cow is called steak, beef, or hamburger. We use other words to dissociate from animals. We don't tell it like it is, that we are eating flesh from a murdered cow. We dissociate in this way for all farm animals.

I also grew up in an extremely religious household. This took the indoctrination even further. There are so many religions that impose the obsolete belief that humans are the only ones with souls. That was always perplexing for me. It didn't make any sense. It seemed like an unfair privilege that proclaimed superiority. It degrades animals so that they're nothing but soulless objects created exclusively for human use. I also questioned the whole idea of dominion over animals. I remember hearing that word as a child, and I thought it meant we were supposed to protect animals and give them good lives.

As I grew older, I became disillusioned with it all. My relationship with Boogie helped me see so much more. She was like a good friend, a friend who had emotional responses like a human friend. A friend who knew when I was upset. I went through almost three years of chemotherapy and several surgeries. It was really tough. I had many moments of feeling sad, alienated, and angry. No matter what I was feeling, Boogie would crawl up on my lap to be with me. That was my first time in a relationship with an animal.

When I entered college, my worldview expanded even more. During college orientation week, I picked up a bunch of literature at a table run by an animal rights group at the school. I had never been exposed to this information. It spoke of how animals were used for entertainment, research, fur, and food.

I was eighteen years old and went vegetarian immediately. This was the first phase of my enlightenment, and I was angry at the world. I couldn't believe how this culture was (and still is) built on nothing but lies. My friends and family didn't understand and had no empathy for the truths I was telling them. They went into denial. It was a very trying time. I felt alienated yet again. Nobody wanted to know the truth. They preferred to stay asleep. This prompted me to question everything. I questioned the government and wondered why there was no transparency. I questioned democracy. I wondered why we weren't talking about this in schools. I became increasingly disillusioned with society.

Reading about all of the hidden truths inspired me to take action. I got involved in circus protests. I distributed vegetarian literature to everybody I knew, and I wore T-shirts with animal rights messages plastered across my chest. I ranted about our moral imperative to take animals off our plates and rid ourselves of products tested on animals. I lived with a depth of anger and frustration that consumed me. I distanced myself from friends who wouldn't listen.

Of course these methods were not very productive. Being confrontational and alienating only made things worse. I was so upset with the lies that had been normalized that it filled me with despair. My outlet was my rage.

I realized that this strategy was causing a greater divide, so I learned more effective ways to share the information. Some people are responsive to videos; others respond more to experiential stories. One of the more powerful stories I tell sanctuary visitors is about how mother cows cry for days and days when their newborn babies are taken away by the dairy industry.

Stories like these plant seeds for people. In today's world, we're so disconnected from how animals live and die. We still believe the bucolic images of happy animals grazing in grassy fields, pigs wallowing in mud, and mother hens nurturing their chicks. Sadly, this isn't even close to reality.

No egg farmer allows their chickens to sit on and hatch their own eggs, because they don't want the roosters. So 99.99% of chickens in this country never meet their mothers. They're hatched in massive hatcheries where the males are either ground up alive or suffocated in giant garbage bags because they serve no purpose for the egg industry.

I took a public speaking class in my freshman year of college, and we were to focus on one subject. I chose animal rights. It was a brilliant strategy because it was a subject that I really cared about. I was able to educate myself so that I could talk about it in a persuasive manner. My relationship with Boogie was the catalyst for all of this.

I was studying film at Columbia College in Chicago and landed freelance jobs in film and television pretty quickly after graduation. During that time I met a woman from People for the Ethical Treatment of Animals (PETA) and documented a fur protest that she had organized. We became fast friends. I did a couple of undercover animal rights activist things with her, and this led to some undercover work for PETA. That was in the early '90s. It had a profound impact on me that continues to this day.

After working in film and television for a decade in a myriad of positions, I worked my way up the chain. I was producing and directing television segments and eventually an entire film for the Discovery Channel. During that time, I learned about an organization called Farm Sanctuary. Their focus was specifically on food production animals. There's so much suffering and cruelty inflicted by humans on all animals, but the worst cruelty of all is perpetrated on farm animals. Ninety-eight percent of the animal cruelty on this planet is imposed on farm animals. In the United States alone, ten billion farm animals are killed annually, and fifty-six billion are killed worldwide every year. These numbers don't even count the number of aquatic animals killed. When we include aquatic animals, the numbers skyrocket into the trillions. The statistics are staggering.

When I discovered these horrifying facts, I began to grasp the absolute magnitude of animal suffering. I was heavily influenced by the work of Farm Sanctuary and became friends with the founders. I told them about the undercover work that I'd done for PETA and mentioned that I'd be more than willing to help them anytime. I'm a pretty bold gal who's willing to take risks.

Next thing I knew, they flew me to Texas for a week to document downed animals. I had some experience with rigging undercover video equipment. I figured out how to rig a small DV cam that mounted to the bottom of a purse with a lens hole. I used this method to secretly document animals known as "downers," which are those too weak or sick to stand up and walk onto a slaughter-bound truck without assistance. At the live-animal auctions and stockyards where I was filming, there's typically a big indoor area where terrified animals are pushed into an auction ring with an electric prod. The men who work there continually prod the animals so that buyers can see their bodily condition. There were typically young heifers, veal calves, dairy cows, and dairy goats.

Outside the ring, the downed animals would wait in big holding pens without shade or water. The animals would bake in the heat. They were living among animals that had died from the heat or dehydration. The non-ambulatory animals would sometimes languish for days without access to water, food, or much-needed veterinary care until they could be loaded onto the trucks in the most horrifying, despicable ways. It's what nightmares are made of: cows dragged with chains, repeatedly electrically prodded, hoisted by a single leg into the air with audible sounds of bones and hips breaking—all so they would arrive at the slaughterhouses alive so they could then be murdered for human consumption.

During the week-long trip where I traveled from auction to auction, I was able to get some powerful footage that made it to congressional hearings in efforts to pass the Downed Animal Protection Act—a campaign that Farm Sanctuary had been working on for years.

As someone who had not yet become vegan, I was beginning to see the light. The first thing I saw was a truckload of skinny little veal calves being unloaded into holding pens. I began to make the connection that veal wouldn't exist if it wasn't for the dairy industry. That realization hit me like a ton of bricks. There were about thirty little calves coming off this truck, some with umbilical cords, and some still wet from birth fluids, having been born that day. Witnessing these calves being unloaded, dragged by their ears, dragged by a leg, treated as inanimate objects, while the workers just chewed their tobacco and laughed with each other, made me sick. They were treating these innocent little beings like sacks of potatoes. The calves would desperately try to suckle the fingers of their abusers in an effort to seek comfort.

I wanted to jump out of my skin and cause some damage, but I had to keep my poker face on to get the undercover footage needed to help them. The reality of all this cruelty hit me like a ton of bricks. Where were their mamas? I realized that their mamas were being forced to be milked for the cheese I didn't want to give up, and their babies were nothing but the tragic byproducts.

That's when it really hit me. I wanted everyone to witness the gut-wrenching pain of a calf being torn away from its mother. I wanted everyone to hear the heartbreaking bellows of despair as mothers and calves were separated. It was harrowing. All for the trivial pleasure of my taste buds and a deeply-rooted belief system that normalized the consumption of the breast milk of another species under the guise of "health." This couldn't be further from the truth.

In that week I began to truly understand the injustice. I saw how these animals were treated. I saw animals with cancerous eyes and cows being forced to stand and walk with broken legs and hips. These animals exist only to be exploited by, controlled by, abused by, and killed by humans for nothing but profit and to feed the collective addiction to meat and dairy. It felt like I was on another planet. Nobody was feeling anything for these innocent beings—except me. It was surreal.

Each day after filming, I went back to my hotel room and cried. It was a week that transformed me. It also scarred me for life. Being around those animals made me realize that they're no different from cats and dogs. They're no different emotionally or intellectually. Their suffering was as real as it is for all of us.

We're such a selfish culture not to consider them. They're longing for life, they're longing to be with their loved ones, and they're longing to be free from pain, exploitation, and a premature death. We've lost our way. Until we realize that all of this violence happens because of our excuses, our greed, and our selfishness, nothing will change. To me this is the biggest social justice issue of our time.

Fortunately, we're making great strides and the number of caring people is growing. Studies show that when 10 percent of the population grabs onto an idea, the rest of society opens up to that idea. People come to our sanctuary and tell us how meeting the animals transforms their lives. I feel ecstatic when I hear of the profound changes happening because people have finally made the connection.

It's also beautiful to witness the healing of the animals we rescue who have come from abuse, neglect, and abandonment. Their spirits and bodies are so broken, but we provide a safe, loving, and nurturing place for them to heal physically and emotionally. There's no greater joy for me. I can't imagine ever doing anything else for any amount of money.

Recharging with Hope

After witnessing so much cruelty toward animals, it's easy to fall into despair. What recharges my soul is how so many people who visit the Woodstock Farm Animal Sanctuary leave here changed, simply from having the opportunity to meet the animals, hear their stories, and see them for the unique individuals that they are. This is a real eye-opener for people. When they meet these animals in a setting where they're loved, where they're viewed as friends, where they have names and not numbers, and where their personalities shine so that real connections can be made—that's how great transformation happens. It's a really powerful form of activism where the culturally conditioned short circuit between the brain and the heart is instantly repaired.

When I lead sanctuary tours, I speak about how we can't base compassion on perceived intelligence. People understand what I mean once they meet the animals. They realize that every animal thinks, feels, and suffers just like we do. This is really transformative. I've heard things like, "My eyes have been opened and my mouth is shut to eating animals," or "We left your sanctuary and my family and I haven't eaten any animal products since." When I hear things like this, I know that we're fulfilling our purpose of opening hearts and minds to greater compassion.

There's growing concern and awareness about our industrialized food system, and people are waking up. We can't go anywhere without seeing news articles about the wrongs of factory farming, the mistreatment of animals, and the industrialization of animals in the food system—not to mention the negative effects on our health and the world in which we live.

We're not there yet in terms of the philosophical debate about why we have any right to eat these animals in the first place. But for those of us who fight for animal rights and are working toward elevating consciousness, we live in an age where eating meat is beginning to take on the same stigma as smoking. A growing number of people are realizing that perhaps animals are here *with us* and not *for* us.

We can change the way we think. By doing that, we can change the world. That's when we can heal the wrongs we've committed toward other beings, as well as toward ourselves.

We could also feed the world if we converted the food we grow for animals into food for people instead. As Colleen Patrick-Goudreau says, we can eliminate the "middle animal" and eat plants directly, rather than eating them through the flesh of animals. We could feed billions of people with this change alone.

There are more and more people who are living proof that we can live happy and healthy lives without causing harm to others. So why wouldn't we eliminate the violence from our diets and our lives? With that one powerful choice, we can all feel a deeper connection to ourselves and to all of life. I know I certainly do!

If You Had a Magic Wand …

I would create a world where we regarded all animals—human and nonhuman—as equals, where we treated each other with compassion and kindness. These would be the guiding principles in our society.

Maybe we'd have some devices that allowed us to share our knowledge and connect with people across the world. But as Joni Mitchell sang, "We've got to get ourselves back to the garden," referring to the Garden of Eden. We need to live more natural lives—connected to the land and to each other. In my world we'd make time for our families and grow our own food. We'd open our doors to other living beings and help each other out as good stewards of the land.

I want that magic wand. If you know where I can get one, I'm in the market for one of those.

Learn more about Jenny's work at woodstocksanctuary.org.

EIGHT

Roz Savage

An Inspired Life of Courage, Happiness, and Meaning

"What would life be if we had no courage to attempt anything?"

– Vincent Van Gogh

Imagine a world where a powerful beam of higher consciousness alters the minds of humanity. This beam of higher consciousness ignites the pure potential of love, unity, and compassion previously dormant in the hearts of the masses.

Citizens around the globe rouse from the slumber caused by centuries of separation. Conformity, consumption, judgment, fear, selfishness, apathy, and indifference are replaced by authentic expression, simplicity, acceptance, love, selflessness, passion, and inspiration. Kindness and community are restored.

A deep love for the natural world returns to the hearts of the collective. The appalling planetary mess created by a once-crude species becomes the greatest priority for all to resolve—together—united in solidarity with the singular mission of healing planet earth.

Imagine …

Okay, take a deep breath and return to reality.

There hasn't been a powerful beam of higher consciousness to alter the minds of humanity. Separation is still the prevailing mindset. And nobody is coming to save us. But what if your thoughts, choices, behaviors, and actions have a greater impact on planetary healing than you could possibly imagine? What if the powerful beam of higher consciousness already exists within your heart, patiently waiting to be activated? What would the world be like if we collectively activated this higher potential?

When our actions align with the truth of our essential nature, we become the change that the world needs. Individual actions multiplied by many have the very real potential to heal this planet. We often forget how powerful we can be, and all it takes is the activation of the truth that never leaves our hearts.

This is the story of Roz Savage, a former British management consultant snapped out of her materialistic ways into the inspiring role of ocean adventurer and passionate environmental advocate.

It was prompted by a simple personal development exercise that involved writing two versions of an obituary. Version one would be the obituary of her dreams. Version two reflected the direction she was actually heading in.

Obituary one revealed the life of an adventurer, a risk-taker, a woman who lived out loud guided by her passionate soul. Obituary two revealed a conventional life of normalcy trapped within the confines of perceived safety. The differences were startling. She knew that something had to change.

And so the adventure began. Roz embarked on a journey of personal transformation. She courageously ventured into the unknown, aligning her life with the obituary she craved.

She discovered the importance of a life congruent with her core values. She realized an inner, ardent desire to better the world. And she discovered her authentic Self along the way.

Roz Savage became the first woman to row solo across three oceans: the Atlantic, the Pacific, and the Indian. She used her ocean-rowing adventures to engage critical thought and inspire action on the most pressing environmental issues in the world today.

Confined to a twenty-three-foot rowboat, Roz has rowed over fifteen thousand miles, spent over five hundred days of her life at sea, and taken more than five million oar strokes.

She capsized three times in a twenty-four-hour period, faced death by dehydration, encountered endless sea life, and was graced with the breathtaking beauty of untarnished sunrises, sunsets, and star-filled skies.

What prompted her to do this? In her own words, "There came a time when my convictions became more important than my comfort."

The powerful beam of higher consciousness was activated and the authentic Roz Savage emerged, an inspiring adventurer and fierce defender of planet Earth.

As she states on her website:

> I believe that if you don't keep pushing the boundaries, keep expanding your comfort zone, your comfort zone actually gets smaller and smaller, until you're shrink-wrapped in such a tiny comfort zone that you can't move, you can't achieve anything, you can't grow. And so I keep pushing, keep developing, keep evolving. I keep showing what an ordinary person can do when they put their heart, mind and soul into it. I am proving that anybody can achieve the extraordinary, if only they have enough guts and determination and sheer bloody-mindedness to see it through.

Roz Savage is a courageous status quo crusher whose adventures inspire within us the best of what it means to be human.

***

Roz's Story

Unplugging: Path to Purpose

I grew up the daughter of Methodist preachers with very little money. On a trip to California when I was sixteen, I saw the lifestyle in San Diego and said, "Wow! I want this! I'm tired of being poor." I was lucky enough to be born in the right country at the right time, where I could get a good education free of charge. I went to Oxford University and got a law degree.

I graduated in 1989. It was a time when everyone wanted to be an investment banker or a management consultant. I wanted that, too. I was so materialistic. I followed the crowd into the City of London and thought it was exactly what I wanted. I felt like I was on track. I got the big house, all the stuff. It was great.

Eleven years later, I realized that that life wasn't making me happy. I thought there was something wrong with me. All the people I worked with seemed perfectly happy with their long hours, high pay, and materialistic lifestyle. But I felt that there was something missing. I turned to self-help books, and one of the books prompted me to write two versions of my own obituary—the one I wanted and the one that I was heading for.

What I wanted was to be a fearless, intrepid person living according to my values with great faith and confidence in life. The person I was at that time was constrained by self-limiting beliefs. I lived by the demon words, "must," "should," and "ought." I also believed that I needed a certain amount of money to be happy.

The obituary exercise blew the whistle on my whole life. I realized that I'd been climbing the ladder of success, but I had put it up against the wrong building.

I wish I could say that I went into the office and told my boss what to do with his job. But I wasn't that courageous. I was still constrained by societal norms. So I put the two obituaries in a drawer and tried to forget about them.

But once you know something, you can't pretend you don't know. From that moment on, the writing was on the wall. I knew I was living a sham, but it still took a couple of years before I reached a low point that forced me to break out of my box. I had to break through all of the self-limiting beliefs and the social norms that were holding me in that box.

Once I made the decision to change my life, things happened quickly. In a fairly short space of time, I quit my job, and although I'm not particularly proud of this, I left my husband. I left behind everything that represented security. I was in a sort of free fall, which might sound terrifying, but in fact it was incredibly liberating. Up to that point, I'd been cursed by my own success. I was good at school, I got good grades, and I jumped through all the hoops. When you're in that position, failure becomes scary because you've never really failed at anything.

Many people regarded what I'd done as failure. But I realized that the world kept turning, the sun kept rising, I kept breathing, and a thunderbolt from heaven didn't strike me dead. I said to myself, "Wow! I've done scary things and survived. If I can do these scary things, what else can I do?"

Suddenly a whole world of possibility opened up in front of me. It was so exciting. I was absolutely in love with life and the world. I could see the beauty in a flower. I felt the warmth of the sunshine on my face. I loved not going into an office for twelve-hour work days. It was almost like I was reborn. It sounds kind of cheesy, but it really felt like that. I wondered why I hadn't figured this out earlier.

I was so grateful for everything. The more grateful I was, the happier I became. I was very fortunate in those nervous early days that I had an amazing selection of people in my life. I felt like the universe was reassuring me that I was on the right path. It was a very spiritual and magical time for me.

I was very inspired by a book called *Cave in the Snow* by a British woman who became a Buddhist nun. She went on to live in a cave in Tibet for twelve years.

I decided that I was going to have my own little cave in the snow. I went off to a cottage in Ireland and started reading books about many things. Various themes emerged. One of the themes was our ongoing environmental challenges. I was reading a book about the Hopi tribe of North America. Like many indigenous people, they understand on a very deep level that we need to have a symbiotic relationship with the earth. It must be a give-and-take relationship between ourselves and nature. Our current model of consumption is not sustainable.

I was shocked. I had what I believed was a high-quality Western education, yet nobody had pointed out this fundamental fact. I felt ashamed of my former materialism. It was a real epiphany for me.

I think it was because my parents were both Methodist preachers that I absorbed their attitude about having a higher calling in life—that we should have a purpose, a legacy, a message, a mission, and a reason for our existence on this planet.

So when I read that book, I found my calling. I knew that I had to tell people about this. At the same time, I was reading *Conversations with God* by Neale Donald Walsch. It encouraged readers to be the grandest version of the greatest vision they've ever had for themselves. That phrase struck home with me. Having come from a humble, very modest British family, this phrase gave me permission to dream big and to actually believe that I had something important to say.

There were many ideas buzzing through my mind. A few months after I returned from Ireland, I met a man who had rowed across the Atlantic Ocean with his mother. I really admired adventurers. I loved reading books about people who climbed mountains or sailed around the world. I never thought I could be one of them. I thought that a big bushy beard was required. So after hearing that someone's *mom* rowed across an ocean, I thought, "I know how to row. I rowed at Oxford. That's something I can do. I can row across oceans to raise environmental awareness."

It sounds like a bizarre confluence of ideas, but it actually made perfect sense to me. It was my calling. It struck me like a thunderbolt when I was driving along in my camper van one day. It was like some great Intelligence provided the answer to the burning question about what I would do with the rest of my life.

Action for a Better World

On one level, the ocean rowing was epic. But the mental images that flicker through my mind are remarkably mundane. Yes, I was alone in a twenty-three-foot rowboat, sometimes in big waves and high winds, and at night with no support boat. There were times when it was deeply scary.

But a lot of what I remember is the mundane stuff like cooking meals, my bathing routine, and the sheer tedium of rowing for twelve hours a day without driving myself crazy.

What I love about ocean rowing is how it taught me to be humble in the face of Mother Nature's power. My journey was never about the world records. It was about helping our planet.

On dry land we tend to be overly confident about our ability to control Mother Nature. We only have to look at the ways in which we've succeeded in controlling aspects of her with our pesticides, herbicides, and the way we've killed off so many perceived competitors for food. The way that we've terraformed, drilled, and mined—we've really exploited nature.

When you're out on the ocean alone in a storm, one thousand miles from land, feeling absolutely petrified, you're very conscious about who's running this show. I would love to get some of our big industrialists out there, alone in a twenty-three-foot rowboat for a few months, to see how they feel about the world when they come back.

My biggest mission exceeds that of my role as an environmental advocate. It's about advocating for how we can all live life to our highest potential. When we live from that perspective, we naturally make kinder, more informed choices.

We don't have to row across oceans to do something really special in the world. In fact, rowing is largely irrelevant. It's a metaphor. It was my way of getting people's attention for the important things I had to say.

I've become so aware of the vital importance of the blue parts of this planet. Seventy percent of this planet is covered in ocean, and yet for most of us, the ocean is out of sight and out of mind. For far too long we've regarded it as a cross between a sewer and a garbage dump. Since the advent of plastic, which really only went into mass production about fifty years ago, we've run into big trouble. We use it for everything. It's so ubiquitous.

When I was rowing from San Francisco to Hawaii on the first stage of the Pacific, I rowed around the outskirts of the North Pacific garbage patch. Depending on who you listen to, it's the size of Texas, five times the size of Texas, or the size of the whole continental US. Regardless, it's massive. It's one of the many rotating ocean gyres where plastic accumulates. On the outskirts of the North Pacific garbage patch, scientists are finding six times as much plastic as plankton. In the middle of the garbage patch, there's forty times more plastic than plankton. That's just at the surface, because different plastics have different buoyancies.

It's pretty appalling that in such a short space of time, we've so fundamentally altered the chemistry of the ocean. Plastic doesn't biodegrade, it photodegrades. The sunlight weakens it and breaks it into smaller pieces. This ends up being even worse, because it ends up in the food chain. It accumulates in higher levels as we go up the food chain until it ends up in the apex predator. That's us.

So it's a significant example of how we live in the ultimate closed-loop system. What goes around comes around. Now that there are over seven billion humans consuming more than ever, we can't keep pumping out plastic, pesticides, herbicides, and estrogens.

All of these things are messing up the entire planet, and they're increasingly coming back to bite us in the backside. We've put so many toxic substances into the environment that our bodies are poisoned. All of these manmade chemicals are making us sick. Pollution is not good for the health of any living being.

Many of our systems are broken. Environmentally, we really need to do things differently. We're supposed to be an intelligent species, which means we have created the technology to do a lot of amazing things. Hopefully, we can also be intelligent enough to know when to stop using technology and stop being so destructive.

I really believe that every time we choose what to buy, what to throw away, or how we travel from place to place, we're making a difference. We have the choice of what kind of difference we make. Most of the damage that we've done to the world has been the accumulation of billions of tiny individual actions day after day, year after year. We can turn it around the same way. I know it sounds like an impossible task, but we can't allow ourselves to be trapped in that mindset.

I have to remind myself that every time one of us does the right thing, we get closer to the tipping point. By doing the right thing, we then inspire others to do the right thing. We keep adding another straw onto one side of the balance. The more straws we add, the closer we get to where one of these days the scales will tip. I hold faith that one day we will have a massive outbreak of common sense.

Recharging and Reconnecting

I think we are all looking for happiness. For me, happiness and meaning go hand in hand. The things that generally make people happy are connection and community. It's about being generous and relating to people.

One of my pet peeves is the advertising industry. I think that our desire for happiness has been misappropriated by the advertising industry. They've succeeded in presenting us with images of perfection and happiness that make us feel inadequate. Once they've hooked us into unhappy, they persuade us that if we buy their stuff we'll be happy and look like a supermodel; or we'll have perfect kids or white pearly teeth. It just doesn't work that way. It may be cliché, but happiness comes from within. It's more about paring life down to the basics and not getting sidetracked by all the *stuff*.

Having been so materialistic, I love not having stuff. I've now gone to the opposite extreme and it works so much better for me. It frees up so much head space to focus on the more important things in life.

This has been a really big transformation for me. I used to run on the materialistic treadmill, and I was never happy. Because no matter how big the house, or how many beautiful things there were, there was always someone with a bigger house and more beautiful things. When we opt out of that insanity, it feels great.

Hope ... and Reality

I do have my moments of existential despair. When we care, I think it's difficult not to, but there's not much point in lying around in a depressed heap on the sofa. We've got to get out there and do something to remain optimistic. It makes me feel happy to engage with problems rather than run away from them. It gives me a tiny sense of control. One of the most stressful things in the world is to see big, scary stuff going on and not have any control over it. What helps me remain hopeful is to find something I can do that helps me feel like I'm making a difference. It might be small in the face of a very big problem, but it's something.

Of course hanging out with positive, optimistic people also really helps. I think we tend to underestimate how important it is to choose carefully who we allow into our headspace. Jim Rohn said, "You are the average of the five people you spend the most time with." Their attitudes and values are contagious. We have to choose our company carefully, and I'm very fortunate in that I know so many amazing people who support each other. When we surround ourselves with good people who also have a sense of optimism and hope, it's very powerful and motivating.

If You Had a Magic Wand ...

I would ban advertising so that we're all happy with what we've already got.

As Marianne Williamson says, "We are all beautiful, glorious beings." Why can't we just accept this and love ourselves for who we are? We are all amazing. Through self-awareness and self-acceptance, we are so much happier. I'm not exactly as I'd like to be, but I'm happy. Having gotten to know myself through all the solitary time on the ocean, I like who I am.

People are good. We're all good and I think when we understand that on a really deep level, the world will be a very different place.

For more information about Roz and her work, please visit rozsavagecoaching.com.

NINE

Rae Sikora

Sowing the Seeds of Compassion

*"The purpose of human life is to serve, and to show compassion
and the will to help others."*

– ALBERT SCHWEITZER

One of the many ways I stay grounded in faith is to surround myself
with inspirational people who care deeply about our planet, heart-driven
revolutionaries who pave the way toward a higher level of consciousness.
I'm blessed to have many such beautiful souls in my circle of compassion.

Rae Sikora is a dear friend and a well-known champion of compassionate living.

I've known Rae since 1999, a time when she was fully immersed in
her role as cofounder of the Center for Compassionate Living (now the
Institute for Humane Education), a place that profoundly changed my
life. In a single weekend workshop, I learned the transformative power of
critical thought. I discovered how our words, choices, thoughts, and actions are not without consequence. I realized how every one of us chooses our impact on the planet and all of her life systems—consciously or
unconsciously. In a mindless world of consumption, this is an empowering awakening.

To use the metaphor of the movie *The Matrix*, I've never feared the
red pill of truth. Because of this, my hunger for awakening has always
been fierce. This is what led me to the Center for Compassionate Living
so many years ago. It was a time in my life when I self-identified as a

passionate vegan environmental activist. I figured this meant that I was already living a commendable and conscious lifestyle. It wasn't until my transformative weekend with Rae that I recognized the gaps in my life where separation still existed. I was humbled.

Unlearning the life we've been taught and reclaiming the truth within is an ongoing process. As Chinese philosopher Lao Tzu once said, "The key to growth is the introduction of higher dimensions of consciousness into our awareness." In other words, once we allow ourselves to know, we can't un-know. Expanding consciousness occurs through knowledge, experience, self-reflection, and truth. Without this self-awareness, personal growth is no more than an elusive dream. As disheartening as it was to see the gaps in my life, I'm eternally grateful for the gift of this awareness. Rae Sikora was a catalyst for powerful personal transformation.

Rae is a woman who exemplifies compassion. She's a passionate world citizen with a heart so big, so open, and so giving that one cannot help but feel loved, simply from being in her presence.

Rae moves with her spirit. Although she's lived throughout the world, her roots are firmly grounded in her heart. Wherever she goes, she devotedly spreads the seeds of compassion. Rae Sikora is an embodied agent of change.

Rae and her partner Jim Corcoran share a website, Plant Peace Daily, on which they boldly declare, "We should live our lives as a message of peace every day." They also state, "Our choices as individuals are the solution to the many challenges facing the world. Our own health, all people, the environment, and other species benefit when we live in alignment with our most compassionate values."

Ultimately, as a collective, we must ask ourselves if we are ready to take action on what we can no longer ignore. Are we willing to think more critically and act more lovingly so that we show up in ways that, thanks in part to Rae's tireless efforts, sow the seeds of compassion?

We are all agents of change. We need only choose to be so.

***

Rae's Story

Unplugging: Path to Purpose

It all started for me when I was five years old. I was terrified of all animals, including humans. If I saw a dog outside, I'd run into the house and not go out —for hours. I was so fearful. My father, for better or worse, decided my childhood was not going to be about fear—definitely not fear of animals. One day he came home from the animal shelter with a small puppy. He said to me, "You're going to sit every night for an hour with this puppy on your lap until you get used to animals." I was terrified. I would sit with my back pressed against the refrigerator with this dog on my lap. I think the puppy was as scared as I was, because I wouldn't pet her. I would just cry out of fear.

I remember the moment when it all changed. I looked into the puppy's eyes and everything shifted. In those eyes, I saw a dear friend and the least threatening being I had ever locked eyes with.

That moment changed everything for me, and that little dog became my best friend. We were inseparable. We talk about gateway drugs—this was my gateway animal. Her name was Sandy. She was the gateway that connected me with all beings. Sandy became my confidante for sixteen years. She was the only one that I really trusted. Because of Sandy, I opened up to all animals—wild and domestic, it made no difference. Every animal became family. It's amazing how one little being can change a life.

After that, my awareness continued to expand. One day when I was fifteen, I was in Chicago with a friend and I'd just finished eating a hot-dog. I don't even think I chewed it. Then we walked into a leather shop and there were skins hanging everywhere—from the ceiling and on the walls. It hit me hard. I said to my friend, "Don't buy anything in here. It's dead animals." The woman behind the counter asked me a question that changed my life. She asked if I ate meat. My first thought was, "What does meat have to do with dead animals?" Then the light bulb went on and I made the connection. I turned to her and said, "No, I don't eat meat."

When we left the shop, my friend asked me why I'd lied. After all, she'd just witnessed me gulp down a hotdog. I said to her, "Because I don't anymore." From that moment on, I never ate animals. I stopped eating animal flesh, but I was still eating eggs and dairy. I was also still wearing leather. I hadn't yet made those connections.

I had no one to turn to. I didn't know the word "vegetarian." It would be a few years before I met my first vegetarian. When I finally did, I was so excited; I finally had a label that I could identify with.

My world was once again turned upside down when I was twenty years old studying at the University of Wisconsin. Wisconsin is considered America's Dairyland. I was renting a little cabin from a dairy farmer, and one day I heard an alarming sound coming from my landlord's barn. I hopped on my bike to investigate. When I arrived, I witnessed my landlord and another man loading calves onto a semitrailer. Some of the calves still had dangling umbilical cords. Some were still wet and wobbly. Some were no more than a day or two old. I asked the men what they were doing, and they explained that the male calves were being sent to a veal facility. They would be kept there for a short period of time before they were "processed." I learned then that male calves are considered useless by-products by the dairy industry.

It was crazy watching them do this. As I witnessed this horror, I heard other alarming sounds from behind the barn where the calves were being loaded. I went to see what was going on. What I saw broke my heart. The mother cows were crying in desperation to get their babies back. They kept pushing against a barbed wire fence in a pitiful attempt to get to them. There was blood on the chests of the cows as the barbed wire ripped their skin. All they wanted were their babies. It was so painful to witness. In that moment I decided to never eat dairy products again.

That expanded my world and inspired my hunger to know the truth about everything. I had to know what I was supporting. So I visited an egg facility—I wanted to see it firsthand. I was shocked to learn of the cruelty in that industry. Like the dairy farm, it was a small place, but still they got their eggs from a hatchery that killed the males.

Author's note: Commercial egg hatcheries have no use for male chicks. They are destined to die on their first day of life because they cannot produce eggs, nor do they grow large or fast enough to be raised for profitable meat. They are either thrown into oversized garbage bags and left to suffocate or they are dropped alive into a grinding machine. This is standard industry practice.

This small egg facility was not much different from a factory farm. They employed the same practice of slaughtering any birds that were not producing "enough" eggs. We often think that factory farms cause the most suffering to animals, but it's all farms. It doesn't matter how big or small they are. It doesn't matter if they call themselves organic, free-range, or industrial. If animals are being exploited for food, they are only as worthy as their body parts.

Once I saw the reality for myself, it became very clear. I would not be someone who supported it. Instead, I would share the truth with everyone I met.

Unbeknownst to me, this became my life path. I said yes to anyone who was willing to hear me speak the truth. I did this in a way that didn't create division. I didn't want to tell people that they were wrong or that they were bad. Instead, I wanted to share the reality and invite a kinder alternative. I wanted to show how we can cocreate a compassionate world. We don't have to support things that we don't believe in. I knew that the only way to sustain this work was if I could do it from love.

This has been powerful work. I used to think that one day I would be a finished product: a compassionate being totally aligned with my values. Instead, it has been an ongoing process of surprises and openings that lead me to more of the person I want to be.

Anger, Understanding, and Compassion

I had no idea that I was filled with unexpressed anger until my first meditation course in 1984. It was my first time sitting in quiet. I had never been alone with myself enough to feel what was really there. I was shocked at how much anger I carried. It was like Darth Vader emerged when I first sat down. It was really important for me to understand this, because I could then see myself in others, and I could see others in me. From then on, it was impossible to see an enemy. This realization has helped me so much in my work. It's also helped me realize the patience required to do my work in a loving way. It's not about forcing people into "different-land," it's about gently shifting awareness through critical thought.

I continually learn from others. For me, this path isn't about needing people to understand me and my choices. It's about wanting to understand their choices and where they're coming from. I ask a lot of questions, even in the most confrontational situations. I want to know. I want to understand. This natural curiosity has made the difference in my work.

For me, compassion is about connection. This is how compassion grows. If I look at another person and start blaming, then I'm creating conflict. Compassion is about being able to really connect. The definition of compassion is "to suffer with." I like to extend that definition to mean "to suffer with, to feel joy with, and to connect with." There's so much pain when we see someone as "other." It feeds the separation that has caused so many problems in today's world. Who is the other? I think that's the key to compassion. How do we define other? It doesn't have to stop with other humans. It doesn't have to stop with those of our own culture, and it certainly doesn't have to stop with animals or nature.

I think it's really powerful to be open to the possibility that each of us is an integral part of a greater whole. I know that this can be a really far-out concept for a lot of people. But think about it, I'm just a bunch of subatomic particles bumping into your subatomic particles and we're all part of a greater whole.

What we can do together is very powerful if it's based in love. It's also very powerful if it's based in hate. At some of the places I've worked, people are so angry; but I get to choose how I respond. If someone comes at me with anger or hate, I see it as an opportunity to repaint the picture. "Oh, you're coming at me with this package filled with hate. Oh, no, thank you. I'm not interested in your package. But I have one for you. Maybe you will like mine. Here's what I have for you. It's based in love and caring. What do you think of my package?" We always get to choose. We don't have to accept the fact that just because someone is coming from anger, we have to be in anger as well. It doesn't have to be that way. We can't open other people's hearts for them. We can only live our lives as an example of compassion. I think a lot of burnout comes from believing that we have the power to change people, that we can close the gap between what they know and what they act on.

We can't close the gap for people. They have to do that themselves. We can share the reality and be living examples of compassion. But we can't force people to close the gap between what they know and what they're willing to act on. It's impossible. I think the most powerful thing that we can do is keep loving them. The people we think are the least open and the least loving are the ones who need loving the most. That's a really important thing to remember in this work.

It's also important to remember that there are no lost causes. I've seen so many people who I thought were lost causes become spokespeople for other species and for the earth. It's really important to remember this when we're angry, because inside most people is a gigantic, compassionate being. The part that appears callous or cruel is actually a thin external veneer. There are no lost causes. We could all have been lost causes if our lives hadn't taken a turn for the better.

Recharging and Reconnecting

There are times when I can barely handle doing this work. On a recent trip, I witnessed some horrendous things that broke my heart—beyond broken, it felt like it damaged my heart. I witnessed things that I didn't want to share with anyone, even my partner. I couldn't come out of it. I felt like I'd been hit with a spiritual two-by-four that knocked me on my butt. I went to someone who specializes in posttraumatic stress and found out that I had something called compassion fatigue.

Compassion fatigue can happen to anyone in a helping field. It can be social workers, medical people, any people who give their lives to serving and helping others. Do this work for any length of time and there's a saturation point where compassion fatigue sets in. I'm not normally the type of person who needs to find ways to return to myself, but I developed compassion fatigue from my own negligence. I stopped doing the things that keep me grounded.

I stopped meditating, which I'd been doing since '84. I stopped eating healthily. I stopped getting regular, hard exercise. I just stopped caring for myself. I gave up on my life. I gave up on the planet. I just gave up. It took a nudge from a person who works with posttraumatic stress disorder, to say to me, "Forget everything except taking care of yourself right now."

So I stepped it up. I not only got back into meditation, I doubled it. I wanted to get my Self back and I want to show up loving. I didn't want to show up as a tired, hopeless person who couldn't function in the world. What kind of a compassionate living representative is that?

So I stepped it all up. I started swimming a mile a day. I felt like I was swimming for my life, and for all of the living beings I can only speak for if I'm healthy. Now I swim three times a week, and I hike with the dogs every day. I've woken up and got myself back. Not only am I back, but in a new way, in an even bigger, more loving, more confident way.

I felt like I was in hell when I was in that dark place. It seemed like such a negative thing at the time. Now I look at it as a positive thing. Obviously, I had to bottom out to find my way once again. I realized that neglecting myself is selfish because it takes me away from my calling and what I'm supposed to be doing in life.

We often forget that caring for ourselves equals caring for all life. We cannot be effective spokespeople for compassion if we're tired, sick, or depressed. We're no good for anyone then. We don't do the animals any good. We don't do the earth any good. We have to take care of ourselves first. This has been a real eye-opener for me, a good reminder that I have to be a healthy, strong person if I'm going to be consistent in this work and effective in how I present it.

Simplicity

I live very, very simply. I don't have fancy things. I have a home that is light-filled and I have gardens. I have a lot of time. I have the freedom of time. I get to choose what I do with my time. For me, that's more valuable than all the stuff and money in the world. It's more valuable than anything. I get to choose what I do with every minute of my day.

So I'm able to really focus in on what's important to me. I don't have the latest, coolest stuff. I'm not dressed in the latest fashions. When I go to yoga, I'm not in the coolest spandex stuff. I'm not cool. I'm a thrift store person. I've not had to worry about money, though. I trust that if I live with strong, loving intention, I'll always be provided for with everything that I need. It's a peaceful way of living.

I live on very little in terms of what I have in the bank. I believe that we need to redefine wealth in our lives. What does a rich life look like? For some reason, I know a lot of millionaires, and I can guarantee that lots of money doesn't automatically bring happiness. In fact, it often brings misery. Some of the most joyful people I know have a lot of time, and a lot of freedom, but not a lot of money. I'm one of them.

I've redefined wealth. I have such a rich life. I have my health. I have a loving family. My family relations are amazing. I have loving friends. What else can you ask for? I have a refrigerator full of organic food. I have gardens, and I feel like I'm like the wealthiest person in the world. You wouldn't see that on my bank statement, though.

If You Had a Magic Wand ...

That's pretty easy. A world where we didn't see any separation after that wand was waved. Every being would come from a place of pure love. There would be immense gratitude for the beauty of all life. From the smallest little spider to the largest elephant, all we would see is their beauty. I can see it now, living in such gratitude with everyone wanting the best for everyone else on the planet. Yeah, it's a beautiful place. If you find that wand, could you send it by overnight mail?

For more information about Rae and her work, please visit plantpeacedaily.org

TEN

Barbara Marx Hubbard

Radical Evolutionary New Thought for a Brave New World

"It is our duty as men and women to proceed as though the limits of our abilities do not exist."

– Pierre Teilhard de Chardin

Barbara Marx Hubbard is blessed to embody an infinite wellspring of passion. Her life is a testament to an unshakeable commitment to the creation of a better world. Born in 1929, she's been witness to startling changes in our global civilization; most notably, a degradation in consciousness that has many of us wondering where we went wrong. Barbara is a sanguine futurist, however. She holds a powerful vision for a new humanity, a humanity aligned with essence—the paradigm shift from head to heart.

Barbara is contagious in her enthusiasm for life. She's an author, speaker, and educator who has produced, hosted, and contributed to numerous documentaries seen by millions of people around the globe. She's tireless in her commitment to global awakening.

Barbara is a staunch believer in "evolution by choice, not chance." In her heart, she knows that a collective working selflessly for the greater good will create global transformation. I wholeheartedly agree. In the introduction to her book, *Emergence: The Shift from Ego to Essence*, Neale Donald Walsch writes:

"We can become something that we never were—and always have been. We can create something that we could not have imagined—and that we've always dreamed. We can produce something on this planet that we never thought possible—and that we always knew was probable, sooner or later."[6] Barbara Marx Hubbard is a powerful catalyst for the emergence of the universal truth from within.

Barbara has influenced the likes of Deepak Chopra, Michael Beckwith, Ken Wilber, Bruce Lipton, Marianne Williamson, and the late Buckminster Fuller. Needless to say, when my heart prompted me to connect with Barbara for this book, my mind fussed about how I would make it happen. This is where the power of faith intersects with belief to create miracles.

This book has been an interesting journey. I've gone to great lengths to meet each interviewee personally. The accurate portrayal of their essence, through my essence, to your essence has been of prime importance. The end result is a collection of heart-to-heart personal connections communicated through the written word to ignite soulful transformation and activate inspired action.

My meeting with Barbara is a story that bears repeating.

It started with one question: how would I meet her? I lived in Ottawa, she lived in California. I'm not Marianne Williamson, I don't have a jet-set budget, and she's a busy woman on an important mission. How could I be noticed with so many others vying for her attention? My mind tried to reason my way out of this mission, but my heart would not let go.

I resigned myself to faith. If this was meant to be, my heart would lead the way.

I've been on the Omega Institute mailing list for a number of years. The event catalog has often served as browsing material in quiet moments of calm. I mention this because synchronicity has a way of expediting purpose.

Barbara's presence was in the forefront of my consciousness, and the Omega catalog arrived the following week. Two seemingly unrelated occurrences, but there was more to come.

Perusing its pages one afternoon, I noticed a workshop titled, "After

2012: Manifesting Change: Rebirthing Self and Community." Interesting, I thought. That is, until I read that it would be cofacilitated by John Perkins and, drumroll please, Barbara Marx Hubbard. I signed up immediately. My soul vibrated with delight. I knew that this was my gateway to connection.

The workshop commenced on a Friday evening and ended late Sunday afternoon. I had two and a half days to overcome the next hurdle: an intimate opportunity to share my co-creative vision with Barbara. With sixty participants in the workshop, the odds were definitely better than a random email exchange from a stranger in Ontario, but the challenge still remained to find a quiet moment alone. The last thing I wanted was to appear pushy. After all, I'm Canadian, eh.

Saturday would be our first full day together. That morning I set the intention for my heart to present the perfect opportunity to connect with Barbara for this book. When passion and intention align for the highest good, synchronicities abound.

The morning commenced with an ice-breaker exercise to set the stage for group connection. Intimate lighting and soft music created the mood for heart-opening unity. It was a lovely way to start the day. As we flowed around the room chatting quietly with each other, I found myself instinctively moving closer to Barbara, magnetized by a force greater than myself. Before I knew it, I was standing directly in front of her. In that very moment, John Perkins announced that we were to partner with the person in front of us for the next exercise. Without thought, I raised my arms, looked up at the sky and whispered "thank you," as tears clouded my eyes. Barbara smiled warmly. We sat on the floor face-to-face, knees touching, and holding each other's hands. I looked into her beautiful wise eyes and knew that I was looking directly into her soul.

My heart pounded with an excitement that could barely be contained. With moments to spare before the exercise began, I pounced (that seems to be the way I roll in these circumstances). I told her everything: why I was there, how I was guided to her, and what my mission entailed. I spoke from my heart—and she heard me with hers. It was clear that she felt the depth of my sincerity and the strength of my passion. She said yes; and the rest, as they say, is history.

Incidentally, the partner exercise was a powerful guided shamanic meditation to expand consciousness and open the heart to a greater potential for ourselves and for the world. I never would have dreamed that this is how I would meet the "Mother of Invention" herself, Barbara Marx Hubbard.

Never doubt the power of intention.

***

Barbara's Story

Unplugging: Path to Purpose

My father was Louis Marx. He was a type of Horatio Alger American who, for a year of his life, was known as the toy king of the world. By an accident of chance, Hap Arnold of the US Air Force lost part of a toy train from his collection. My father was the man who gave him the part that he needed. They befriended one another, and this led to other friendships with military generals of the Second World War—including General Eisenhower. Many of these men became godfathers to my half brothers, so I saw them regularly as a child. I had great admiration for them.

The defining moment that started me on my path was when the US dropped the bombs on Japan in 1945. That was the end of my happy childhood. I was fifteen years old and thought that everything we did was good. I thought power was good. America was good. Military power was good. Winning the war was good. When the bombs were dropped, I realized that this power could destroy everything. If we used this power in the same state of self-centered consciousness that created it, we could destroy the whole world. That prompted me to ask a simple question of President Eisenhower, "What is the meaning of all this new power that's good?"

I began searching for answers to where the human species was going. I discovered that nobody knew. The church didn't know. The universities didn't know. When I asked President Eisenhower about the meaning of all this new power, he answered, "I have no idea."

This became my life quest.

The second big jump for me was reading the work of Pierre Teilhard de Chardin, the Jesuit Catholic paleontologist who was censored by the Catholic Church. He discovered God in evolution. He discovered the law of complexity consciousness. As systems become more complex—from single cell to multi-cell, to animal, to human—they jump in consciousness and develop a more synergistic order. We know this as love. Instead of evolution being in one place, and God being an external creator, he saw the entire process of evolution as an expression of divine intent leading to higher complex order. He saw it leading to the noosphere, or the thinking layer of earth getting its collective eyes; the awakening of the planetary consciousness. When I read this, I knew that this was the meaning of our power that was good.

By this time, I was a somewhat depressed and disoriented housewife in Lakeville, Connecticut, with five children. I was seeking more. I knew that my purpose was to help create the global consciousness. I also knew that I was an expression of this universal process of creation. We all are. Instead of the discontented housewife, I was the universe in person, because the universe in person has an impulse toward higher consciousness, greater freedom, and more complex order. In other words, we are the universe evolving. This changed my identity. In the 1960s, there was no such thing as an evolutionary woman. Feminism was just beginning. But I leaped over feminism and feminine empowerment and became an evolutionary cocreator. So in a way, I jumped the culture and become a futurist. I also became a pioneer experimenter, investigating our participation in evolution. Because I'm a journal writer, I feel that one of my jobs in life is tracking the evolutionary process—particularly of the feminine.

Out of this came the idea of conscious evolution: that we are the first generation on earth to be conscious of evolution, that we are part of evolution, and that we are affecting evolution. We can destroy ourselves or evolve ourselves by choice, not chance.

I believe that this is a great wake-up call for the next stage of human consciousness. We had self consciousness about fifty thousand years ago. Now we have evolutionary consciousness.

I was turned on by what I call the impulse of evolution. It became my vocation to communicate the evolution of human potential. I feel that I'm getting newer rather than older, because the planet is going through a new era of its own culture. The new culture is currently being born on this earth. There are millions of us now. I am attuned to the new. What that actually does to you personally when you get to be my age is what I call "regenopause."

A lot of older women, instead of dying, are evolving their authentic self into the world. As the global crisis deepens and the evolutionary potential becomes more apparent, particularly with mass communication and the internet, the possibility of entering a phase of evolution where the body responds to this newness becomes very real. It presents in a form of regeneration. It actually feels like the cells are being informed by consciousness. They know that we have something new to express. Life force is incarnating in a more intense way to those who say yes.

The way it has been is that when a woman no longer chose to procreate, the life force would drain. She looked older, felt older, and much of her beauty and vitality was lost. But we're moving from the procreative phase to the cocreative phase. We can't have large numbers of children anymore and survive as a species. That's not just cultural, it's biological. In the emergent new world, many women are internally ignited and giving birth to the greater self. It seems to me that the procreative, reproductive body is igniting this greater capacity at not only the psychological and spiritual levels, but also at the physical level. Many women no longer feel like they're aging, they feel like they're renewing. They're animating.

They're possibly extending their lives. I don't feel age-specific, actually. I don't feel younger, I feel newer. I was not like this when I was young. It's very different than trying to look young. It's actually wanting to be new. Evolution creates newness, and not in a superficial sense. It's new like from Neanderthal to Homo sapiens, or from single cell to multi-cell, or from Australopithecus africanus to the two of us speaking today. Every turn in the spiral is radically new.

So if we're at a turn in the spiral of evolution—on the one hand possible destruction of civilization, and on the other hand creating a new co-creative, cooperative culture—what would the full-scale use of the power of humanity look like if we became a cocreative culture? Then we'd begin to see real newness, because it's not about fixing our mistakes. It isn't even about repairing the terrible things we're doing to the environment. It's about restoring the earth. It's about freeing ourselves from poverty and disease. This is what a creative species could do if it mobilized its new power and explored the dimensions of its next stage of evolution. That's where I am.

Accessing the Higher Self: Reconnecting

I'm still experiencing what my higher Self really means. It started with my journal writing. This has been the magnum opus of my spiritual practice. I have 190 journal volumes. It's truly phenomenal. I learned to meditate, be silent, turn off my mental mind, and allow what I called my higher Self to come through.

Often the higher Self is so much wiser than my mental mind. I notice that when I focus on my higher Self along with a specific feeling, that frequency enters my heart. With that frequency in my body, I actually incarnate my own higher Self. Putting my attention on it allows it to come in. This has made me realize that I'm an expression of that Self. It's my essential Self. The biggest issue is turning off the local selves, which are compulsive: "Get this done, do this, do that." This is an ongoing process.

Everyone has local selves. Sometimes they're called "ego" and we try to destroy them. I don't do that. I treat my local selves like compulsive little children.

As my own essence empowered me, I would invite the local selves to come into their own essence, because the higher Self is the essence of who the ego would prefer to be. I would say that my local selves fell in love with their own essence. This is when I began incarnating my own higher Self.

I'm going even further than the incarnation of my higher Self now. I have contacted what I call a universal Self. When I observe at a certain level, I feel a presence that is free of the earth field. It is universal and non-local. This is the joy that I feel. It has its own ecstatic joyfulness, and it's post-transition. It already knows that we're getting through this planetary crisis. It knows that victory is assured because it's already been through it. It says to me, "Keep your attention on me. I'm coded with your evolution." My practice now is to place attention on this universal Self, which enters my essential Self, and then I bring the local selves in so that I become an integrated human being.

Recharging

I have a deep practice of getting up very early, like around 5:30 a.m. I get a cup of coffee, sit in my little green chair overlooking the sunrise, and meditate with my journal in my lap. From time to time, I connect with a certain group of people and we go into a higher state together. We call it the "Evolving We," or the formation of a Universal Human Pod.

There's a lot of talk these days about going "from me to we," but there's a level of "we" that is cocreation, cooperation, and unity. If we go further with "we," we go to revelation. This is when real breakthroughs happen. This can only happen with an extremely resonant group. It's actually beyond resonance because it's revelation. Our "Evolving We" group is not aiming for power over something, or even to fix anything up. Instead, we're aiming for metamorphosis. We're aiming at evolutionary potential to restore the earth and free ourselves from the terrible separation that we've been facing for far too long.

A New Story of Evolution

Having seen the picture of the new story of evolution; having seen the cosmogenesis, the fourteen billion years, as a continuous expression of higher order, higher complexity, and higher consciousness; having seen the lessons that breakdown precedes breakthrough, and that problems are evolutionary drivers, I'm interpreting every crisis we're facing as an evolutionary driver.

Nobody knows how this is going to turn out, but it's very different if we interpret the crises as evolutionary drivers toward the emergence of a cocreative universal humanity in a universe of trillions of planets.

This is when we need a "strange attractor" to move us forward. When a system is far from equilibrium, it seeks a higher system. If there is no higher system, it turns to diabolical structures like Nazism or Communism. Out of disorder, we can get terrible systems. There must be some type of system, because nature will not remain in chaos. It will move toward a patterning structure.

What this means is that every one of us can move ourselves, our message, and our essence into the strange attractor of the emerging whole system. This begins to activate the system. That is the direction of evolution. You might say that the Force is with us. When it hits a crisis, it seeks the higher order. I feel that everyone who is living from their higher potential is cooperating with a divine impulse of universal origin. The greatest blessing we can have as a person is when the divine impulse incarnates and moves through us. Life then becomes an expression of this. There's a trust factor here, though. We can give ourselves fully to the impulse, but we need to trust that we won't be able to do everything for everyone.

We often think that what we're doing is so urgent that the entire world depends on it. First of all, it doesn't. Second, we can't do it all. Third, it will destroy our capacity to do anything, because that very feeling is demoralizing. Part of the internal practice is saying yes to the particular part that is ours to do. If we're in alignment with the highest purpose of our own being on any given day, it will shift. It's never exactly the same. According to the life pulse in each moment, we self-calibrate to the highest degree that we can. Everybody is unique in that respect.

Every vocation is unique, like every cell is unique and every thumbprint is unique. It's quite amazing. When I know that I'm doing that which is uniquely mine to do, that perhaps I do it better than anyone else because it's uniquely what I can do, then I'm okay no matter what. The internal chemistry inside me gives me that sense of joy and hope.

If You Had a Magic Wand …

I would manifest a cocreative world in which each person's unique creativity is activated. They would join others and share their gifts to create a world that we have never seen before. We would resonate with the higher intelligence of the universe. That's what I see, and by seeing it, I'm being it.

For more information about Barbara's paradigm-altering work, please visit Evolve.org.

ELEVEN

Gene Baur

The Conscience of the Food Movement

"The voice of conscience is so delicate that it is easy to stifle it; but it is also so clear that it is impossible to mistake it."

– MADAME DE STAEL

We are all born compassionate. The seed of compassion resides permanently in our hearts as a reminder that we are all connected. Compassion is the greatest expression of love.

As we move through life conditioned by parents, teachers, authority figures, and culture, compassion is squelched, fragmented, and compartmentalized. We're taught to hear but not listen, speak but not act, think but not feel. We're taught to conform, consume, comply. We label, we fear, we judge … we separate.

This is not who we are.

The human heart has the capacity to hold an enormous amount of love and compassion. By our very nature, we are compassionate. Anything less than that is the lie we've bought into to separate us from life. The reason we do what we do to those we perceive as "other" is because we're asleep at the wheel.

But we are not separate. We're autonomous expressions of a greater whole in an interconnected world. We have a choice: to live the lie or not. We're the ones who created it. We're the ones who can un-create it. Just as we've chosen ignorance, so too can we choose truth. The most important thing we can do in our lifetime is to dare to care about the sacredness of life for all living beings.

Gene Baur is a compelling reminder of who we all can be, should we choose to live from the depths of compassion in our hearts.

Gene is the president and cofounder of Farm Sanctuary, my Ironman raison d'être. He's also a bestselling author, activist, environmentalist, humanitarian, and a talented runner and Ironman triathlete to boot.

Gene is a man on a mission—a mission of compassion and love. He's a man who is deeply connected to his calling. As a result, he's had a tremendous impact on the lives of human and nonhuman animals alike.

The defining moment of Gene's life arrived in a rather unlikely place. While documenting a live animal stockyard in Pennsylvania, Gene's calling emerged from a "dead pile." As grisly as it sounds, a dead pile is exactly that—a pile of dead and dying animals considered useless by the profiteers of this madness.

As Gene approached the pile of dead animals, a sheep raised her head. She was still alive. Without hesitation, Gene removed the sheep from the mound of lifeless beings and took her to his vehicle. Thinking euthanasia was the only humane option, Gene took her to a veterinarian to prevent further suffering. Much to his surprise, she needed only vitamins and fluids to bring her back to health. She not only recovered, she went on to thrive for many more years.

This is the condensed story of Hilda, the sheep who touched the heart of a dedicated activist, who in turn created an international movement of compassion.

This was the inception of Farm Sanctuary, America's leading farm animal protection organization, with locations in New York and California. Farm Sanctuary invites visitors to connect with hundreds of rescued farm animals and see them for the emotional, intelligent, and loving beings that they are. Gene has dedicated his life to promoting compassion and advocating on behalf of the billions of forgotten beings in our world.

I've had the honor of hanging out with Gene on more than a few occasions, and I can honestly say that he's one of the kindest, most compassionate and dedicated men on this planet. He's a tireless voice for the voiceless and a shining light of hope and optimism for a kinder, more compassionate world. He also happens to be movie-star handsome, which bodes well for the company he often keeps. Celebrities such as Alicia Silverstone, Ellen DeGeneres, Daryl Hannah, Moby, and Denzel Washington are dedicated supporters of Farm Sanctuary.

Time magazine hails Gene as the "conscience of the food movement." I take this a step further and hail Gene the conscience of a new paradigm.

***

Gene's Story

Unplugging: Path to Purpose

I grew up in the Hollywood Hills, where I often saw wild animals like deer, coyotes, and skunks. Like most kids, I was awestruck and very curious about them. I remember seeing the human impact on these animals at a very young age.

One of my earliest memories was of a deer caught in a chain link fence in a neighbor's yard. Sadly, the deer had to be killed. Another early memory was of a beautiful oak tree across the street from where I lived. It was cut down for the expansion of a house.

Both of these incidents bothered me on a visceral level. I didn't like witnessing the human encroachment and disrespect for nature and animals. I was upset by the harm that humans were causing, and I knew that I didn't want to be part of it.

My parents were conservative Catholics, so I went to Catholic grammar school and was hit with a strong dose of "thou shall" and "thou shalt not" morality. I'm not a fan of the dogma and judgment attached to religion, but some of the basic kernels, like the Golden "do unto others as you would have done unto you" Rule, stayed with me.

I always wanted to make a positive difference. I didn't want to just get a job to be a cog in the wheel of a system that I knew was causing harm. My parents encouraged me to become an engineer or to join the military, but it didn't feel right, so I took a different path.

I started volunteering at a children's hospital with terminally ill kids. I went to college, studied sociology, and started working with adolescents who were having problems. I also started learning about consumer and environmental issues. I worked at Greenpeace for a while.

As I learned about the various issues, it became apparent that factory farming was a huge problem causing great harm to animals, the earth, and consumers. It was an issue that was not getting very much attention.

Over time I learned more about factory farming and its impacts on animals, the earth, and humanity. I decided that it was an issue with profound consequences that needed to be addressed. So in 1986, I cofounded Farm Sanctuary, and I've been working at that ever since.

I felt that it was important to bear witness and see firsthand what was really going on. I started visiting farms, stockyards, and slaughterhouses to become more familiar with the reality of animal production systems. In August 1986, I was behind a stockyard in Pennsylvania and came upon a pile of dead animals—dead sheep, dead cows, dead pigs. They were covered in maggots and flies that were so thick you could hear them buzzing.

From the dead pile, a lamb lifted her head. I was shocked that a living animal was discarded like garbage. We took her off the dead pile thinking she would have to be euthanized, but when the vet examined her, she perked up. She went on to live with us for ten more years.

That was Hilda. She was our first rescued animal. Her story is one of transformation and healing. It was so important for my Farm Sanctuary colleagues and me, because witnessing the cruelty of factory farming over and over again takes a real toll on the heart and soul. Sometimes you feel like it's so big and nothing can be done about it. It can be very challenging.

Rescuing Hilda was good for her and it was good for us. It was something that we were able to do that made a real difference.

Back in 1986, we funded Farm Sanctuary by selling vegan hotdogs at Grateful Dead concerts out of our Volkswagen van. We were a very small volunteer organization and didn't have a long-term plan or vision of what we would become.

Farm Sanctuary has really just evolved in response to various needs. When we first started rescuing animals, we were living in a little row house in Wilmington, Delaware. Eventually, a farmer in Pennsylvania let us use some of his land. We lived in a school bus on his tofu farm for a couple of years.

We finally acquired the farm in Upstate New York. But during the early years, we recognized that people were interested in the animals and their stories. So we started telling the animal stories, and the animals became the ambassadors for the organization. They also became ambassadors for the billions of farm animals who continued to be exploited by our culture.

Over time, people wanted to visit. They started asking where they could stay. In response, we built bed-and-breakfast cabins. Then we created programs and events, because people wanted to participate in bigger ways.

So we've really done things in response to people's needs and interests, and it continues to grow from there. We now have about 250,000 supporters. We have three farms: one in Watkins Glen, New York, and two in California. It's great to see people visit the sanctuaries and connect with the animals and other people. When they visit, they feel validated.

Farm Sanctuary is a place where vegan is normal. For vegans, it can be pretty tough living in a world where one's perspective and lifestyle is misunderstood and not supported by colleagues and family members. Farm Sanctuary is a place where vegans are supported. It's also a place where non-vegans can learn about the plant-based lifestyle in a friendly, nonjudgmental way.

I feel really good about the sanctuary work, as well as the outreach and advocacy work we do. One of our most important organizational values is to speak to people where they're at on their journey. We encourage people to take steps on the path toward more compassionate living.

We recognize that each person has to make their own choices, but I really believe that people are humane and want to make humane choices. I think that when they realize this, ultimately it makes sense to become vegan. All of us are imperfect, and I think it's important to recognize that change happens over time.

I feel very lucky and grateful to do work that I believe in, and that's having a positive impact in the world. I feel glad to be part of this movement toward a more compassionate world.

Recharging: Connecting to Compassion

I think it's important to slow down. One of the biggest problems in today's world is how fast we move. People are trapped in their own worlds of doing, doing, doing.

They don't live in the present moment, so they don't recognize that we are all interconnected. I think it really boils down to empathy and recognizing that we are all part of one global community. When anybody suffers, we all suffer.

Rather than being in our own world, it's important to understand that we are all part of each other's world. How we think and act has ramifications beyond ourselves.

I think compassion is about empathy. It's about helping others. By helping others, we help ourselves. We are part of one large community. I think we sometimes forget that.

It's a natural tendency for children to be curious about animals and to be empathic when they see anyone being hurt. That speaks to our true humanity. But as we grow up, we're often discouraged from having these feelings. Instead, we're encouraged not to care. We're taught to focus on our own personal interests, whatever they might be.

I think when we remember that we're all connected and recognize that we all suffer, that's when we can help each other get through the tough days and soar on the good days. That is compassion.

Hope

Positive changes are happening all over the world, and this gives me tremendous hope. Hope also comes from witnessing individual animals heal when they learn to trust for the first time. Watching their fear transformed into love is such a beautiful thing.

There are also so many people in various communities around the world who are making a difference. Wherever I go, I see individuals doing really great things. I prefer to dwell on that. I take heart from the good in people rather than dwelling on the horrible things that are happening.

I think it's important to be aware of the bad things in the world to be able to challenge and educate people about important issues. But I also think it's important not to dwell on the bad things until they pull us down. Instead we need to be pulled up by the good things that are happening.

So I try to dwell on the positive. Thankfully there's a lot of this happening. There's more awareness than ever before about the cruelty of factory farming. There are also more plant-based alternatives available than ever before. So it's a very good time to be vegan, and this makes me feel very optimistic.

Reconnecting

For me, reconnecting is as easy as slowing down, being in the present moment and just breathing. I have the tendency to impatiently rush from place to place. When I stop, breathe, and just focus on what's happening now rather than what I have to do next, I'm happier. I'm also more centered and connected with everything, including myself.

Sometimes I'll go for a run, blow off some steam, and get the blood moving through my brain to think through challenges and gain new perspectives on things. Spending time in nature, appreciating the trees, mountains, rivers, and oceans, also helps. There's so much healing power in the gratitude that comes from being in nature.

I travel a lot for all of the public speaking I do. Sometimes when I'm traveling by plane, I just close my eyes, breathe, and become very present. I don't formally meditate, but I guess that's a simple form of meditation. Presence is the most important way to reconnect to my heart and feel what's true inside.

There are times when I think about the state of the world and feel quite upset about what's happening. Knowing about the needless suffering that happens every day because of our consumptive ways is deeply troubling for me.

I try to recognize that people are responsible for their choices. Sometimes we do bad things, but I believe that most people want to do better. Most people don't want to be part of a cruel and violent system and would much rather make peaceful choices given the appropriate knowledge and opportunities.

When people stop eating animals, whether it's for athletic performance or for health, they become less defensive about the ethical issues. They become more open-minded. I'm noticing how many people who were initially attracted to a vegan lifestyle for health reasons are embracing the ethical issues as well.

The plant-based athlete movement is playing a very positive role in demonstrating that we can get all the protein and nutrients we need by eating plants exclusively. We live in a society that bombards us with messages and marketing campaigns that tell us we need to eat meat for protein. This is absolutely not the case. It's one of the myths that needs to be debunked, and I think vegan athletes are doing a very good job of challenging the notion that plant foods are somehow deficient.

I'm excited about the growing interest in connecting health and athletic performance with ethical concerns. I think we have a number of really compelling spokespeople, and I'm very excited about that. So for me, it's also about reconnecting to the sense of optimism that comes from knowing that there are so many positive changes happening in today's world.

If You Had a Magic Wand...

It would be a vegan world. It would be like a Garden of Eden where killing was not known, where violence did not exist, where no one had to be afraid of harm from anyone else. Now the big question is this: "Could such a world actually come to be?"

I don't know. Sometimes, with struggle, we learn and evolve. So whether this perfect world that I dream about could ever manifest is anyone's guess. It's certainly an aspiration to move toward. I've been told many times that I'm a dreamer, but I think that dreaming is okay. In fact, I think it's necessary. How can we create a better world if we can't imagine it?

I often look at things in terms of aspirations. Aspirations recognize that we are all works in progress continually striving to be and do better. We are trying to live in a way that is aligned with our better selves. But we're human and we will make mistakes.

So I think waving the wand would also include having a planet full of open-minded people who were receptive to new ideas and who were willing to consider other possibilities for how we could live on this planet more kindly.

To learn more about Gene's work with Farm Sanctuary, visit farmsanctuary.org.

TWELVE

Brynn McLennan
Choosing Life and Love

"We are our choices."

– Jean-Paul Sartre

Life is a series of one-time-only moments never to be replicated. Every moment, every circumstance, every thought, every breath, every heartbeat—yours and yours alone. How you feel. How you deal. How you heal. This is what makes you real.

Who we are is shaped by a culmination of lifetime experiences. Some we perceive as good, some we perceive as bad. But often the most transformative gifts arrive in ugly packages: the unforeseen events and experiences that reveal the frailty of our humanity. These are the defining moments that forever alter our lives. Do we choose to grow or do we choose to shrink?

On a collective scale, the endless cacophony of whining and complaining from the self-pitying victims of their own life circumstances clearly shows the damage caused by a cultural paradigm that does not support growth. The self-perpetuating cycle of PMS, or Poor Me Syndrome, ensures the illusion of smallness.

But here's the deal, we all have our own stories to tell. We all have our own worldviews. We all have the power of free will. The power lies not so much in the choices we make, but more in the *knowing* that we have choice. Unless we choose to be, we are not victims of our circumstances. We are growing, evolving beings every moment of every day. We have the choice to nurture this growth or stunt it. We have the choice to become our stories or evolve from them. Therein lies the ultimate choice.

While many choose the rut, others choose to rise.

I thrive in the presence of "risers," people who own their lives—everything—the good and the bad. People who don't pretend to be someone or something that they're not. People who are as comfortable with their vulnerability as they are with their strength. People who are loving, humble, honest, selfless, caring, passionate, inspiring, raw, and real. People who are openhearted and awake.

This brings me to the story of Brynn McLennan, a story of courage, tenacity, faith, and love. Brynn is an inspiring woman with a fierce passion for life and a powerful faith in the human heart.

At the age of twelve, Brynn was given a wheelchair sentence by doctors for a rare form of muscular dystrophy that stripped her of the ability to stand fully upright. Not one to be easily deterred, Brynn refused the bleak prognosis and remains upright to this day. Despite the medical odds, she's built a rich life for herself. The mind, when coupled with the heart, is an unstoppable force for paradigm-shifting transformation.

Brynn is someone who could easily fall prey to Poor Me Syndrome with her physical reality. But instead, she refuses to define herself by the disease that has robbed her of what many people take for granted—the ability to move freely, uninhibited by the miraculous temple we know as our body. In Brynn's own words: "I had two choices, I could wallow in self-pity and make my own life miserable or I could focus on all the things I could do, all the love from family and friends and even the kindness that I felt from strangers." The combined forces of loving support and Brynn's natural fighting spirit led her on an extensive search for alternatives. Though mainstream medicine disappointed, stem cell therapy opened the doors of possibility.

Through Brynn's own healing journey, she's become a passionate crusader for stem cell therapy—an exciting advancement not only for human health but also for the elimination of archaic and cruel animal testing. Through her grassroots, nonprofit, fundraising community, Stem Cells for Brynn, she's been able to raise the needed funds for costly biannual treatments in the US. She's also actively working to raise awareness and bring stem cell therapy into her native country, Canada.

Brynn is proof positive that our wounds, tragedies, and life circumstances can become our greatest teachers. She also shows that the depth with which we're willing to heal and expand from the circumstances in our own lives gives us the capacity to inspire healing and expansion in others. By accepting the circumstances that altered her life, Brynn has embraced a calling that will heal so many others.

Brynn's brother Ryan wrote a heartfelt song in honor of his sister. "I'm Strong" is a musical masterpiece that inspires powerful emotions. In the chorus, Ryan sings, "This life is worth fighting for. I know … the heart's a muscle so … I'm strong. I have the power to love … to love." His words speak to an important part within each of us. Stripping away the layers of human complexity reveals the truth that never falters: love is the greatest healing force of all.

There are only two reasons people make changes in their lives: inspiration or desperation. In the end what matters is not what happened, but who we become as a result of what happened. The more we allow ourselves to be, the more we can become. The more we become, the more we can still be. Life is not a process of discovery, it's a process of creation. It's not about finding ourselves, it's about deciding who we wish to be. We are not here to create ourselves from the opinions or prognoses of others. We are here to design life as we choose, so that we can live it on our own terms. We are here to shape our world, not be shaped by it. Each time we expand beyond our perceived limits, there is endless room for growth to discover who we have the potential to still become.

Imagine if, by accepting our own life circumstances as Brynn McLennan has, we began to feel needed rather than needy. What a different world this would be.

* * *

Brynn's Story

Unplugging: Path to Purpose

I've always been feisty. Even as a little girl, I didn't take no for an answer. My mentality is that if I can't do it, then I'm going to keep on trying until I find a way. I've never been the type to just give up.

Having this core quality was a definite asset when I was diagnosed with muscular dystrophy. I refused to let the muscular dystrophy define me, because I've always been the one who called the shots in my life.

I first discovered that things weren't right while playing hockey. I noticed that I wasn't able to skate as fast or shoot the puck as hard. There was no visible evidence that anything was wrong, but I just couldn't do it anymore. I kept pushing myself even though I was asking my body to do something it was no longer capable of.

Then other things began to show up. I'd hurt my back and it would be exceptionally sore. I could no longer lift the laundry basket. Simple things were not so simple anymore. But other than the fact that I could no longer do certain things, there was no evidence of anything wrong. It was so frustrating.

As human beings, if we can't figure out why something isn't right, our imaginations run wild. We get overwhelmed. For instance, we can do a Google search for the causes of a sore throat and end up with life-threatening possibilities that spiral us into despair. When I finally got the diagnosis, my response was, "Well, at least I now know what it is." Once I knew what was going on with my body, I could figure out how to overcome it.

When I was born, my right tear duct was blocked. Apparently this is quite common in infants, so nobody was overly concerned. I was able to run, play hockey, do kid stuff—I was a little tomboy. Over time, my eye did clear somewhat, but it never closed tightly or teared as much when I cried. I found out later that the type of muscular dystrophy I have affects the face, arms, legs, and hip muscles. A blocked tear duct with an eye that doesn't close properly can be one of the first symptoms out of utero.

I was a really active kid, and I loved playing hockey. Of all the things that I can no longer do, such as running, walking, and going up stairs, what I miss the most is hearing the sound of my hockey blades on ice. Otherwise, I've adapted.

When I was ten years old, my mother noticed that my right shoulder blade was winging out. Shoulder blades are covered by a thick piece of muscle that holds them down. They're not supposed to wing out. When my mother noticed that it was winging out, she paid close attention. When my left shoulder started to wing out, she was very concerned. That's when we went to the hospital to figure out what was going on.

There's a common phenomenon where, once someone knows they have a disease, they start going downhill. Like when you cut yourself and you don't notice, it doesn't hurt. But when you finally notice that you've cut yourself, it suddenly hurts. Even though it helped to finally know what was going on with my body, there was an initial deterioration.

I'm not sure at what point I decided not to let it take me down. I feel like it happened unconsciously. Being diagnosed at twelve meant that I still had innocence. I hadn't had my heart broken. I didn't know about the negativity in the world. I had innocence on my side, and this allowed me to remain positive.

My mother started searching for alternatives to prolong my independence, because the doctors gave me a debilitating wheelchair sentence that I refused to accept. That's when she discovered the exciting possibility of stem cell therapy.

Stem cells are unprogrammed cells found within our bodies. We have billions of dormant stem cells stored in our fat tissues. In stem cell therapy, the unprogrammed cells are removed via liposuction and are then activated. Once activated, they're injected intravenously, or, as in my case, directly into muscles. They can become anything—lung tissue, muscle, skin, brain—anything. They actually *become* that tissue, so to speak. They go to areas of the body that are in need. Wherever there's distress or inflammation, that's where the stem cells go. The cells have their own intelligence. Stem cell therapy uses the body's own intelligence to heal itself. It's quite remarkable.

After the first treatment, I noticed that the signals from my brain to my muscles were quicker. I also noticed that the muscles that weren't affected by the disease were getting bigger and sturdier. I rarely fall, but when I did, I noticed that my falls were more "normal." There are continual changes, and the great thing is that they are lasting changes. I space the treatments out because the positive effects can take up to six months to become noticeable to me.

Just because I'm getting these treatments doesn't mean that my work is over, though. I have to ensure that I'm eating healthy, that I'm exercising, and that I'm creating the best habitat I can within my body for the stem cells. I can't just sit on the couch eating chips all day.

I'm not going to say that this is a cure, but I am saying that it's helping me. I'm being the test subject. I'm trying to figure out the best way that it can help with the muscular dystrophy. So far it's working. It's allowing me to focus on all of the good things in my life.

If I wanted to, I could wake up every day and focus on everything that I can no longer do. I could focus on the things that cause struggle or that I have to do differently. People look at me differently now, and I could focus on that. I'm aware of all these things, but I don't let them bring me down. I'm not defined by these things. Instead, I focus on the good things that I can still do and all the things around me that bring me so much joy. Playing the victim may provide the attention that some people crave, but it's disempowering. It doesn't work for me.

I'm human and I have my days, but those days are few and far between. Some days I feel quite sad for myself, because I'm grieving a profound loss. But by allowing these feelings to move through me, I'm able to return to my sense of optimism. I don't allow myself to remain stuck in self-pity.

I feel that every disability, every disease, has its pluses. There are a lot of growth moments. I recognize that there are also certain privileges I have that I wouldn't have if I didn't have this disability. I need to remain focused on the loving things in my life in order to combat any sort of victim mentality or sense of entitlement that could prevail if I focused on the disabled privileges. The most important thing for me is to focus on healing and loving my body so that ultimately I get better.

Recharging and Reconnecting

Whenever I find myself falling into any sort of despair or negativity, I give my body and heart what it needs. I laugh. I look for the humor in situations. It's so much better than seeing the negativity all the time, don't you think?

There are other times when I need to yell and cry. I just express whatever emotions need to come out. I never stop them from emerging because expressed emotions help us grow and heal. Why would I want to trap any of that stuff inside of me? I want it out and gone. I want to expel it so that I can ground myself and refocus on what I need, where I need to be, and what I want to see for my life.

I constantly remind myself that I'm the only one in this body. I'm the only one living this life. So I have the choice to make it miserable or make it happy.

It's totally okay to have days that suck. As long as we bring ourselves back to what is real in our hearts. The most important thing for all of us to remember is that we have the power to be whoever we wish to be in every moment of every day. We should never identify with any of our emotions, because they're supposed to move *through* us. We're always changing anyway, so why remain stuck? We're allowed to feel it all. We're supposed to feel it all. We're just not supposed to suppress our feelings or remain stuck in them.

If I suppress any emotions, then I'm living in them. I'm keeping them inside of me, when in reality I want them gone so that I can return to all of the good things around me. Whether it's the sun coming out, the green grass, whether it's seeing someone smile … whatever it may be, I take it in and feel it. I can't do that if I've suppressed an emotion that I'm now stuck in. I won't be able to see beyond that.

So, for me, recharging is about allowing emotions and feelings to move through me, and reconnecting is about returning to what matters once I feel emotionally cleansed. I can then bring the good things into my heart and really feel them without the unconscious heaviness of un-expressed emotions weighing me down. This way, the good things can fully replenish me.

There's so much liberation when we learn to just accept ourselves as we truly are.

Passion and Purpose

I want to empower people to get out of their victim consciousness and take ownership for their lives. I want to help them go inside and tap into their individual strength. I don't want to be their strength for them; I want to inspire them. I believe that everyone has this strength in their hearts, and if I can help people access it through my story, then it's all worth it. Once they access their own inner power, then they go on to inspire others. This ripple effect has great potential for large-scale transformation.

As far as stem cell therapy is concerned, there is profound potential for incredible healing for so many people. We really need to stand behind stem cells. We need to donate to stem cells. We need to back them up, because stem cell therapy is the wave of the future. It's something that can help so many people suffering from many different ailments and injuries. Stem cell therapy is being done all over the world, and we need to step up to the race line here in Canada. We need to really start pushing it because we, the people, are the only ones that can make this go faster.

I'm doing my best, but I need others to rally with me. We need to start getting more funding toward this and really push it. Sure, there are drugs out there. There are all kinds of things that people take for their ailments. But it's time to start moving toward something that can actually help someone's life rather than just medicating it. It's time for progressive treatments that offer people independence. We need other avenues. We need to stop putting Band-Aids on things and instead, create real transformation.

Stem cell therapy is good not only for people, it's good for animals too. It can actually eliminate the perceived need for animal research. With stem cells, there's no longer a need to test on monkeys, rats, dogs, cats, rabbits, or any other animals. Ricky Gervais said it best when he said, "Don't get soap in your eyes. It stings. Now can we stop testing on animals?"

I'm passionate about this for so many reasons. Because of my own experiential healing journey, I feel very much on purpose when I inspire others to explore alternatives such as stem cell therapy, and also when I inspire people to take charge of their own lives. There's no greater gift than this.

The Power of Self-Love

I can't stress this enough: it's so important to just live in your heart, to remind yourself of the love that you have, to remind yourself of how much you love yourself. The word for the day, for every day, is "love." Love others. Love yourself. Love is stronger than everything. Love is all about being in your heart. It makes you the rational one.

Loving yourself makes you feel powerful in the sense that it makes you feel good. When you enter a room feeling good about yourself, you command attention in a good way, in a way that makes people flock to you because they see your light. They want to be in your bubble. They want to be with you. Being in a state of love is the strongest, most powerful thing out there. Loving yourself in whatever body you're in is the key to it.

Truly loving everything about yourself is key. Someone may say, "Well, I don't love myself because I have this or that. I don't love myself because I'm in a wheelchair." I've thought of this in the past. I've thought of how I didn't love myself because I didn't like the way my body looked. But those thoughts only led to self-loathing, which caused a lot of damage. Once I took it back and started loving again, all the little things that I judged or didn't like were loved by others as well.

If we don't love ourselves, then we will think that others don't love us either. It then becomes a self-perpetuating cycle of self loathing that turns into victim consciousness. Self-love is everyone-love!

If You Had a Magic Wand ...

I would create a world of acceptance. The acceptance would be so broad. Accepting others would mean that we accepted ourselves. Accepting everything would mean that there were no more struggles because everything was accepted. There would be no more judgment or opinions about what is nobody's business.

Now by that, I mean acceptance of all good, acceptance of all things that are pure, that come from the place of the heart, of goodness, that help our higher being and help us to be better people. That's what I mean by acceptance. I should clarify that. Not accepting all the negative, cruel, violent things in the world, but accepting all of what is true in our hearts. I think that would be a really great world.

For more information about Brynn and her work, please visit stemcellsforbrynn.com.

THIRTEEN

Colleen Patrick-Goudreau

Authenticity is Born from Compassion

"Our task must be to free ourselves by widening our circle of compassion to embrace all living creatures and the whole of nature and its beauty."

– ALBERT EINSTEIN

In a world where advice, opinions, and judgment run rampant, it's refreshing when wisdom arrives to save the day. Wisdom promotes a sense of ease. Wisdom has soul. Wisdom is truth. Wisdom changes the world.

Today's fast-paced world is inundated with knowledge but absent of wisdom. The dictionary defines wisdom as "the ability to discern what is true, right, and lasting." Knowledge, on the other hand, is defined as "knowing facts, information, and skills through experience or education." But life is not about what we know or what we've learned, it's about who we become as a result of what we know and have learned. Wisdom is knowledge embodied.

Wisdom differs from advice. Advice is the product of knowledge and seeks to demolish uncertainty. Advice is black or white—my way or the highway. By contrast, wisdom rises above one's own perspectives and explores the greater meaning beyond the limitations of knowledge. Wisdom inspires critical thought.

If we peel back the curtain on advice, we see it more clearly for what it is—a belief or opinion imposed on another under the guise of guidance.

Advice is never without bias. Advice is judgment in drag.

Advice is a filtered worldview based on personal opinions, fears, beliefs, unhealed wounds, insecurities, perceptions, thoughts, and experiences. It is often relayed as gospel—with a pinch of arrogance here and a dash of superiority there.

When we impose a worldview on another under the guise of advice, we encourage conformity to our beliefs, strategies, or mindset. We diminish the self-worth of the recipient by implying that they are incapable of discovering their own solutions. Advice is a form of projection, a devious avoidance tactic designed to "fix" the problems of others while avoiding the limitations within ourselves. Advice creates the illusion of eminence in areas of our lives that are otherwise unexamined.

Advice is surreptitious in its ability to infiltrate consciousness in ways that bring us down.

Advice imposes. Wisdom empowers. Advice speaks. Wisdom listens.

Wisdom communicates through acceptance, understanding, empathy, and compassion. In the presence of wisdom we feel safe, empowered. Wisdom has been there. Wisdom comes from the heart.

In a cultural paradigm where mass distraction is so pervasive, it takes courage to explore the truth in a world gone sideways. A wise person desires to know life from all perspectives: the pain, the joy, the lies, and the truth. Wisdom knows the limitations of knowledge and gracefully accepts that there is no greater teacher of truth than life itself.

What better teacher of compassion than one's own experiences of pain? What better teacher of humility than one's own mistakes? What better teacher of life than one's own experiences of loss? What better teacher of love than one's own capacity for forgiveness? What greater teacher of kindness than one's own connection to suffering?

Wisdom is not for the faint of heart. It means actively seeking truth in a world filled with lies.

The blind eye of ignorance may still be the cultural default, but the seed of awakening lies dormant within the hearts of everyone. We all know that we can be better. We all know that we can do better. When we say "yes" to better, we transform ourselves; we transform the world.

Our world is shifting. More and more people are actuating the seed of awakening by questioning beliefs, systems, knowledge, institutions, and industries. Wisdom is rising as powerful questions replace conditioned thought patterns. Many are asking themselves, "How do we change all that's gone wrong?"

The unfolding new paradigm is emerging as a leaderless movement inspired by a collective awakening that no longer tolerates the absence of truth. The provocateurs of higher thought in the unsettled world of today exemplify kindness, compassion, presence, and joy. With eloquent wisdom they expunge the line in the sand that separates us from life. Colleen Patrick-Goudreau is one such person, who boldly speaks to the love in our hearts that returns us to truth. She's dedicated her life to inspiring "better" by reminding us of who we truly are—compassionate beings with a love for life—all life.

Colleen is an award-winning author, engaging speaker, long-time podcast host, and tireless advocate for compassion. Her message of plant-based wellness is breaking down barriers, shifting perspectives, and indelibly altering our perception of animals.

As Colleen states, "I want to be remembered as someone who inspired people to be the best they could be: the healthiest, most joyful, most articulate ambassadors of compassion possible in order to prevent animals from being used, violated, and killed. I want to be remembered as someone who shifted the paradigm."

Shifting the paradigm is exactly what she's doing.

Colleen has a way of telling it like it is without creating division. She's passionate, compassionate, feisty, and funny. Most importantly, she's inclusive. She knows that we can all be better and speaks to the light within that is desperate to emerge.

By thinking more critically and acting more compassionately, we embody the wisdom that changes this world. As Colleen so wisely says,

"Don't do nothing just because you can't do everything. Do something. Anything."

***

Colleen's Story

Unplugging: Path to Purpose

I walk the line of guiding people and offering skills that I believe are necessary to be authentic in this world, while also acknowledging that we all have different personality traits. A lot of what I do comes from my own personality. That's what I encourage for other people as well.

We all have different paths with different hallways. Sometimes we travel down one hallway and have to turn back. We try another one as we continue to learn along the way. It's all done imperfectly, but that's what the journey of life is all about. Everyone is on a different path. There are no mistakes.

I've always been really good at listening to my intuition and being true to myself. This comes with its own pitfalls, because we live in a world where we're told that we should live according to our joy and do what we love, but there's so much pushback from family, society, and status quo, that it's not easy. Sometimes we have to plow through despite what people say—even if it's not popular.

I've always felt that I've had a kind of wind behind me pushing me forward, protecting me if I fall, but always pushing me forward. I always knew that I would be okay with this force behind me.

I've also had many defining people in my life who've supported me and made it possible to stay on course. Whenever I felt unsure, they were there to hold me and tell me exactly what I needed to hear. The defining people were the women in my life who were like mother figures. I had many wise women in my life who helped shape me. Nowadays, I take it very seriously when young people look to *me* for guidance. It's a real honor.

We have to take personal responsibility for who we choose to listen to. We're bombarded with messages from everywhere—including within ourselves. We have the choice to listen to the truth of our inner world or the noise of the external world.

The external world can sometimes be a positive influence, but because of the way it has taught us to disconnect from ourselves, we've strayed really far from our inner guidance. Fear stops us from doing what we know is right because we've lost trust in ourselves. We need to get really clear about what the fear is, because once we name it, we know the difference between what is and what isn't true.

Someone once said to me, "I'm a private chef and I've since become vegan. I'm getting more and more uncomfortable cooking meat for people. What should I do?" I replied, "When it gets uncomfortable enough, you'll stop. You know what you need to do, and when you can't do it anymore, you will stop."

Once we're really honest with ourselves, we can listen to our inner truth and the right path shows us the way.

The Foundation of Compassion

I believe that compassion is the foundation of who we are. It is so powerful because it's when we feel the most connected. When we're compassionate, there's no separation; no us and them. The work that I do is all about expanding our circle of compassion to include the animals we've commoditized and separated from.

Once we realize that we're not disconnected from anyone else, the rest is effortless. The effortless part is that we care and don't want to hurt anyone anymore. That's the truth of who we are. That's our core nature.

I talk about vegan as a means to an end because that's the most powerful way to get to the core of who we are—deep, all-inclusive compassion.

I believe that nobody wants to consciously contribute to violence or hurt others. The best way to cause no harm is to live a vegan lifestyle, because it's so broad. It's not just about eating tofu instead of chicken. It's about manifesting our deepest compassion. If I were to whittle down what it means to be vegan, I'd say it's literally the physical manifestation of our core values of compassion. We can't manifest our core values of compassion and still participate in behavior and industries that intentionally harm others. If we're still eating animals, wearing animals, using products tested on animals, or paying to see them perform, we're not honoring our core values of compassion.

Many people who consider themselves compassionate but still eat animals are indignant about this fact. I do believe that they are compassionate. But they're not living in the fullness of their compassion if they're still making choices that cause harm to others. Their compassion has been compartmentalized.

I believe that people know, at their core, that they can be and do so much better. If they're honest with themselves, they already know that better exists within. That's what I speak to. I speak to that part of everyone. Vegan is so much more than a diet. It's who we authentically are when we're connected to our deepest core values of compassion.

I can't promise that the dietary part of veganism will mean weight loss, boundless energy, or perfect health—many of the things that vegan organizations and authors promise. I think that's problematic. But I can promise that if someone becomes vegan, they will be more connected to their compassion. I can promise that they will have a new perspective on the world. I can promise that they won't be consuming saturated fat, dietary cholesterol, and animal protein. I can promise all of those things, and to me, that's what really matters because it gets to the essence of who we are. My message is compassion.

Hope for a Better World

I'm a consummate optimist. I'm seeing big shifts happening. There's a desperate desire for authenticity. I can speak anecdotally about this. This is what I hear from people who connect with me. This is what I see from people. The stories that I read from people who write to me are stories about finding truth, speaking truth, living from the heart, and finally feeling authentic. It's very moving.

Many more people these days are wanting to feel good and healthy so that they operate from their highest selves. Quite frankly, animal-based meat, dairy, and eggs are a great metaphor for what is spiritually and physically wrong. The consumption of animal products is like coating ourselves with death and fat.

More people are seeking out what it feels like to live authentically and to eat authentically. It's really a beautiful thing because once they know how it all feels, they want more of it and they want to share it. That's what evangelism is, right? There's a natural instinct to want to share with everybody how good it feels to be so real. Once we feel what it's like to be removed from separation and to live authentically, it becomes contagious.

I really believe that our thoughts create our reality. I really believe that people are good and that compassion will prevail. I believe that. If I'm wrong, then what do I have to lose?

But if I'm right, then this will be a completely transformed world, and I want to live in that place rather than the other place.

An Inspired Life

I practice what I preach and I preach what I practice. I mean, this all comes from a place of me trying to do the best that I can.

I'm always asking myself what I can do better. How I can be a better daughter, wife, friend, citizen, neighbor, advocate, mother to my cats, or a better part of my community?

An inspired life is about being really honest. It's about being able to look at myself and see where I need to improve and always being willing to say that I made a mistake. I can always do better.

I'm not perfect. But in every aspect of my life, I try to make decisions that have the least harmful impact and the greatest helpful impact. I don't always succeed, but since that's my goal, I tend to do a better job striving toward that.

I know that I'm never going to be perfect. I'm never going to do it all right. I'm going to make mistakes. But if the direction I'm looking is to be the best that I can be, and the most compassionate that I can be, I get better and more consistent results.

Recharging and Reconnecting

I'm a very ritual- and habit-oriented person. I do really well with routine. I always have.

Every morning I work out to start my day feeling grounded. I find that if I don't, I feel ungrounded and disorganized. I'm up at 5:30 a.m. Working out is the first thing I do. I start with some core work or resistance training. It feels so good to move after sleeping for seven hours or so. After that, I meditate. I'm not very good at sitting still because I have a huge amount of energy. So meditation is an ongoing practice for me. It's really good for keeping me still in my body and for focusing my mind. Part of my meditation is about problem-solving. It's not just sitting around in stillness. It's also making mindful decisions about who I want to be that day, how I want to be that day, and how I want to treat other people that day.

That is the most centering part of my day, when I literally invite all of the people that I'm going to interact with into my heart and commit to being the best, most compassionate person I can be. It becomes the touchstone for my day. I really believe in the power of mindfulness practice to remain centered throughout each day.

It's a lot easier for me to be kind and compassionate to other people than it is to be kind and compassionate to myself. That's the truth. I mean, it just is. But meditation and mindfulness have helped me shift that. It's an ongoing practice to be mindful in every moment, but it's worth it.

I also love spending a lot of time in nature. If I can't get outside, I feel loopy. It's essential for me. I spend as much time as I can outside. Running and hiking are really important for me to recharge and reconnect to myself.

At the end of every day, I take stock and check in with myself to see how I did. Some days are better than others, but the mindful intention is always there.

If You Had a Magic Wand …

Maybe it's a bit cliché, but I would create a world where we recognized the beauty in every single being that crosses our path—their flaws and their perfections. I speak about wanting to change our collective perspective so that we no longer see animals as commodities for profit and abuse. I prefer that we see animals as the autonomous and wondrous beings that they are. Not as higher beings, but as fabulous as they are with their quirks, flaws, and imperfections. If we could celebrate the differences as much as the similarities, that would be the most powerful thing to shift our perspective in how we treat one another, how we treat animals, how we see animals, and how we eat and live in this world. It would be such a beautiful place if we saw the sameness rather than the differences.

For more information about Colleen and her work, please visit joyfulvegan.com.

FOURTEEN

Louise LeBrun
A Catalyst for Accelerated Evolution

*"The key to growth is the introduction of higher dimensions
of consciousness into our awareness."*

– LAO TZU

There are many Universal laws that govern our life on earth. One such law is the Law of Gravity. Without it, we'd float aimlessly about. The Law of Free Will empowers us with choice. How we choose is how we live. The Law of Action manifests our thoughts, hopes, and dreams. No action, no results.

The Law of Resonance states very simply that like attracts like. Think about it: when you feel creative, you attract inspired thoughts. When you feel agitated, you attract annoying situations. When you feel happy, you attract positive interactions. This isn't new age fluff; it's just the way it is.

We are energetic beings. What we transmit reflects back to us. Gandhi knew this. "Be the change that you wish to see in the world," he once said. If we want more peace, love, passion, joy, and truth in the world, we must first *be* that ourselves.

At its most basic level, quantum physics explains that the world is composed of vibrating energy. Dogs, chickens, trees, pigs, flowers, water, you, me—we all exist as the same energy. This is the web of life. Quantum physics describes the universe as nothing more than vibrating strings of energy. On a molecular level, vibrational frequency is all that differentiates us.

Our quality of consciousness determines the vibrational intensity of the energy we project. Toxic, fearful thoughts equal toxic, fearful, low-vibration energy. Peaceful, inspired thoughts equal peaceful, inspired, high-vibration energy. It's that simple. When we live from a higher state of consciousness, we resonate with higher-vibration thought energy. When we vibrate at a higher frequency, we resonate with others who vibrate at higher frequencies.

Sometimes the Universe coordinates the meeting of two resonant souls in creative ways. Many call it fate, chance, or destiny, a random occurrence at play. I believe it's much simpler than that: the Law of Resonance at work.

My circuitous journey of healing inspired immense transformation. As I expanded into more of who I was meant to be, I developed a hunger for more of who I was yet to become. Enter Louise LeBrun, a passionate catalyst for accelerated human evolution. In Louise's words, "Transformation requires safety, science, and a touch of the sacred. Anything less, and what we get is incremental change." Louise and I both agree—incremental change sucks! Voila, resonant energy.

I was turned on to Louise's body of work at a coffee shop on a beautiful summer day in 2013. A patio, an iced soy chai, and an engaging conversation with an inspiring friend. "There is someone whose work you must get to know," she said. The Law of Resonance in action. "Tell me more," I replied. The Law of Free Will in action. This led to a paradigm-altering audio program, an inspiring book, and an insatiable desire to meet Louise. The Law of Action in action.

It is commonly believed that when the student is ready, the teacher will appear. I've been blessed to have been inspired by many wise teachers along the way, but few have resonated as deeply as Louise LeBrun. Louise articulates what many cannot set to words. She speaks with a resonant intensity that ignites what is aching to come alive from within.

Louise is the founder of the WEL-Systems® Institute and creator of the WEL-Systems® body of knowledge—a gateway to the paradigm shift essential for quantum global transformation. The WEL-Systems® approach to transformation awakens the core of our greatest potential.

Louise is a visionary, activist, cutting-edge thinker, writer, speaker, educator, and coach. She's also a deeply respected mentor who continually expands my world. There are no words to articulate the depth of gratitude that I have for her wisdom, her work, her kindness, her generosity ... her Self.

We all have the power to transform our lives. The shift often begins by simply telling the truth—by expressing who we are and what we really want. The baffling question, then, is why do so many of us stick with the status quo rather than risk change? Why do we remain loyal to who we have been rather than discovering who we can become? It takes great courage to seek the truth of who we are, even more so to live it. But as the saying goes, courage is not the absence of fear, it's the willingness to act in spite of it.

The time has arrived to claim the truth of who we are and expand into who we've always been meant to be. We're at a pivotal time in the history of our existence where we desperately need a revolution in consciousness. What will it take to come fully alive? Allow Louise LeBrun to show you the way.

***

Louise's Story

Unplugging: Path to Purpose

I was eighteen years old and suicidal—far too young to die. When I realized this, I knew I needed to change. This is how it all began for me.

I relied heavily on my intellect and believed that if I had the right knowledge or enough knowledge, this would be my gateway to inner peace.

Being born in the 1950s, I was at the cutting edge of the emerging self-help movement. I was a voracious reader. I read all the psychology books I could get my hands on. I also started therapy in my late teens. I loved reading the same books that therapists would read for their training. This made for great intellectual duels with my therapist.

I noticed that despite my intellectual prowess, however, I still felt crazy. When my life was working and everybody behaved the way I thought they should, everything worked really well. But despite my vast repertoire of knowledge, when things didn't go well I would spin out and wonder, "Where did I go? What happened to me?"

I began to pay close attention to myself, and I noticed that there were things going on in my body that defied my intellect. I expanded my realm of knowledge through the study of NLP (neurolinguistic programming). I became a master practitioner, and eventually an NLP trainer. This also included the study of hypnotherapy.

My curiosity led me to the gaps in NLP. When things didn't work, I wanted to know why. When they did work, I wanted to know how they worked—what caused the change, and what was being said that caused the change. They were very different things.

I eventually recognized within myself that there was something happening with my body. I noticed that my body was far more powerful than my formidable intellect, because it could stop me in my tracks. I realized that I would never find the right book, the right knowledge, the right people, the right group, the right training, or the right community. It just wasn't out there.

In a moment of total and utter despair, I literally fell back on my bed, sobbing with tears. I let go. I gave up. It was a pivotal moment in my life, because something profound happened in my body. It was rage, outrage, disappointment, despair, and the exhaustion of a search that always led to nowhere.

This intense letting go took about three minutes. At the end of it, my body felt very stable and I finally felt peaceful. I was about thirty years old then. I'd been searching for years for what happened in those three minutes of total surrender. This experience changed my life, and it led me on a mission to discover what it was all about.

Fast-forward a few years. I'm a single mother and I discover that one of my children has been abused by a babysitter. There's no greater guilt than to know that, as a mother, I had not protected him from this violation. Despite my expansive knowledge and insight, I didn't understand what had happened to him. I couldn't relate to it.

I began to realize that the abuse he experienced was not a child's problem. It was an adult's problem, and no amount of incarceration could change that.

That was really the starting point for my exploration into how I could empower adults to realize that they no longer had to live as byproducts of their parenting. There's a high correlation between people who abuse and the history of their own abuse. I wanted this to end.

That became the platform for everything that has evolved over the last twenty years in my work. It's a journey into the Self. In my world, it starts with me, just like in your world it starts with you. If I don't change the identity that I carry, I will not change the way I think. If I don't change the way I think, I won't change the way I choose. If I don't change the way I choose, my world remains the same. It's not about changing what's outside, it's about changing what's inside.

Changing what is outside is like moving the deck chairs around on the Titanic. Unless there's an internal course change, the ship goes down.

Personal Transformation

I've worked with both men and women for over thirty years, but I've chosen to devote my attention to working with women.

As women, we tend to be terrified. We're terrified to be wrong. We're terrified to make a mistake. We're terrified to not know. We're terrified to come to a realization inside of ourselves that we are innately broken—that we're insufficient. It doesn't matter how many degrees we have, how much money we make, how many cars we drive, or how big our house is.

Deep down, we believe that we're a fraud.

The blockage and the release are unique to each person. Transformation emerges from within as we relax into a process of inner discovery. People must be able to find a safe place to come face-to-face with themselves and move into their truth, and that's when they can finally discover the deep, deep magic of who they really are. The willingness to engage with this process is what brings about transformation.

It's been scientifically proven that we are all beings of energy. Yet this is something that is profoundly negated by our culture. We talk about how we are spiritual beings having a human experience, and how we are beings of light. But the question nobody seems to ask is, "How does a being of light live in a world of matter?"

There's so much scientific evidence that we are beings of light, from endless stories of near-death experiences, from Bruce Lipton's work, and from so many others. But we don't know how to live in a world of matter. Essentially, we are all living god-forces expressing ourselves through tissue.

Sadly, that's a far cry from what and who we've been told we are. We've been conditioned to believe we're everything that we're not. We must remember that we are a god-force expressing itself through physical tissue.

Every morning I ask myself this question, "How does the god-force that I am choose to live my life today?" We all need to ask this question. When we ask ourselves this question, we don't live a life that's rooted in fear. We don't live a life that's rooted in scarcity. We don't live a life that's rooted in anger and separation.

There's a massive internal shift that occurs. This is what inspires higher-level choices. By embracing this higher-order identity, we're supported by higher-order thoughts—all because we've remembered the god-force that we are. It all starts with breath. So many people have unconsciously trained themselves to not breathe properly. This only serves to lock things down in their bodies so that their pain doesn't interfere with their ability to function.

As a species, we've become adept at managing our physiology so that we can tolerate the intolerable. By managing our physiology, we're able to do work that depletes us, remain in marriages that hurt us, and allow ourselves to be denigrated verbally, emotionally, and sometimes physically within our family systems. After all, blood is thicker than water.

These are the things that make us crazy as a species. You don't have to be a rocket scientist to see how this cultural conditioning has led to choices that are destroying the very biosphere that supports our existence. This is a deep, deep intergenerational, thousands-of-years-old coma. The only way to penetrate the coma is to provide a space of safety where powerful conversations can be had that interconnect new knowledge, new information, and an entirely new way to consider the truth of our own experiences without the filter of our conditioning. I do this through my Decloaking and Living Authentically™ program, and the in-person programs that follow.

I've written five books and created multiple audio programs. There's also a lot of free content on my website that can be accessed anytime. It's profoundly life-altering.

The more important thing to note is that transformation happens through the body. If we stop and think about the most pivotal and significant moments in our lives, they're always preceded by sensory cues that feel like a wave moving through the body. There may have been goose bumps or hair standing up on the back of the neck that resulted in a curtain of tears, hysterical laughter, or some other emotional response. But there is always a wave of information that moves through the body. Quantum TLC™ is a process I created that allows this wave to move unhindered through the body without the need to slow it down by talking about it or trying to understand it. We just get out of the way and let the body do what it's designed to do.

In the moment that the wave moves through us, there's a curtain of cascading white light moving through the body—a trillion bazillion cells talking to each other. It's all electricity and energy. That's what Quantum

TLC facilitates. It's similar to what we see in science videos that show cellular activity when information is moved through the body. Once we move through this natural process, the body stabilizes, and the neurological pathways are altered. Quantum TLC shakes things up. It shuts down some neural connections and opens up new neural connections. These new neural connections inform the body, and this allows for new insight, new discovery, and a new way of being.

When people leave a Decloaking and Living Authentically experience, they don't just leave with new knowledge, they leave with a more expansive sense of personal identity. There's no return to a conditioned life after this transformative process.

Global Transformation

We already have a critical mass in a coma. What we need now is the critical mass of awakening. I believe that an awakening is happening all around the world in many different ways.

We can all make simple choices that bring an end to the systems that have caused so much destruction. For example, if I want to see an end to factory farming, I stop supporting it. I don't have to picket or walk up and down the street with a protest sign. I just say no by voting with my choices and my wallet. End of story.

Imagine if a billion people did this. It would bring a grinding halt to the brutality that profoundly affects those who ingest the flesh of animals that are full of antibiotics and other drugs. More importantly, the chemical signatures of terror and pain that come from consuming this brutalized flesh would no longer be an issue—all from simply saying no to this violent system. Things didn't change because we went out and did anything extraordinary. They changed because we stopped doing what we've been mindlessly doing for decades. I think we'd be amazed at the instant effects of these choices. We don't have to spend exhausting hours trying to figure anything out. We just have to stop doing it. News travels fast through the internet, so there's no excuse for ignorance anymore.

If we don't redirect on a scale that is significant enough to be recognizable, Gaia is going to do it for us. I really believe that. We know that ignorance and fear does not define a culture in any way that is life-supporting, so the only way to transform this world is to awaken our Selves.

Reconnecting

My commitment is to the process of discovery, not to any particular practice, just an ongoing process of self-discovery. I started when I was eighteen, so I'm well-practiced in this process. Where I'm most vulnerable is around my kids. They're living in a world that I'm very concerned about. They're the generation who will pay the price for our cultural ignorance.

In the moments when I feel despair over the destruction caused by generations of collective ignorance, I allow myself to have my tears. I allow myself to feel what is authentic so that I fully own the power of these feelings in my body. That's how I stay connected to my Self. That is what allows me to remain passionate about the intention that I carry. Surrender is not an issue. Walking away from despair isn't going to happen. Pretending it's not occurring isn't going to happen. This means that I have to be willing to have my moments, knowing that that's all it is. It's just a moment. It's not my identity. It's not my future. It's just a moment. Live it and get on with it.

Recharging

I'm formidable in many ways, but I know that the world I am seeking to create cannot be created alone. I'm reaching out and looking for the women who can no longer deny the higher vibration within themselves. I'm looking for the women who are seeking not just to be able to claim and express this, but to go beyond by asking, "How do I now become the most magnificent living expression of the god-force that I am?"

In a time and in a world that is absolutely screaming for an awakening of consciousness, how do we do this as part of a collective? How do we do this in a way that encourages the continued evolution of our capital S Self?

I think that's a challenge for women, but we have to rise beyond our histories and our experiences to discover that we're so much more than any of that.

If You Had a Magic Wand ...

From a biosphere perspective, I would certainly make some adjustments to the systems. Realistically, I do believe that every single one of us not only has the magic wand to be able to create something better, but I think we actually *are* that wand. If we were willing to reveal that within ourselves, we would have paradise on earth. We would think differently, choose differently, and we would behave very differently. Our world would look very different, and I don't think it would take long to clean up the planet, either.

To learn more about Louise's extensive body of work, visit WEL-Systems.com. Check out her transformative eBook on iTunes, New Paradigm—New World: Awakening the Quantum Biological Human™

FIFTEEN

Steve Pavlina
Daring to Care in an Uncaring World

"Be daring, be different, be impractical, be anything that will assert integrity of purpose and imaginative vision against the play-it-safers, the creatures of the commonplace, the slaves of the ordinary."

– CECIL BEATON

Humanitarian Harriet Tubman once said, "Every great dream begins with a dreamer. Always remember, you have within you the strength, the patience, and the passion to reach for the stars to change the world."

The word "passion" is derived from the Latin root *pati*, which means "to suffer, to endure." Passion is the powerful force that compels us to persevere despite pain, uncertainty, or fear. Passion weathers the storm no matter how tumultuous it is. Passion is our passport to greatness.

With our collective aversion to pain, it's no wonder that today's world is devoid of passion. No passion, no purpose. No purpose, no life-force. Under the guise of "busy," the prevailing culture of distraction fosters a complacent mindset that blindly accepts the status quo. By not challenging ourselves to be and do better, we negate the passion in our hearts. We search outside for something to spark us, forgetting that we already *are* that which we purport to seek. Sadly, since we already have what we're looking for, the search always turns up empty. The key is to stop long enough to be found. When we remember who we authentically are, passion flows with ease.

Passion is life-force. It's the outspoken renegade in a culture of conformity. It's what carries us, lifts us, and fuels us with the courage to challenge the status quo, demolish boundaries, speak out against injustice, and ultimately, create a new world story.

Passion is love on fire.

Passion is at the very core of Steve Pavlina, a man with a voracious hunger for truth, love, and life. Gandhi once said, "Where there is love, there is life." Where there is love, there is also truth. Love, life, and truth are essentially interchangeable. Passion is what drives it all.

Steve Pavlina is a warrior for truth who is widely recognized as one of the most successful online personal development bloggers. He's a prodigious critical thinker who fearlessly alters paradigms, a man on a mission to inspire within each of us the best that we can be. He's written over 1,300 articles on topics ranging from productivity and relationships to spirituality and higher consciousness. He's been quoted by *The New York Times*, *USA Today*, the *Los Angeles Daily News*, and *The Guardian*, with many of his articles translated into languages that inspire readers in over 150 countries. He's an author, a speaker, and a man who dares to care in an uncaring world. His message is simple: never stop growing as a conscious human being.

Steve's passion for personal betterment was spawned after being arrested for felony grand theft. He chose a better path, a path aligned with his heart. Steve has since become one of the most inspiring growth-oriented individuals in the public eye.

Steve is fearless in his approach to life. He lives out loud and boldly shares his essence with the world. He's passionate, compassionate, courageous, and loving. He knows that the only way to meet today's challenges is not to use yesterday's solutions, but to dare to think the previously unthinkable, speak the previously unspeakable, and do what was previously out of the question.

Steve Pavlina dares to dream big, and in the spirit of Harriet Tubman, with strength, patience, and passion, he is indeed changing the world—one heart at a time.

Steve's Story

Unplugging: Path to Purpose

From the time we're babies to the time we die, we experience growth in our lives. But we all start off on a path of unconscious growth. Most of us eventually experience some form of life-altering catalyst that forces a deeper examination of life. This is when we have the choice: to cooperate and be a conscious participant, or remain a victim of life. It's a lot more empowering to cooperate.

My life began with twelve years of Catholic school, from grade one through to high school. I was raised in a pretty strict environment. My mother was a college math professor and my father was an aerospace engineer. They had the same jobs for thirty-five years. It was like being raised by two androids, but two religious androids. It was a very stable, linear existence.

There was no objection from my parents when I told them that I wanted to major in computer science. It made my linear-thinking parents very happy.

I was one of those people who knew what I would study in college before I even started high school. When I got into computers, there was no doubt that it would be my path. As long as I didn't stray from that path, I was well supported.

We lived in a nice middle-class neighborhood in Los Angeles. All my friends and family members were Catholic. Everybody was married. There were no divorces in our families. I didn't know anything outside of that insulated environment. In that sense, it was very structured.

When I went to college at UC Berkeley, it was an entirely different experience for me. I began questioning my religious beliefs to the point where I didn't believe in anything anymore. I explored alternative beliefs through the friends I made along the way. This led me to experiment with everything that was the opposite of what I grew up with. My first semester in college, I tried alcohol. I also started playing weekly poker with my friends.

My first month in college, I began shoplifting. I got into a lot of trouble. I was arrested four times and barely escaped a long jail sentence for felony grand theft. I got off with community service because of an administrative glitch, but I should have spent a year or two in prison. I'd taken a crazy detour in life, but there was a part of me that was lit up by this detour.

Because of the self-destructive nature of my choices, my life was really chaotic. I stopped going to classes. After three semesters, I was kicked out of school.

After my explosion against the rigid structure that I grew up with, I went through a contemplative period. I began wondering, "Who am I now?" After destroying the path that was laid out for me, I couldn't go back. One part of me was asking why I'd sabotaged myself, and the other part felt liberated from all of the previous cultural expectations. I finally had the ability to choose my life. This gave me a profound sense of freedom.

For the next year, I didn't do much. I moved back to LA and got a job working for six dollars an hour in a video game store. In an eight-hour shift, I'd do about sixty minutes of real work. When customers came in, I'd talk about video games. It was so easy. It gave me a lot of space to think. I wasn't making much money, but it kept me out of trouble. In my spare time, I started thinking about personal growth. I read a lot of books, including *The Seven Habits of Highly Effective People* by Stephen Covey. That book inspired the exploration of who I really wanted to be.

Up until that point, I didn't know that I had a choice, because the Bible tells us what we're supposed to be. There are so many rules, and everyone is taught to be essentially the same character. I was really excited to find that there were so many other alternatives to choose from. I could choose to be an adventurous risk-taker or someone more security-oriented. The possibilities were endless.

This led to a lot of deep questions about myself. I went through an experimental phase that eventually led me back to school. This time it was with a newfound sense of purpose, and a mission to learn more about myself. I was eager to sculpt the person I really wanted to be.

I realized that I didn't have to be who my parents taught me to be. I could choose. But at the same time, I didn't have to automatically reject everything. I could keep the good parts of my upbringing, shed what I didn't like, and replace anything that didn't feel right. I realized that I wanted to really stretch myself. I didn't want to live like everyone else. I wanted to set goals that I knew I was capable of, but that other people wouldn't believe. I think we all have this inside of us. We all have our special strengths and talents. I knew that there were things I could probably do that exceeded cultural expectations if I really pushed myself.

So I went back to school and did a double major in computer science and mathematics. I started over as a freshman because I had flunked out at UC Berkeley. This time I went to Cal State Northridge and started with a clean slate. I managed to get through the entire four-year curriculum in just three semesters. Within a year and a half, I graduated with two degrees by taking a triple course load. I ignored everyone's advice and just went for it.

While I was at school, I would feed my mind with positive, growth-oriented material for a couple of hours a day. This was before iPods and iPhones. I'd listen to audio cassettes on my little Walkman tape player. I didn't have a lot of money at the time, so I listened to the same tapes over and over again. I'd also borrow tapes from the library, listen to them for a couple of weeks, and then get more. It was my own personal coaching program. I kept pumping my mind with positive information. I finally felt like I was figuring out who I wanted to be.

There are many more steps along the journey, but that was the launching point for my discovery that I didn't have to be what society told me to be. I empowered myself to consciously choose from the myriad of possibilities for who I wanted to be, what skills I wanted to develop, and what kind of character I wanted to create for my life story.

Being so aligned with growth has made me feel much more connected to life. This is how I evolved into doing the work I do today.

The Spiritual Path of Veganism

I didn't actually set out to become vegan. It started as an experiment that was inspired by a vegetarian friend in college. I always found it interesting that he ate cheese pizza while I ate pepperoni pizza. He was never pushy about trying to convert me, but I was curious about it. I wondered what it would be like to be vegetarian. I grew up eating a pretty standard American diet: meat, potatoes, and a few vegetables.

One day I decided to do a thirty-day trial to experience things from the inside. I realized that an inside perspective is very different from an outside perspective. As any vegan knows, the way meat-eaters think about being vegan is very different from the actual experience of being vegan. The way meat-eaters think their lives would be if they became vegan is not at all how it is as a vegan. Because most vegans remember what it was like to eat meat, dairy, and eggs, they have both perspectives. Unless people actually experience something, they're ignorant. The interior perspective is always very different. I knew this because of the shift I'd had in religious beliefs—from being Catholic to no longer being Catholic. I experienced both sides and knew how different they were.

So, having gone through that kind of shift with religion, I thought, "What if it's like that with vegetarianism? What if the interior perspective of a vegetarian is different from how I imagine it to be from the outside looking in?" That's one of the reasons I decided to do a thirty-day trial. There's nothing like personal experience for true understanding.

That was back in 1993. It wasn't nearly as difficult as I thought it would be. It was actually really easy. I would go running each morning and noticed that it felt easier. I was getting a little faster without really trying. I had more energy and I was breathing easier, and I could also concentrate better. When I arrived at day thirty-one, I had only vegetarian food in my apartment, so I decided to just keep eating that way.

Pretty soon, six months had passed and I was still eating vegetarian. I realized at that point that I no longer wanted meat. I no longer had a taste for it, and the thought of having meat turned my stomach. It wasn't for ethical reasons that I got on this path. It was more of a personal growth experiment.

I realized that as I explored the interior perspective of vegetarianism, I began thinking differently. It changed my thoughts around animals. I could now look at a chicken, cow, or pig and not feel like I owed them an apology. I was no longer paying anyone to kill them, cage them, forcibly impregnate them, or steal their babies from them.

That surprised me. It was an unexpected side effect. I had no idea that it would increase my sense of caring or compassion. For me, it was always just a growth experiment.

As I kept going down that path, I started thinking that maybe I should go vegan. Maybe I should expand my relationship with animals. I realized that because I was buying cow's milk and eggs, I was still participating in the system. So now it was becoming an ethical issue for me. I was vegetarian for about three and a half years before I finally decided to go vegan.

Once again, it started with a thirty-day trial. But this time it was a little different. This time I decided in advance that if the thirty-day trial went well, I'd stick with it.

That was in 1997. I've been vegan ever since. After I went vegan, I really started to wake up. I started feeling a sense of oneness and connection with animals. I shed that sense of human superiority and dominion that I was taught when I was growing up. I began thinking of animals as equally valuable beings on this planet. As I progressed further down this path, I got rid of all my leather and wool because I didn't want to relate to animals on the basis of force in any way. I realized that I wanted to relate to animals as more like family.

I think the reason we control animals the way we do is because we think we can. But is that a good reason to do what we do to them? What's the real reason for eating them? Because we like the taste of their flesh? I don't think that's it. It's almost like there's a special power trip from having a sense of dominance over them. And really, ten billion animals slaughtered for food each year in the USA alone? That's insane. The relationship we've created with the animals of this world is insane. It's not just damaging to the animals, it's damaging to us. I believe that our relationship to animals affects how we feel about ourselves, our place in nature, and what we think we deserve as a human being. I think it affects all of our relationships, including how much love we experience with each other.

When I allowed myself to love animals and connect with them in a deeper way, it changed things across the board. I experienced a profound heart-opening that changed how I feel toward people as well. To me, being vegan and doing service work in the world go hand in hand. I don't think I would be doing the work I do today if I wasn't vegan, because I wouldn't care. I wouldn't have the deep sense of caring for life that I do.

If I can't care about a cow, I can't care about humanity. To me, they're inseparable. I know some people might argue otherwise. But to me, caring applies to all life.

As many vegans already know, it's easy to see how much better the world would be if we eliminated animal products. Life would be so much better for everyone. We would have more resources available, a lot less scarcity, a lot more abundance, a lot better health. We would practically empty our hospitals, and so many resources could be diverted to better use than caging and killing animals. We'd also drastically reduce greenhouse gases. Across the board, it's so much better for everybody.

The larger body of existence wants harmony, not just for humans, but for all species. It wants us to express our creativity and achieve our greatest potential. It really wants us to care more—about all living beings.

If I had a message to share with vegans, I would say, let people know that you care. Don't hide your caring. Don't let society tell you that caring is wrong, or that you're an extremist or a radical because you care too

much. Put that part of yourself on display. You don't have to be belliger-
ent or turn people against you, but you can let people know how you feel.
You can express your caring more openly. I think if anything has a chance
to transform the way society relates to animals, it will be people openly
expressing how much they care.

Vision for a Better Self

My ultimate vision for my Self is to become a man that I absolutely
love. It's to be the person that I admire. So the questions that I ask myself are: "What kind of man must I be to ridiculously love myself?" and
"What kind of qualities do I admire?"

Some answers are obvious. I have to be vegan. I wouldn't love myself
as much if I weren't. If I had a relationship with animals where I treated them as products and consumables, that would not be the best me. I
know that I can be better than that.

I also have to be brave enough to tackle challenges. If I fear public
speaking, for instance, that's not me. I should be totally comfortable in
front of an audience, because the fear isn't rational.

Life is impermanent. When we die, if we take anything at all with us,
it's an aspect of our consciousness. All the physical stuff remains here.
Even our human relationships remain here. If we attach our sense of security to what's temporary, we'll always feel insecure. But if we can root
ourselves to something that lasts, like our best self, then we have a deeper
sense of security in life.

Recharging and Reconnecting

Most mornings I'm out running at 5 a.m. When I've completed my
run, I cool down and relax in a nearby park. There's a grove of trees where
I like to sit and enjoy the birds. I'm usually there around sunup when the
birds are really active.

I feel a beautiful sense of joy and connection with the birds, just listening to their songs. It's really interesting to watch how they begin their

day. I feel a deep connection with these beautiful beings—fellow species on this planet Earth. It really lights me up and gives me a deep sense of unity. Animals always help me feel connected.

If You Had a Magic Wand …

I would create a world where everybody cares about the planet as a whole, where everyone feels a sense of responsibility for making the planet a better place for all living beings. If everyone thought about how they could serve the planet, it would be an incredible world.

I don't think we need a magic wand to accomplish this, though. If more and more people wake up to this level of thinking, eventually there will be a critical mass that changes the way people think in society.

If people stopped thinking in terms of what they need to learn in school to get a job, raise a family, buy cars, homes, and stuff, and instead thought about their mission for a better world, they'd be inspired by a greater calling to do the work that they're meant to do in the world.

Life gets so easy when you say yes to it … and keep on saying yes to it!

To connect with Steve and his work, please visit stevepavlina.com.

SIXTEEN

Janette Murray-Wakelin
Conscious Choices Change the World

"Learn from yesterday, live for today, hope for tomorrow.
The important thing is not to stop questioning."

– ALBERT EINSTEIN

My first meeting with Janette Murray-Wakelin was filled with tears. It was the autumn of 2004 in the small Vancouver Island town of Courtenay, BC. Janette was the featured speaker at an Earthsave Canada event. The evening was lighthearted and festive—great food, great conversation, and a hall packed with like-minded souls.

When Janette took the stage, the room fell silent. "Festive" became "focused" as anticipation filled the air. With raw authenticity, Janette shared her heart and held the crowd riveted with her transformative story, leaving a teary-eyed trail of inspiration in her wake.

In 2001, at the age of fifty-two, Janette was diagnosed with a highly aggressive carcinoma breast cancer. Medical doctors gave her, at most, six months to live. After recovering from the shock of the initial diagnosis, she chose "not that." Unwilling to accept the medical death sentence, Janette resolved to take matters into her own hands. Not only did she reject the life-destroying solutions championed by the allopathic medical system, she also rejected their bleak prognosis. Janette turned her back on modern medicine with an intentional power that supplanted all fear.

She dove head first into an intensive mind-body-spirit journey of healing. Her healing path consisted of infrared detoxification therapy, holistic immunotherapy, ozone treatment, conscious breathing, aerobic exercise, visualization, meditation, spiritual awareness, and maximizing her nutritional intake through juicing, wheatgrass, and living raw vegan foods.

Within six months of this rigorous regime, Janette was given a clean bill of health with no signs of cancer anywhere in her body. Janette is quick to mention that this miraculous time was filled with love, laughter, and ample support from her family and friends.

I had the honor of befriending Janette while living in Courtenay. I was impressed by her bountiful energy and exceptional joie-de-vivre. At the time, she owned a small juice shop with her life-partner, Alan. I became a regular customer, hungry to learn more from this dynamic woman.

As a long-time athlete, I was also impressed with Janette's running prowess. With ease, she'd set off for hours-long running excursions into the mountains. Upon return, she'd casually carry on with her day, often with no mention of her epic daily pursuits.

I lost touch with Janette when my partner and I moved from Courtenay, but Janette's story of defiant courage remained permanently etched on my heart.

Janette and Alan eventually returned to their roots Down Under. Originally from New Zealand, the pair now lives near Melbourne, Australia. We reconnected in 2013 when I discovered that they would embark on a record-breaking journey of passion, purpose, and compassion. Despite the many years that had passed, their joie-de-vivre had not wavered.

Now well into their 60s, the dynamic duo inspired millions of people around the globe with their Running Raw Around Australia adventure. By running a marathon a day for 366 days straight around the perimeter of Australia, they logged an incredible 15,782 kilometers, fueled entirely by raw fruit, smoothies, and vegetables. This incredible feat was motivated by a deeper sense of purpose: to inspire conscious living, promote kindness and compassion for all living beings, and raise environmental awareness for a sustainable future.

Janette and Alan run their talk and lead by example. By completing a marathon every day for 366 days (they did a bonus marathon on January 1, 2014), they inspired millions of people to believe in themselves, to follow their dreams, and to achieve their goals with simple lifestyle choices. As Janette states on her website, "We can be living proof of what can be achieved by making conscious life choices. Inspiration is what motivates people to 'Never Stop Pushing' for what they believe in and for what they want to achieve. We believe that the survival of the human species is dependent on our kindness, compassion and caring for all living beings, and that this is achieved by making conscious lifestyle choices. By doing so, we can make a difference."

There's a common misperception that epic feats are accomplished only by epic people. But what defines an epic person? There really are only four factors: passion, drive, conviction, and love—qualities that reside within each and every one of us, ready to be activated with the flip of a perceptual switch.

Lao Tzu once said, "A journey of a thousand miles begins with a single step." Every great accomplishment begins with a single step. Every painting begins with a single stroke; every book begins with a single word; every life change begins with a single decision.

Janette and Alan prove that anything is possible—one step at a time. We're never too young, we're never too old. Most importantly, they show us that we can all be exceptional. When we open our hearts, say yes to life, and leap over the hurdle of fear, we emerge stronger than we could ever imagine. We shift our perspective from head to heart and everything changes for the better. It's that simple.

***

Janette's Story

Unplugging: Path to Purpose

I have memories of my mother's generation being filled with a persistent fear of cancer. There was so much hype about cancer becoming the new epidemic. Rather than thinking about cancer prevention, they just lived in fear. It was a large industry in the making. We now know it as the biggest money-maker in the sickness industry.

When I was diagnosed, I was on the edge of that mindset. It was devastating to get a diagnosis with such a poor prognosis. At that time, the cancer statistics were one in nine. When I published my most recent book in 2014, the statistics had risen to one in two.

There's so much fear-mongering tied to the pharmaceutical industry, because there's a lot of money to be made from "researching the cure." People don't know about other possibilities because they're not given any choices. They may be given a few options that treat the symptoms, but that's not what it's about. It's about taking care of ourselves, preferably with a preventative lifestyle.

If a person is in ill health, whether it's cancer or a cold, there's an imbalance in the body. And there are varying degrees of imbalance. There's always a reason for it. Once the reason or cause is discovered, it can be eliminated. It's very, very simple. Because we've been brainwashed to believe that something is incurable, or that the only treatment option is chemotherapy from a doctor, we perpetuate the belief that it's incurable.

When I first got the diagnosis, I had to know why it happened and how I could change it. When we think of how the body works for us twenty-four hours a day, even in the womb, we realize how miraculous it is. Until we die, it never stops working to maintain an optimal state of health. It highlights for us when things aren't right, but it never works against us.

When I think of the cancer treatments perpetuated by the status quo, they make no sense. They hinder the body's natural healing abilities. It's illogical to further compromise the body by giving it treatments that only make us more ill and that we may not recover from.

After my diagnosis, I did a lot of research into alternatives. With the support of family and friends, I came up with a plan that I felt comfortable with. I found natural ways to support the body so that it could heal itself.

I started looking at the food I was eating. I was already vegetarian. I thought this was pretty healthy, but I found out that I could be even more healthy by eliminating everything that compromised my body and well-being.

I eliminated everything negative and replaced it with everything positive. I switched to a raw vegan diet; I meditated and began living more mindfully. Since switching to a raw vegan diet and a more conscious lifestyle, not only am I healed from the cancer, my mind is clearer, and I'm more spiritually aware. I feel that this simple lifestyle shift can help anyone.

I've come to the conclusion over the last few years that the most important thing people must know is that they're worth it. Most people don't place enough value on themselves to even consider doing something that is outside of the cultural box of thinking. They don't believe in the natural healing ability of the body, so they resign themselves to a system that clearly doesn't work. They don't take responsibility for their own health. Most people don't take ownership and they throw all of their belief into a narrow-minded medical system. In most cases, they're looking for something that will cure them immediately. The medical system perpetuates this mindset. Most people aren't willing to change their entire lifestyle. They prefer the quick fix instead.

We need to think differently. Instead of being "in remission" or being "survivors," we need to become thrivers. I consider myself a thriver. I have vitality and I'm in a state of optimum health. I know that health is limitless, and I see how my health continually improves as I live in a way that is more connected to life and the earth. People need to recognize that they have the ability to heal themselves.

I've had so many people ask what my secret is. The secret is easy: we need to take care of ourselves. Every person is worth it. We also need to remember our connection to the earth and the animals if we are ever to realize the deepest connection within ourselves. Through a plant-based diet, we not only make a significant difference in our own health, but we contribute to the well-being of animals, the planet, and humanity as a whole. It's also very life- and health-affirming not to have the energy of suffering and fear in our bodies. Animal flesh and secretions are full of bad energy, chemicals, and toxins. It's insane. With runaway climate change, it's also getting to the point where it will be imperative to no longer eat animals, because we're very quickly running out of time.

There are other important lifestyle changes for optimal health as well. How we think, our emotional states, our stress levels, where we live, how we live, our conscious awareness—there are so many factors that contribute to our health from the inside out. This sort of information isn't commonplace in modern medicine.

We all have the choice to thrive or not. It all starts with taking back our personal power and believing in ourselves. I'm living proof that this works.

Running Raw Around Australia

Running Raw Around Australia was the culmination of many years of learning how to live well through personal experience. For many years, I've been teaching and sharing this information with others. By running a marathon every day for 366 days, Alan and I were living examples of how simple choices lead to a more conscious, life-affirming lifestyle.

We live simple lives. The food isn't complicated. I mean, there's nothing easier than unzipping a banana. It's the ultimate fast food and it's not boring. You can make it as exciting as you want. What people don't understand is that when we eat nutrient-dense, vibrant, living foods, that's what we become ourselves. What we put into the body is what we get.

So if we put dead food into the body, that's what we get back. Processed food, junk food, and animal products are all dead. No wonder people are sluggish, sick, obese, and diseased. It's impossible to get something live out of something dead.

I mean, if we're eating something out of a box that says it's organic and natural, we may as well eat the box, because at least the box has fiber. Once it's processed, there's little nutrient value anymore.

But if we pick an apple off a tree, it's alive and straight from nature. All of the nutrients remain in the right balance because only Mother Nature knows how to do it right.

Alan and I never worried about whether we were getting enough nutrients or calories, because our bodies tell us what we need. We knew that we would need to eat a lot of fruits and vegetables to sustain us in a marathon a day for a year. But we never had to think about it. We would sit down to a pile of oranges and eat until we got the signal. It's not a signal of being full. It's a signal of being nourished. That's the difference with eating this way.

When someone eats a diet that is deficient, they have to think about it, analyze it, and try to figure out how many calories they need to lose weight. The way we eat, we don't have to do any of that because the body gives such clear messages.

It's not until people actually experience this that they will understand what I mean. It's actually quite easy, because the body is very clear with its direction. That's a really important message. People don't need to be told what fruits and vegetables to eat and how to combine them, because the body already knows. It's so simple when we just trust the body's innate wisdom.

When Alan and I ran around Australia, we wanted to share a positive message of truth and hope from the experiences and knowledge we've gained through living consciously. We wanted to inspire others to make their own informed choices. We knew that the best way to do that would be to walk, or in our case run, the talk. Inspiration is what motivates people to keep moving toward what they believe in and for what they want to achieve. By running a marathon distance every day for an entire year—together—we hoped to inspire others to think more consciously about the choices they make in life.

While we were running around Australia, we had the opportunity to show that by eating raw, living, plant-based foods, we're healthy, physically fit, and have unlimited energy at an age that most consider "old." We wanted to prove that it's never too late to make choices that enhance life and health. Living a conscious lifestyle ensures optimum health and happiness—the two things that everyone is ultimately striving for.

We finished the run, but that was not the end. It was just the beginning. Because running a marathon a day around Australia is not about Alan and me, it's about a positive and inspiring message that will help to bring about a shift to a more sustainable future for ourselves, our children, our grandchildren, and future generations … before we run out of time.

It's a simple but powerful message. We reached so many people around the world with this message, and there are now many people who are starting to think more consciously and in ways that support life and health.

That's what we hoped for. We feel really blessed to have played a part in getting out this important message. Ultimately, what we're advocating is for people to eat well, exercise, and think more consciously about their lifestyle choices. This can change the world.

Hope For A Better World

In the early '70s, there were a lot of things going on in the world that led to feelings of deep despair. Everyone was worried about nuclear threats—including me. There was a lot of negativity and not much hope. At the same time, there was a movement toward bringing more peace, love, and happiness into the world. It was the hippie era and there were some pretty significant changes that came out of that.

I think that although the world of today is in a greater state of disarray, there's more hope now because people are starting to think more consciously. There's definitely been a huge shift in conscious thinking over the last ten years. Once it starts, there's no stopping it. Once we start thinking and acting consciously, it multiplies. When love endures, truth always wins. But we need that element of hope for it to actually move in the right direction.

For instance, more people are seeing more clearly how the pharmaceutical and sickness industries aren't working. Even though there are more treatments, more drugs, and more technologies, people are sicker and fatter than ever before. Many people are now questioning this and looking into more holistic alternatives. With more access to information, it's easier to find alternatives. The only problem is that there's so much information out there. It's really important to be discerning. But I think that today, there are more people bringing their light into the world because of their own healing experiences.

We need to understand the consequences of the choices we make and how they can affect the planet and our very being. I truly believe that the survival of humanity is dependent on our kindness, compassion, and caring for all living beings. We can only achieve this by making conscious lifestyle choices. That's how we can transform this planet.

There are millions of people out there who are now making positive changes in their lives. There's a tremendous ripple effect that comes with this that can totally alter consciousness. I feel very excited about it.

If You Had a Magic Wand ...

I see a world where all people, adults, children, all races, all creeds, all animals, wild and otherwise, live in harmony together in heaven on earth. Everyone would be compassionate and loving. We would remember that love is unconditional and act from that place. If we didn't eat animals, peace on earth would come quickly. So I really wish for a world full of people who are unconditionally loving toward each other, animals, and the planet. If everyone was vegan and acting compassionately and kindly toward each other, wars would stop. Crime would stop. All the negativity in the world would just go away and the world itself, Mother Nature, would come back to her own. It would be the paradise on earth that this planet deserves.

To learn more about Janette's work, please visit rawveganpath.com.

SEVENTEEN

Sierra Bender

Reclaiming the Goddess, Unleashing the Warrior

*"God may be in the details, but the goddess is in the questions.
Once we begin to ask them, there's no turning back."*

– GLORIA STEINEM

Love. A word so freely used and so greatly misunderstood. The "love" that drives our culture is fluffy, sweet ... passive. Hollywood love, fickle love, the emotion of love. But Hollywood love is romantic love is ego love. Ego love separates who and what is worthy, when they are worthy. Ego love judges. Ego love falls in. Ego love falls out. Ego love bypasses those it perceives as "other." Ego love conforms to a fantasy-driven culture. The foundation of ego love is separation. This is the whimsical "love" of a spiritually vacant world.

Ego love exists within the realm of the mind, for it is the mind that separates. Spiritual love exists within the heart, for it is the heart that knows no separation. The heart cannot be broken, for it is omnipotent. The ego can be broken, for it is an illusion.

Jane Goodall once said that we only protect what we love. Collectively, we've fallen short in this area. With widespread reliance on pharmaceutical numbing agents to ease the pain of our internal disconnect, it's clear that the precarious state of today's world is a direct reflection of the inner self-loathing projected by the masses. No self-love equals no love for what truly matters.

Ego love disconnects us; spiritual love awakens us.

Love is unity. Love is action. Love is purpose. Love is fierce. Love is tender. Love is peace. Love is grief. Love is joy. Love is a powerful force that transcends the culture of separation and unites us with all life.

"Love is not just an emotion, but the most powerful force and source in the universe grounded by action and responsibility; a commitment to one's true, authentic self." The wise words of Sierra Bender, author, speaker, activist, and leader in the female empowerment movement.

In Sierra's five-star Amazon book, *Goddess to the Core*, she writes:

> Our health, children, and relationships are suffering; how can we, as the wealthiest country in the world, have such a high percentage of sexual abuse and addiction issues? A recent study shows that the number of Americans using antidepressants doubled in only a decade.
>
> Doctors are now medicating unhappiness. Too many people take drugs when they really need to be making changes in their lives. According to this government study, antidepressants have become the most commonly prescribed drugs in the United States.
>
> Depression is anger turned inwards. We have the right to be angry and sad because of the abuse of the feminine. There is relief if we choose to stand in our core female essence and fight from the place of self-love and self-worth. The true definition of female empowerment is what I call Fierce Love. "I will no longer allow my environment to dictate my future."[7]

Sierra's life has had its fair share of challenges. She's a survivor of childhood sexual abuse. At the age of thirty-two, she was pronounced dead from a rare tubular pregnancy. After surviving this near-death experience, she realized that modern medicine saved her life, but it didn't heal her.

This experience inspired a ten-year inner vision quest and outdoor adventure across the globe. Along the way, she discovered the body's innate ability to heal itself.

She approached her quest with equal parts humbled confidence and defiance. By the end of it, Sierra had absorbed the teachings of many of the world's sages and leaders. This spawned the Sierra Bender Method for Personal & Professional Empowerment (SBM).

The Sierra Bender Method for Personal & Professional Empowerment (SBM) is at the core of the Sierra Bender corporation's work to empower and awaken emotional intelligence and leadership. It's been clinically researched by the American University Department of Psychology in Washington, D.C., since 2010. It has also been published in medical journals.

The SBM is a unique multimodal method infusing clinical studies with holistic intelligence. It works to break the cycle of stress and disempowerment by synthesizing the disciplines of modern medicine, science, indigenous wisdom, holistic health, exercise physiology, quantum physics, nutrition, yoga therapy, and the psychologies of trauma, addiction, and sexual abuse. The SBM is a method of self-realization, self-empowerment, and self-love that leads to a dramatic inside-out transformation of the whole person.

Sierra's work has been featured internationally in media outlets including *Marie Claire, Shape, Whole Living, USA Today*, Univision TV, and Oprah Radio. Her mission is to empower women to rise above their wounds and claim the Goddess within. Her passion is fierce, her love unwavering.

As the power of the feminine rises, it's time for women to be bolder, not in the hubristic way that men are bold, but in a way that speaks from the heart. It's time for women to reclaim their power, speak their truth, and take action without fear or judgment of who they are. Women are the force of nature that will change our world and return the balance we so desperately need.

Let's face it: gender aside, the patriarchy has hurt us all. We think too much and we feel too little. As a result, we're asleep at the wheel.

The patriarchal mindset has removed us from the life-force of love. The feminine has been cleverly edited out of history in order to support the oppressive nature of the patriarchy, a.k.a. the consumptive, destructive machine. Women have been viewed as a great threat by many men. The evidence is clear in our culture of objectification and sexism. But let's tell it like it is. Sexism is fear. Fear made manifest is often violent. As a result, women have been silenced in their voices and their power. Fortunately, this is now changing. There is a greater opening to the power of love as the collective consciousness shifts from patriarchy … to balance.

In a culture that profits from the low self-worth of women, love is the ultimate act of rebellion. Love creates existence. Love is the power of life.

It is the work of women like Sierra Bender that brings into consciousness what has long been denied: the Goddess, the warrior, the transformative force of love. Fierce love.

***

Sierra's Story

Unplugging: Path to Purpose

I knew my true authentic self when I was seven years old. I had a conversation with my mother, and I told her that I would never get married; I would travel the world and not have children.

In a circuitous way, that's exactly what happened. At seven, I was already a little warrior who saw the injustice of how women were treated in the world. I had no idea what that would eventually mean in my life.

As I grew into young womanhood, I suffered through many experiences of sexual abuse. It affected my identity, my body image, and my self-esteem.

I became a high-end personal trainer and semiprofessional athlete. I used my body as a weapon. I would beat it to a pulp. As an athlete, my goal was always to defeat the opponent. That meant putting my body through extremes. Being hyper-competitive, I often competed with boys. I was trained at a young age to be a warrior, but I was never trained in how to be a girl—or a woman.

Although I had all of the womanly "goods," I didn't know how to be a woman because of the past abuse. I had disconnected from my feminine essence to survive.

Eventually I felt the pressures of society and followed its rules. Society expected me to get married, have a baby, and start a family. I could still have my career, but I had to do what was expected of a woman in our culture. Even though I knew at seven that this wasn't my path, I tried it anyway. These choices only took me further away from my true self.

I ended up getting married, but it didn't work out. I got pregnant, but I had a rare tubular pregnancy that ruptured my uterus. I needed four emergency blood transfusions and wasn't expected to survive. I actually had a near-death experience, and what I experienced during that time was the most truthful part of my life. When I was revived, I didn't have any way of communicating what happened because it was beyond words. It was passion. It was purpose. It was contentment. It was joy. It was love. I felt it in every cell of my being.

When I had the near-death experience, I experienced the power of love. God's words permeated every cell of my being inside and out. I felt the surge of this love move to me, and through me. I was asked four questions by what I knew as God:

1. "Spiritually, where did you disconnect from the source of my love?" I realized that I'd stopped praying. I'd stopped listening and asking for help. I used to pray all the time as a child. I was really connected to nature.

2. "Mentally, what were the belief systems from your culture, religion, family, and media that took you further away from the source of this love?" I remembered that it was the first day of confession, when the priest told me I didn't know how to speak to God. It was such a contra-

diction. If God is everything and everywhere, why do I need a priest to speak to God? This created a lot of fear and doubt about not knowing how to speak to God, my God. Nature was always my greatest source of connection. I didn't trust human beings because what they said and what they did was often a contradiction. I didn't know how to trust them. I trusted nature, though. Nature was my savior. I knew how to speak to God through nature. The priest's words confused me.

3. "Emotionally, why do you continually punish yourself, not feeling worthy of this love, through the eating disorders, drugs, alcohol, and other addictions?" That was an easy one to answer. I felt like I needed to numb out the emotions because it was too painful to be in my body.

4. "Physically, why do you consistently resist this love, doing the same things over and over again? Why do you keep attracting the same actors and actresses in your life?" Again, it was an easy answer. I didn't feel worthy. I kept attracting people who told me I wasn't worthy. I existed for their needs and pleasure only.

By answering these four questions, I was able to understand what I was doing, why I was doing it, and how it was affecting me. It was profound. These four questions started the methodology of the Sierra Bender Method for Personal & Professional Empowerment.

My near-death experience changed me forever. My senses, intuition, and awareness were heightened during the recovery process. I could feel what others were feeling and knew what they were thinking before they spoke. I felt stiller inside. I had a renewed sense of purpose. I trusted that the wisdom I'd experienced on the other side was real.

Technically, I died on the operating table. Modern medicine saved my life, but it didn't heal me, so I embarked on a search for answers. What I was searching for was compassion, community, pure core healing, and the ability to look into someone's eyes and not only see myself but also see the God within. I wanted to connect deeply with humanity and spirit. I knew that it wasn't going to happen in New Jersey where I was living at the time.

Being the person that I am, I've always been aware of the injustices in life. I believe in standing up for what's fair and fighting against injustice—the injustice of power and the needless suffering in the world of women, the earth, and animals. My awareness of the injustices was also heightened by my near-death experience. I couldn't take my focus off of them. I knew that there had to be another way. Prayer became the captain of my ship. Through prayer, I asked my spirit where I needed to go to find what I was searching for.

My journey led me to ashrams in India, the jungles of the Amazon, and the mountains of Peru, where I studied with shamans, yogis, and indigenous healers. I was totally open to wherever I needed to go, and I let my spirit guide me. I rediscovered spirituality, reconnected with the earth, and discovered a more expansive worldview.

Searching for and experiencing healing in so many places of wisdom brought me to the faces and places of my true, authentic self. It's amazing. I didn't do it to help other people or get into the business of it. I did it to find my own answers. In doing that, I saw how many other women were suffering with the same problems I had in my own life.

My whole life changed. I discovered my purpose to empower women to reclaim the Goddess within and to be who they authentically are at their core. I learned how to love myself. This inspired the creation of programs to empower other women to love themselves. It meant redefining the twenty-first century woman, redefining fitness, redefining beauty, and redefining power. I've created a number of retreat programs for women who are ready to step up to the plate and stand in their true, authentic selves. These women are ready to do the work to reclaim their femininity, their body, their power, and their voice. I created a safe community where women could heal and feel supported. These programs have changed the lives of thousands of women over the years. They've created leaders, and women lead very differently. They lead with love. They lead with passion, and they lead with purpose, not only for themselves but for their family, for society. They look at the big picture and the future. This is an empowered woman. This is my life's work.

Self-Empowerment

Anger is my best motivator. It sets boundaries. It tells me that something is wrong. It's my radar for injustice.

One of my biggest strengths is my courage to confront things that are not of justice, that are abusive power. I grew up with that all my life. Sports, politics, and family stuff—it was all abusive power, and I don't like abusive power. Whenever I see abusive power, I step in and speak the truth. I'm not afraid of it.

I was also given a voice. We all are. For me not to use my voice because I'm afraid, or for me not to speak my truth, means that the abuse continues. The abuse of power, the abuse of people, the abuse of nature, the abuse of animals, abuse, abuse, abuse. If I deny it or try to walk away from it, it comes at me harder. That's why I can no longer just sit back and watch. I speak out and take action.

I created programs that help women heal because I'm fed up with the abuse. If women do the work and heal in the one week that they're with me, what does that do? It destroys harmful industries. That's what the world needs.

My programs bring women back into their bodies. Because of technology and media, there is so much noise and distraction. Their minds are so full that they're not in their bodies. When they're actually in their bodies, they make their own decisions; they actually heal. I don't heal them, they heal themselves. I just give them information based on the programs that I've created from the discoveries of my own healing journey.

People can't believe that healing can happen that quickly. All they have to do is get into their bodies and feel, so that they can deal with their issues and finally heal from their wounds. Feel, deal, and heal. It's liberating and so much quicker than all of the expensive talking that goes on in therapy offices.

My programs, my book, everything I create is about self-empowerment. Not only is it about empowering oneself, it's about a tribal empowerment that empowers others—our children, our family, the women in our lives, anyone in our inner circle who wants off the wheel of suffering so they can take control of their lives in a way that best suits them. To see women transform, become content and physically present, is a beautiful gift for all of us.

Recharging

The world can be a really tough place, so maintaining my connection with spirit is a nonnegotiable in my life. I do this through prayer—asking God to give me the strength needed to keep going. I also know the importance of feeling what is real, despite how painful it might be. I would rather be in that space than numbed out like I used to be.

I have compassion for both sides, because I've been there. In my workshops, I deal with some of the ugliest things in society, such as rape, abuse, and addiction. It's so rewarding to witness women healing, but it takes its toll.

When I go home, I pray, I meditate, I go to the beach, I take walks. The first thing I do is dive into the ocean. I now live in Florida, because the ocean called to me. It's interesting, because the more intense my work is, the more the ocean calls to me. It's the biggest healing salt bath.

I also allow myself to emotionally break down because I've taken on so much energy. I have a rule of thumb that I won't engage in intense conversations within the first forty-eight hours of my return home, because I don't want to project any negative energy that may still be with me.

Then I go see my horse. Nature is always my biggest filter. I lie down on the ground to pray and meditate. I ask the earth to take away anything that is not mine, that is not resonating with my being, anything that's not of service to me.

It's important to recognize what is ours and what's not ours; what's still lurking within that needs to be healed. So every time I return from my work, I respect the recharging and reconnecting process within myself. I respect the process and realize that I'm not an almighty teacher who is better than anyone, because every participant also teaches me.

This work is very humbling. I have so much responsibility and re-spect for this gift I've been given. I've worked hard for it, but I still have deep gratitude for the fact that I'm being used for a higher purpose that facilitates healing and community for women in need.

There are times when I need help because I feel stuck. That's when I seek out a healer or a masseuse—whatever I'm guided to for wherever I am.

Reconnecting

I have a daily practice where I get up in the morning and set my in-tention for the day. I light a candle. I pray. I cleanse my energy to create a new day, a new opportunity. I sit with my emotions while I'm sipping my tea. I'm fully present in my consciousness. Rather than turning on the television or getting out of bed and moving at one hundred miles an hour, I take the extra time and care to set the daily tone for myself.

It's a practice and it's like a muscle. Like an athlete—a spiritual ath-lete. I get out of bed. I walk into the bathroom. I take a shower. I look at my eyes in the mirror, and ask myself, "Where am I? Are my adrenal glands on overload? Am I exhausted today? What do I need to do today? Do I need to be more tender? Am I filled with fire? Do I need a challenge? Where am I?" That is self-reflection.

Then I go outside, sit on the ground and play with my dog before I start my work for the day. I know when my eyes are fried or when I'm feeling too much mental energy from the computer. I listen. I stop, look, listen, and feel. Rather than being overextended with my energy, that sets the tone for my day. I've learned how to preserve and reserve my energy so that when I really need it for the bigger things, I'm ready.

I run my business with my mind, but what I do is with my heart. The warrior part of me is with my mind, but the Goddess part of me is with my heart. Doing service-based work, the two have to be very balanced. I can't be all love and light, meditate and do yoga all day. That's not realistic. However, I do maintain my body and my health by connecting to nature, and doing all of the things that I teach in my workshops. I live what I teach and I believe that we would all benefit from living this way.

If You Had a Magic Wand …

No violence—verbal, physical, emotional, every aspect. No violence.

For more information about Sierra and her work, please visit sierrabender.com.

EIGHTEEN

Jo-Anne McArthur
Seeing Through the Lens of Truth

"Three things cannot be long hidden: the sun, the moon, and the truth."

– BUDDHA

Let's face it, the world can be an ugly place. There's no end to the violence we commit against one another, the natural world, and ourselves; but the poisoned imagination rages most savagely against those with no voice—the animals with whom we share our planet. We brutalize them for food, fashion, science, sport, entertainment, power … for profit. We brutalize them for no other reason than because we think we can.

It's easy to cast blame at the profiteers of this insanity, but the condemnatory nature of this behavior succeeds only in circumventing the greater problem: indifference, the dangerous detachment from truth. Accompanied by its faithful companion, denial, the poison of indifference separates hearts and minds from all that is compassionate, beautiful, and true.

Political activist, Holocaust survivor, and Nobel-Peace-Prize-winning author Elie Wiesel once said, "The opposite of love is not hate, it's indifference. The opposite of art is not ugliness, it's indifference. The opposite of faith is not heresy, it's indifference. And the opposite of life is not death, it's indifference." I couldn't agree more.

The collective epidemic of indifference perpetuates the consumptive machine that swallows our souls. This is not who we are and yet, as a global population, this is who we've allowed ourselves to become. With so many toxic systems, institutions, and beliefs in place to ensure our mental, emotional, and spiritual slavery, what will it take to shake off the collective slumber? It's not a matter of good versus evil; it's a matter of truth versus indifference.

It takes courage to explore truth, for it means opening our hearts to the pain of the world. But without truth, there is no love. Without love, there is no action. Without action, we're trapped in the machine. We have the choice of talk or action, but actions will always speak louder than words. This is the power of free will. To be conscious or not to be conscious, that is the question.

I feel blessed to have met so many people who move the world in ways that enhance life on planet Earth. These are the revolutionaries who inspire radical change for our world. Although it takes courage to explore truth, it takes greater courage to expose the truth, for it means bearing witness to the suffering and death caused by the darkest parts of the human psyche. Jo-Anne McArthur is a warrior of truth on the front line of consciousness, armed with no more than a compassionate heart and a camera.

If a picture is worth a thousand words, then Jo-Anne's photographic work is an epic novel of revelation. For more than a decade, she's been on the front line of truth documenting the use and abuse of animals. Her mission is to change the way we perceive our fellow earthlings, from commodity to co-inhabitant. Jo-Anne and her work were recently featured in the award-winning film, *The Ghosts in Our Machine*. Directed by Liz Marshall, *The Ghosts in Our Machine* is a moving testament to the lives of animals living within, and rescued from, the machine of our consumptive world. It is one of the few films that I, as a highly sensitive person, can watch with peace in my heart.

It takes tremendous courage to actively seek out what most people fear—the dark and violent places and spaces hidden from view and shrouded in secrecy. The machine reaps such outrageous profit from the feedlots, factory farms, slaughterhouses, fur farms, research labs, hunt camps, fish farms, circuses, aquariums, and zoos that it goes out of its way to ensure their survival. Is it any wonder why the violence inherent in these barbaric industries is cloaked in such impenetrable secrecy?

Jo-Anne's work comes at a hefty price. Posttraumatic stress disorder (PTSD) regularly haunts her consciousness. Bearing witness to what is so blatantly wrong in our world is a heavy burden to bear. This begs the question, what is it that compels people like Jo-Anne to willingly subject themselves to such trauma? The answer is simple. Truth. Compassion. Love. For Jo-Anne, there is no compromise. This is the way it must be if we are ever to realize a more peaceful and just world.

The planet is desperate for a massive upgrade in consciousness that includes a hefty dose of radical compassion. No longer can we turn a blind eye to what we know in our hearts is so wrong. No longer can we justify the choices and behaviors that destroy the most sacred gift of all— life. The evidence is clear. It's not working: for the animals, the planet, or our souls.

It is the work of courageous warriors of truth like Jo-Anne McArthur that brings light to the darkness and reason for change. We are all so much better than what we've allowed ourselves to become. It's time for us to remember.

***

Jo-Anne's Words

Unplugging: Path to Purpose

I'm a storyteller by nature who is endlessly curious about what motivates people throughout the world to do the things that they do. It's been a lifelong passion. One of my mentors, Larry Towell, a Magnum photographer, helped to sharpen my focus during an internship many years ago. I would search for stories without focus. He would ask me, "What's your point? You have to first look at your point, then do what you love and a project will flourish."

He would tell me things like, "Don't just go to Afghanistan because there's a war there and it will be interesting to shoot. That's not you. What do you love the most?" What I've always loved most is helping animals. That's the essence of who I am.

I started my work close to home, photographing meat markets, zoos, and circuses. Because I'm a traveler, I began shooting internationally— from sanctuaries that rescue animals, to the bush meat trade in Africa, to factory farms in Australia. Unfortunately, the subject matter is endless.

I spend a lot of time traveling wherever I'm needed, or anywhere I can find an interesting shoot. By interesting, I mean cruelty that needs to be exposed. I also shoot beautiful stories of rescue and sanctuary, because these stories must also be told. Showing the antidotes to the problems we cause is very important.

Inspired by Larry's advice to follow my passion, I started a project called *We Animals*. It's been around for over ten years now. *We Animals* is a title that intuitively came into my head one day. It simply means that we are all animals. When it's framed that way, there's no separation. The biggest problem is the belief that nonhuman animals are "other."

The *We Animals* project positions us at the center of an ecosystem, not at the top of it. We are all animals, and the photographs I take aspire to make that connection. By photographing the eyes and the expressions of animals, there's a deeper connection that reminds us that we're all sentient. We all suffer and we all experience happiness as well. We're essentially all the same. My hope is that people are able to make this connection so that they reevaluate the treatment of animals with an open heart and mind. The *We Animals* project also has Humane Education programs that inspire a wider circle of compassion that includes animals. It teaches people to care. All the Humane Ed presentations are age-appropriate. I go to schools, universities, photo clubs ... anywhere that's open to my message. The response has been great.

I've always felt a communion with animals. I'm very comfortable in their presence. Because I'm calm and open with them, we're able to enjoy each other's company and be curious about one another. The animals in factory farms, fur farms, and zoos are not used to anyone looking into their eyes and seeing them for who they might actually be. Sadly, they aren't used to gentle voices either. There's a saying that "the eyes are the windows to the soul," and when we look into the eyes of any living being, we realize our connection on a soul level.

When I'm crouching down, speaking gently, getting close, and trying to make a connection with a pig in a factory farm, for example, we connect. I connect with them, and they connect with me. This is crucial for my work because the camera picks up this connection. Through the connection, anyone looking at my photos will also feel the connection. It's quite profound.

The Ghosts in Our Machine was like that as well. There's a lot of eye contact and close-ups of eyes. Looking into their souls, there's no denial of their sentience. It inspires change because it breaks through the resistance. It gets to the heart.

I'm not someone who plans long term. I just follow my nose and do work that's important to me. I jump from project to project and I'm enthusiastic about everything meaningful. When I said yes to the film, I knew it would be an important extension of my work. The collaboration with Liz Marshall was amazing because she and I have a similar aesthetic, and we're both deeply committed to creating a better world.

Things seem to just happen when we're open to life and to saying yes to great opportunities. I'm pretty excited about life and opportunities in general, and because of that I now have a book and the film. Along with the ongoing campaign work I do, and my book-in-progress, *Unbound*, it's all making a difference. It's very exciting.

Recharging and Reconnecting

There are numerous ways that I stay centered and focused. I didn't always know how, and sometimes I really struggle. I have suffered from PTSD and some depression because of the amount of time I spend in the field documenting factory farms, mink farms, breeding farms … you name it. I think it's natural to feel really traumatized by what I see. It would bring down anyone with any sense of compassion. I don't know how people work in those places. I think they must have to put up a lot of unhealthy walls to be able to treat animals and kill them the way they do. But the industries only exist because of consumer demand. That's a whole other story.

Self-care is something I had to learn, because I thought I was invincible, until all of a sudden I wasn't. I would wake up in the morning, and my first thought would be a pig in a gestation crate or something gruesome like that. I realized that waking up with a cloud of sadness around my head was not how I wanted to live, because I'm normally a very joyful person. I went into therapy to learn how to deal with the sadness so that I wasn't stuck in it.

There are so many reasons to be upset. There's a war on animals going on every second of the day for billions of animals confined and killed for food. It's a huge overwhelming emergency. But to dwell in that place in my heart and mind doesn't help the animals, and it doesn't help me. It only causes burnout, which is totally ineffective. As someone who is sensitive to all of this violence, it can be a struggle to be happy. But it's important. I need to have community with family, activists, friends, and people I love. I have to give myself what I need to survive and thrive.

I realized that I had to nurture the things I love. I had to focus on the good rather than spending all my time photographing the bad. Photographing the positive stories uplifts me and provides hope and purpose, not only for me, but for everyone who sees my work.

My goal in life is to save the world, but I can't do it all today. I have to constantly remind myself that I need to take some time out. Maybe by the end of my lifetime …

Luckily I'm not alone in wanting to change the world, and because of that, things are really changing. I know that I will see the end of bullfighting and bear bile farming in this lifetime. That's because we're all working together. But we have to stay focused on the good and not get mired in the sadness, because this is the only way to sustainably effect change.

I recharge myself by going to places of peace. We all need those, whether it's with our dog or cat, or, like me, hanging out in my little reading nook in the bedroom. Sometimes they're farther afield. For me, it's communing with rescued farm animals. At sanctuaries, they're treated exactly the opposite of how they're treated in factory farms and slaughterhouses.

I also do a lot of volunteering. Giving back to others gives so much to me. It helps me feel purposeful. I feel that if we can all give back in small or big ways, it feeds the soul.

The world has become so disconnected. It's like we're not even citizens of the earth anymore. We're not a community. We're in our own little bubbles watching TV, looking at our phones, doing our own thing for only ourselves. It's not healthy for us, and it's not healthy for the environment or the animals.

We're citizens of the world and we have a responsibility to the earth to look after it, especially given our sheer numbers. We're using up so many planetary resources and taking so much away from other living beings. We need to remember this, and act in ways that give back rather than constantly take away.

The most powerful thing that reconnects me is the gratitude that I remind myself to feel every single day for the life that I have, for the animals that I meet, the people that I work with, and for my loving family. Being thankful is absolutely key in my life, and it keeps me sane as well. I've learned what works for me emotionally. Gratitude is the most potent. I know that wallowing in grief is not sustainable.

I once heard that the best way to live life is to think of our eulogy. What would we want said? I've thought about this, and what first came up was that I'd want to be remembered for my animal rights work through my photography. I wanted to simplify this further though, so I asked myself, "How would I want to be remembered in just one word?"

It's a good exercise to work through. So I thought some more and distilled it down to one word that I can work at every day. I now live my life by that one word. That one word is kindness. It's a tough but noble goal. I know that if I can live every day with a focus on kindness, my life will have been worthwhile.

A Heart-Centered Life

Living a heart-centered life is about doing what you believe in and staying true to your course. I do work that goes against the grain and I get attacked for that. But that's okay, because my message is bigger and more important than the criticism. My message is about ending cruelty to animals, and I share that message through challenging, arresting pictures. I've put myself out there for critique. It can be difficult, but I stick with it because it's my calling.

By holding fast, being vulnerable, and doing what I know is right in the world, things have worked out for me. I'm a heart-on-sleeve kind of person and it takes people aback. It scares some people off, but it also draws a lot of people in. It draws great people in, actually.

There's a scene in *The Ghosts in Our Machine* where I say to one of the most famous photo editors in the world, "I want to change the world. I'm trying to save the world." I laughed at myself when I said that because it's just so naïve and ridiculously hopeful. But it's also pretty exciting to hear myself say that. It's so vulnerable. It's so heart-on-sleeve. It opens the door for other people to not feel crazy about wanting to change the world.

I look at Jane Goodall, who is over eighty years old now. She travels three hundred days a year speaking to thousands of people daily. She draws her energy from her audiences because she knows that she's affecting a lot of people. In some ways, she's a heart-on-sleeve person as well. She made it her mission to say the things that she's saying. I draw a lot of inspiration from her.

I've photographed Jane for over a decade, so I've had ample opportunity to study her. I memorize the things she says and the way she says them. She's unflinching in her delivery, because she speaks from her heart. She says things that scare people, and she says them both gently and powerfully. I've learned a lot from her.

If You Had a Magic Wand ...

I'd live in a world where I could go out into the city and do the things that I normally do, but there would be animals everywhere. They would all be living happy lives in trees or wherever they wanted to be. They wouldn't be afraid of humans anymore, because in that world, humans celebrated and respected them.

I would live in a world where this was the norm; where we didn't kill anyone and animals finally felt safe and at home with us. We would nurture community and relationship with them. The "us vs. them" mentality would no longer exist. We've been taught through science and culture that they're over there, and we're here, and that there's a wall between us. That would all be gone.

We all deserve the basic rights to life, freedom, safety, care, and respect. So we would all share the same space in an easy, beautiful way where everyone is free from harm. Everything is safe in my magic wand world. What a beautiful place!

Jo-Anne's important work can be found at weanimals.org.

NINETEEN

Dr. Will Tuttle
Intuition, Truth, and World Peace

*"The time will come when men such as I will look upon the murder
of animals as they now look upon the murder of men."*

– LEONARDO DA VINCI

Although this book was not conceived with a vegan agenda, I believe that vegan living is one of the most effective ways to connect us with our deepest core essence. Food is a portal to the soul—a gateway to wholeness. Veganism is a compelling launching point that invokes a more expansive perspective on the self, the natural world, and our place within the web of life. It's an essential aspect of honoring our connection with life.

Veganism is so much more than a way of eating; it's a lifestyle rooted in life, truth, and love. The essence of veganism is non-separation: an expanded state of consciousness that excludes no living being from one's circle of compassion. Gandhi once said, "The most violent weapon on earth is the table fork." He spoke to a startling truth that clearly shows how our conditioned food choices contribute to staggering global violence. To believe otherwise is the lie we've bought into to separate us from life.

Our consumptive ways have led us astray. Mindless lifestyle choices have contributed to the irreversible destruction of life. The physical manifestations of our separation-based choices are painfully obvious in today's world. Obesity, heart disease, cancer, war, depression, addiction, anxiety, climate change, mass extinction, violence, and the ruthless slaughter of billions of sentient beings annually to feed nothing more than a culturally created addiction to the flesh and secretions of animals is hurting us all. Leo Tolstoy once said, "As long as there are slaughterhouses there will be battlefields." I believe his words speak to the many battles we wage—on animals, on the natural world, and on each other. Perhaps the most destructive battle of all is the one we wage on the truth that lives in our hearts.

We are all prisoners, subjected to a sentence of conditioned patterns and beliefs. Programmed since birth, our minds are infected by generations of antiquated thought systems imposed on us by parents, teachers, religion, media, and culture. We're taught to run with the pack, think like the herd, conform to culture, consume like there is no tomorrow, and believe everything we're told by those who perpetuate the status quo. We conform, we consume, we comply. We label, we judge, we fear ... we separate.

The truth is that we were never meant to be the voracious consumers of all things living that we've allowed ourselves to become. We've learned this behavior. And just as we've learned it, so too can we unlearn it. We have the choice to live the lie or not. The most important thing we can do in our lifetime is to remember the sacredness of life. Vegan living is an expansive lifestyle transformation that plugs us back into the web of life.

This is the life path of Dr. Will Tuttle, vegan evangelist, spiritual activist, author of the bestselling book, *The World Peace Diet*, and recipient of The Peace Abbey's distinguished Courage of Conscience Award. Will is a former Zen monk who knows how to bring us home ... to the heart. He works extensively in intuition development, spiritual healing, meditation, music, creativity, vegan living, and cultural evolution. His passion for transformation is tireless. He knows that we can all be and do much better than our accepted cultural programming permits.

He states on his website:

I believe that we are all born into a culture that forces us to participate in rituals of violence (meals) from infancy. We are injected with a mentality of reductionism, exclusion, privilege, and might-makes-right: seeing others as mere instruments to be used for our own pleasure and gain. I teach that veganism is coming home to our true heart, and seeing beings as beings, and respecting them as equally sacred manifestations of divine life.

My message is that veganism is a philosophy and practice of radical inclusion, and that going vegan is the most positive, uplifting, and transformative action any human being can make in our culture today. I see it as a profound and effective questioning of the core violence of our culture. I believe that veganism is a loving response that makes us part of the solution to the crises that beset us, rather than being part of the problem.

Vegan living, in its purest form, connects us with our essential nature. We can never reach our true potential if we selectively exclude living beings from our conscious awareness. When we shift the paradigm from head to heart, we extend our circle of compassion to include all life on this planet. Then we can embrace a more passionate, loving, and interconnected world.

Non-harming choices toward others equal non-harming choices toward ourselves. The result: a kinder and more harmonious world for all.

***

Will's Story

Unplugging: Path to Purpose

I was born into a family eating typical American meals in the early 1950s. Living in Concord, Massachusetts, I was born in Emerson Hospital, learned to swim in Walden Pond, attended Thoreau School and

Alcott School, and through all this, perhaps unconsciously imbibed the Transcendentalist spirit of radical inquiry.

When I was in my early teens, I went to a summer camp in Vermont that was affiliated with an organic dairy. I remember participating in the killing of chickens and cows. The slaughters and dismemberments were done as educational group projects. Though it was violent and somewhat shocking, at the time I didn't think there was any alternative to killing and eating animals for food.

I'd been so completely indoctrinated by the mealtime rituals of reducing animals to things, that the actual killing didn't bother me. I knew that I'd die of a protein deficiency if I didn't eat animals, that they don't have souls like us, and that they were put here specifically for our consumption.

My worldview began to expand when I was in college during the early 1970s. I experienced the cultural sensitization toward the violence in the Vietnam War, and this prompted many questions. I began reading about social injustice, war, the domination of women, and the exploitation of natural resources. Though it was enlightening, and I was questioning the underlying assumptions of our society, I never questioned the consumption of animals.

In my senior year at college I started exploring Eastern philosophy, meditation, and yoga. This led me to a book, *Cosmic Consciousness*, written in the late 1800s by Richard Maurice Bucke, that significantly impacted my thinking. He wrote that virtually all of us function at the level of "self-consciousness," which is caring primarily about ourselves. But a few unusual people—founders of religions, great sages, saints, mystics, and poets—attained what he called "cosmic consciousness," which is a qualitatively higher level of consciousness where we lose our self-centeredness and care equally for everyone. He described how these people experienced an illumination of awareness and a moral elevation with a sense of existential joy. They also lost their fear of death and lived lives of benevolence. I remember how deeply this struck me, and how I yearned to devote my life to the quest of attaining this higher consciousness.

This realization sent me into an existential crisis. All the things I had been taught to value seemed like mere distractions. I didn't know what to do about my classes, if I should just drop out or finish college. I ended up completing my studies, and shortly afterward, my younger brother Ed and I decided to leave home.

According to the spiritual biographies of many teachers, leaving home is a metaphor. It means forging an entirely new path, internally. If we don't leave home, we're a mere product of society, robotically following the programming injected into us since birth. Leaving home means questioning the official narratives and relying on intuition rather than cultural conditioning.

When I talked to Ed about cosmic consciousness, I was excited to learn that he had a similar spiritual yearning. Together, we decided to go on a pilgrimage, traveling by foot to California to find a teacher who could help us attain cosmic consciousness. We said good-bye to our parents, walked down the driveway, and journeyed west. We walked and meditated for several months with no money and few belongings in our small backpacks.

When I look back at this experience, it was a defining moment in my life. Leaving home, I discovered that the universe is essentially benevolent and supportive of our quest for meaning. Jesus summed it up well: "Seek ye first the Kingdom of Heaven, (seek first cosmic consciousness, a higher level of awareness) and everything shall be added unto you."

In other words, the details will take care of themselves. We focused on our spiritual practice and discovered that seemingly miraculous synchronicities would occur to open doors and bring us guidance on a daily basis. Food and shelter always somehow appeared. We focused on meditation, service, and healing. For example, I had worn glasses since sixth grade and could hardly see without them. I took them off during our travels. Even though things were initially blurry, I found that my vision improved tremendously, and eventually clarified. I haven't needed glasses since. This was one of many physical and emotional healings that happened during this time.

I also started to feel more self-confident. I was still eating meat, but it was naturally starting to fall away. I remember catching and eating a couple of fish when we were in Pennsylvania. It never bothered me when I was younger because I'd been told that fish can't feel pain. But I was now starting to feel their suffering, and killing them was excruciating. I never did it again.

We eventually walked all the way to Tennessee to a place called *The Farm*, which was the largest hippie community in the world back in 1975. Most of the people who lived there were from California. They called themselves vegetarians, but they were basically vegans. They didn't eat any meat, dairy products, or eggs. This ended up being another important time in my life. I was inspired by this example of people who were living not just for themselves, but for animals, ecosystems, and starving people. They were creating a way of living in harmony with the earth that cared about future generations.

They did big things. They created a spiritual birthing center where women could give birth in a loving, connected way aided by other women. The Farm was all about birth without violence, food without violence, cooperative living, and service. They went into a variety of communities like inner city New York, and places like Guatemala, where they taught people how to live more abundantly, healthfully, and compassionately. This was enormously inspiring to me. We spent several weeks there. When I learned of the misery and violence that eating meat causes, I stopped. I've not eaten meat since.

From that time on, my brother and I lived in meditation centers. We walked to Alabama and stayed in a Korean Zen Buddhist center in Huntsville, and then in Atlanta. A few years later I eventually made it to California and lived in a Tibetan Buddhist center for a few years in San Francisco. I moved on to a Zen center in Oakland, California.

That entire period of my life was internally driven. I did a lot of long retreats and meditative sitting. I did intensive personal silent retreats by myself in nature. I also did group retreats, including living as a Zen monk in South Korea. That went on for about ten years, until I was in my early thirties.

Eventually, I felt that it was time to integrate more into the world. I got my master's degree, and then a PhD at UC Berkeley, and started teaching college. My life was expansive, joyful, and challenging. I believe that when we focus on spiritual development and internal cultivation, there are tremendous unforeseeable benefits. For instance, I was a pretty good student in the past, but with all of the meditation, vegan living, and inner contemplation, I began winning dissertation and achievement awards. Academically I skyrocketed, because I was more confident and at peace with myself. I was no longer just trying to fit into society. I was questioning everything and striving to live according to inner truths.

In 1990, I met my wonderful spouse Madeleine in Switzerland. We started traveling together and have been doing that ever since. We travel around the world sharing the message of compassion and veganism at lectures, conferences, and workshops. This is interspersed with writing and creating music. It's been deeply rewarding. I have to say that even though I'm aware of the terrible human abuse of animals and ecosystems, there's also a precious sense of contribution that comes from working to build a better world, starting from the inside. Though this human life is brief, I've realized that it can have profound meaning and significance— even in the face of suffering.

Becoming a vegan was an expression of spiritual yearning for me. I wanted to wake up. I wanted to attain cosmic consciousness. When I realized our culture's excruciating abuse of animals, I was utterly repulsed. I refused to contribute to the violence with my behaviors or choices anymore. It completely changed my life and helped me realize my calling. I am where I am today because of that one powerful choice of going vegan all those years ago.

Recharging and Reconnecting: Cultivating Intuition

We're born into a society that neglects to develop intuition. In fact, it actively stomps on it when we're kids. We end up disconnected from what is the most important ally that we have in life. I believe our greatest resource is the inner knowing that is intended to guide us through life.

Our intuition opens the doorway to authenticity. Rather than being entranced by the cultural programming that turns us into compliant workers and consumers, through intuition, we take back our power. We no longer support a system that enriches the few at the expense of the many.

Anyone who is waking up to the truth of how things really are must also be cultivating their intuition. I don't think there's anything more benevolent that we can do for ourselves, for humanity, for animals, for future generations, and for the creation of a world where peace and freedom are actually possible.

There are a number of ways we can cultivate our intuition. The first and primary way is through a regular meditation practice. Also, anything that we're authentically drawn to do can be a beautiful expression of meditation, like gardening, walking, spending time in nature, making music, painting, or writing.

Beyond these active forms of meditation, it's important to sit and listen—to be in the silence every day. In the beginning, being in silence for more than a few seconds is difficult, but studies show that even this "noisy meditation" is psychologically healing. It opens space in our awareness, and with time, more space and silence manifest in our inner world. This helps us to realize that we are consciousness, not just a physical object. Within consciousness, there's an arising of thoughts, an arising of feelings, and a passing away of thoughts and feelings. We are the timeless consciousness within which our world arises.

When we begin to understand this, we realize that we are essentially eternal. We then begin seeing this in others. When we don't understand this, we're imprisoned by the belief that we are separate from others and our world. We judge and discriminate by externals like skin color, species, sexual orientation, gender, age, and so forth.

In meditation, we begin to see ourselves and others as the light of eternal consciousness. We no longer judge by outer appearances. Instead, we see beings who are essentially of the same nature as ourselves, and realize our sacred and intimate connection with all. When we reach this level of consciousness, we naturally want to help others rather than harm them. We realize that harming others harms ourselves.

The second way to develop intuition is by consciously cultivating an inner positivity. We're bombarded with so much negativity, not only from the media, but from our experiences growing up.

I think we all grow up in basically the same kind of a culture: competitive, critical, and filled with fears of scarcity. There's only so much to go around. We're not going to get enough. We're not good enough and we need to compete to get our share. We tend to internalize these negative voices, but consciously counteracting this negativity is important for developing intuition. Affirming the truth that we are the eternal light of consciousness, and making an effort to understand this, helps us to trust ourselves, our intuition, and the universe.

The third way to cultivate intuition is to take conscious risks, try new things and expand our worldview. Most of us are creatures of habit. Ingrained behaviors, attitudes, and perspectives condition us. We are called to free ourselves from these patterns by opening to new possibilities by, for example, experiencing other cultures, learning new languages, developing new skills, and looking at life through a broader lens.

A fourth key to developing our intuition is to make an effort to connect with nature every day in a way that is meaningful to us. We live in a society where we spend most of our time in artificial environments. Between artificial lighting, sounds, spaces, temperatures, the online world, and virtual realities, we disconnect from the natural world. Getting out every day to look at the sky, the trees, the birds, and the stars, to feel our bare feet on the earth, and to witness the beauty of nature helps us remember that we're embedded in abundant, beautiful, and intelligent living systems.

The fifth way to cultivate intuition is through creative expression. It can be as simple as dancing around, doing some type of yoga, music, art, or craft, or teaching or writing a poem or a blog: anything that feels like an expression of our creativity. I believe that creativity and intuition are interconnected. The more creative we are, the more we connect with who we are as a unique expression of life. Even though there's suffering on this planet, there's also a lot of joy, beauty, love, and caring. We can see all this more clearly when we connect to our creativity, because it connects us to our true nature and helps us see beyond the material façade of appearances.

The sixth and final recommendation for cultivating intuition is practicing kindness toward other beings. In many ways, we're raised in a society that teaches us to discount the suffering we cause to others. It's no big deal if we eat a piece of meat or dairy. It doesn't matter if we drive a car that takes more resources than are necessary. We tend to discount the suffering of ecosystems, of starving people in faraway countries, and of animals whose lives are being taken for nothing but taste.

To counteract this, we are called to be aware of the ripples that radiate from our lives, and to do our best to ensure that those ripples cause the least harm possible. We can learn to consciously choose to act, speak, and think so that the ripples of our life generate as much caring, joy, and benevolence as possible.

These are some potent practices that can help us connect to our intuitive selves. We can learn to plug in to our inner knowing and extract ourselves from the harmful and limiting programming generated by the society we're born into.

Hope For a Better World

Author's note: In his book, The World Peace Diet, *Will writes, "While it's easy to become discouraged in the face of the immense cultural inertia that propels the continued practice of eating animal foods, it's helpful to realize that it carries within it the seeds of its own destruction." I asked Will about these powerful words.*

This is a nuanced understanding that's hard to articulate because it's more of an intuitive feeling that I have. What's important to remember is that the basic nature of the universe is expansion and growth, interconnectedness and love.

The practice of agriculture that developed about ten thousand years ago caused us to disconnect from this understanding, and from what I refer to as Sophia, the sacred feminine dimension of consciousness that yearns to love, protect, and care for life. We repressed Sophia in order to dominate animals, nature, and each other. We began enslaving other living beings by owning them. We created a warrior society. Men were taught to be hard and tough. Boys were expected to emulate this disconnected male persona, capable of abuse and cruelty toward animals, women, and other people. This violent mindset carries within it the seeds of its own destruction.

We see it all around us. We're cutting down rainforests at an acre per second. We're destroying the oceans in irreparable ways. We've completely destabilized the global climate. We are bringing a hundred species to extinction every day. We may be at the brink of extinction ourselves because of the underlying attitudes that perpetuate this way of living. The earth will not support this much longer. Something has to give.

There's a subchapter in *The World Peace Diet* called "The Last Days of Eating Animals." We're at a point in our human journey where we have a choice: either we continue with business as usual and end life on Earth, or we wake up and move toward a vegan society that respects animals, ecosystems, and all of us. Imagining a vegan world is imagining a completely different world from what we see around us now; it's beautiful and inspiring.

I'm seeing many signs of veganism emerging through an awakening of Sophia: kindness and respect for animals, humans, and our Earth.

Veganism means compassion and justice for all life. As we develop an understanding of our culture as an essentially herding culture that maintains the obsolete practice of enslaving animals for food, we grasp the enormous implications of how this affects every aspect of our relationships and our lives. We can then awaken to what I refer to as deep veganism. This is much more comprehensive than the dietary elimination of meat and dairy for health reasons, or from being personally outraged at animal abuse. It's a profound social movement that transforms both individuals and our culture through facilitating an evolution that embraces the truth of the interconnectedness of all life. Intuitively, I feel that we are on the cusp of birthing a new humanity, rather than falling into complete devastation. The final outcome is very much up in the air, however. These are critical times for humanity.

Deep veganism embraces the whole way we live on this planet—in relationship to each other, to the earth, to animals, and to ourselves. It calls us to evolve beyond seeing others as instruments to be used. It calls to a sense of solidarity, kindness, and an attitude of radical inclusion that excludes no being from the sphere of our compassion and awareness. I feel that significant momentum is building for us as we head in this direction.

If You Had a Magic Wand …

I envision a world that is joyfully vegan: a world where we no longer enslave, own, and steal the sovereignty of other living beings; where we grow our own food in gardens and orchards, and animals live freely. It's a world where humanity no longer sees nature and animals as consumables. I believe this world is not only possible, but inevitable. We have the technology, and nothing is stopping us but fear and inertia.

It's ironic to me how we look to the stars wondering if there's any intelligent life in the universe besides humanity, when we have such magnificently intelligent, resourceful, and fascinating beings all around us. Animals have enormous gifts to share, and I believe that when we are worthy, we will be able to discover these gifts, and much more. The most important thing for humanity is to question the official narratives of our culture, and make peace with the earth and with animals. Through this, we will make peace with each other.

My magic wand would liberate animals. We would then be liberated from the dualistic mentality that separates us from nature. The beauty of this wish is that each of us has the power to fulfill it in our own lives right now, and to share these ideas with others.

To learn more about Dr. Tuttle's work, please visit, willtuttle.com.

TWENTY

Toni Bergins

Dancing Her Way to Freedom

*"There is deep wisdom within our very flesh, if we can only come
to our senses and feel it."*

– ELIZABETH A. BEHNKE

If you could think of one powerful method to release old hurts, emotional baggage, conditioned patterns, and future worries, what would it be?

Typical thoughts include counseling or therapy—an office with a warm ambience and a cozy couch, deep conversations, and endless appointments with a kind stranger who profits from pain. Therapy has its place, but because of its content-driven nature, processing is limited to the confines of the intellect. This makes for sluggish progress with incremental results.

Ah, the formidable intellect. We're conditioned to judge with it, reason with it, think with it, and analyze with it. With false superiority, we revere it. But we don't feel with it, heal with it, and we aren't real with it. Despite the cultural obsession with intellectual prowess, we are so much more than our quick wit and smarts. In service to the heart, the intellect is a worthy ally. On its own, it can be an oppressive adversary.

In simple terms, the intellect/brain, with its short-term memory and problem-solving abilities, can process and retain seven plus or minus two bits of information at any given time. The storage duration of this information is fragile and can easily be lost with distraction and passing time. This is why we make lists. It's also why we resist change. With such meager processing capacity, overwhelm arrives quickly.

Compare this with the body, an impressive processor that moves information at an unfathomable three trillion cellular interactions per second. How this was calculated is beyond me, but suffice it to say, the difference is startling. Imagine if we had to think our way through every breath and heartbeat; if we had to think about digesting our food, blinking our eyes, or growing our hair. If we had to intellectually manage what our bodies innately do, we wouldn't be long for this world.

With its sloth-like processing speed, the intellect is a deterrent to our personal growth. This is why traditional talk therapy can drag on for many years. By talking circles around the content of our stories, we're incarcerated, trapped within the realm of the intellect. We cannot think our way to growth. We may become witty enough to talk the talk, but we're rarely wise enough to walk it. A dear friend once said to me, that attempting to heal through the intellect is like taking the scenic route with many traffic jams along the way.

Transformation does not live in the head.

All right then, what about our feelings?

Emotional circuits are triggered by our memories and thoughts. When this happens, many chemicals are released throughout the body. As emotional energy moves, the body flushes these chemicals with rapid efficiency. Within ninety seconds of the initial trigger, the chemical component of any emotion disperses from the blood and the automatic response is over. This is called the ninety-second rule. Emotions are simply energy in motion.

Why then, do some emotional memories persistently plague us? When we mentally attach to our feelings, the emotional circuits continue to play out. In other words, we fire up an emotional response every time we replay a particular event in our mind. When we replay that moment, we charge up the brain circuitry and release a fresh physiological response. This is when we feel "stuck."

When we trap ourselves in emotional thought loops, we disconnect from our true selves. We can choose the story and remain hooked by the experience, victims of our circumstances. Or we can choose a new path, releasing old emotions once and for all, empowered by what once was. The power is in the choice. As Neuro-Linguistic Programming cofounder Richard Bandler says, "Who's driving your bus?"

When we let go of our stories and lose the need to know "why" (aka content), we expand our consciousness. When we allow ourselves to feel what is real without shame or blame, we open ourselves to new possibilities. This is when we stimulate the shift from head to heart (notice the ongoing theme here).

Our bodies are miraculous creations that facilitate life and help us move through the world free from the cumbersome burden of thought. They're also formidable energy processors that digest old patterns and relay intuitive wisdom at lightning speed. Our bodies are powerful conduits for communication from the soul.

What if by losing our minds, plugging into our bodies, and intentionally getting our groove on, we can rapidly heal ourselves, revealing a more whole, authentic, and passionate person in the process?

As Toni Bergins, founder of JourneyDance™, says, "Embodiment is enlightenment." These words speak to a deep truth.

JourneyDance is a dynamic, conscious dance form that combines freestyle and structured movement to inspire participants to exit the limitations of the mind and enter the limitless wisdom of the body. Through movement, breath, sweat, and self-expression, JourneyDance leads participants on a potent journey of physical and emotional transformation.

I write about this from personal experience. I've been both participant and witness to the incredible healing powers of JourneyDance. Under the inclusive leadership of Toni, I journeyed into the deepest realms of consciousness, releasing emotional "goo" while reclaiming a deeper sense of my Self.

If you think this is new age, hippie nonsense, think again. Better yet, don't think, try it for yourself. Through the JourneyDance flow and the qualities of dance, participants tap into their primal nature—free from judgment and analysis—to become fully embodied and present. With guidance, free flow, and cathartic dance, we make room for long-suppressed emotions to pass through our bodies in ways that can never be replicated in mind-based talk therapy.

Through JourneyDance, Toni has helped thousands of people find a new sense of self-esteem, inner wisdom, emotional health, a spirit al practice, and well-being. By the end of my afternoon with Toni, I felt a deeper connection to my Self and a profound unity with other participants.

In a world that tends to complicate the simple, a return to our primal roots is often the fastest way home. The timeless simplicity of music and dance has the power to radically transform our lives. History has proven this since the beginning of time.

Toni's personal story is one that many women can relate to. Smart and successful on the outside, critical and self-abusive on the inside. Her journey is one of healing, reflection, revelation, and self-reclamation. Dance changed her life. Toni now leads a team of hundreds of JourneyDance facilitators, spreading joy and a passion for life throughout the world.

We live in a society where we experience the world from the neck up, our bodies no more than transportation for our heads. We've disconnected from the natural intelligence of the body and no longer experience the wisdom of our higher intuitive guides—our hearts. We live in our heads, which have been thoroughly conditioned by culture. But we need not fall prey to this disembodied mindset. As Martha Graham says, "Dance is the hidden language of the soul." When we lose our minds and reclaim our bodies, our hearts open, our souls speak, and life is transformed.

Stop thinking, start feeling. Set your spirit free and dance like nobody's watching. Lose yourself to find yourself and reclaim the miraculous gift of your body. As Toni Bergins says, "You have the power to move into a new story."

Toni's Story

Unplugging: Path to Purpose

I grew up in a suburban part of New York, close to Manhattan. There was a lot of pressure to go to college and grad school to become "someone." There was no room to explore who I already was.

With very little effort, I skated through high school on my intellect. I did really well because I was book-smart. Memorization was a piece of cake. But learning ... really learning? That was definitely a problem, because I don't believe that the educational system teaches us how to learn. It teaches us how to function in a fast-moving society. I learned quickly how to navigate this system.

Intellectually, I was great, but on an emotional level, I was miserable. I had experienced my first serious heartbreak, I had "friend" issues, and I went through many of the adolescent dramas that hurt so many kids early on. My coping response was bulimia.

I was very empathic, intuitive, and open. I was also energetically available. I didn't know what to do with my "stuff." I would come home from school to binge and purge before my mother came home from work. I was really good at it. I was good at everything because I was such a perfectionist. I was a perfectionist about my body. Anything I could control, I would. I worked out like a maniac.

I graduated from high school with great marks, but nobody knew anything about me. Bulimia is an easy illness to keep under wraps because no one sees the external results. It's not about losing weight, it's about the binge and purge. It's a very different mindset.

What I discovered is that the binge-purge cycle is an emotional and physical addiction connected to the dopamine and serotonin levels in the body. I developed a parasympathetic/sympathetic nervous system addiction for navigating my emotional life.

I went on to college and did really well. I was Phi Beta Kappa. I did my share of experimentation with drugs and alcohol while keeping the bulimia under wraps. Over the years, I discovered that there were many other bulimic girls who were unsuccessfully trying to manage their emotions.

After graduation, I got a job in New York City. I would rollerblade a hundred blocks to work with my whistle, my helmet, and a backpack filled with a dressy outfit. It was a lot of fun, but the job wasn't doing it for me. I worked as an assistant in a PR firm. I'd spent many years in college learning and expanding my mind, and there I was doing piddly work as a PR assistant. I squeezed myself into the dresses and high-heeled shoes, but I didn't fit into the corporate setting. I never felt grounded, because I had so much energy running though me. This sparked a constant parade of negative chatter in my head.

My outlet was dancing—like a crazy person, not like a sane person. I had a lot of angst. I used to dress in black and wear a hat and dark red lipstick. I was like a vortex. I just didn't know how to deal with the energy of my internal and external world.

I was also an aerobics-aholic. I went to Jack LaLanne and Jeff Martin studios, which were the biggest thing going at that time. I would pay money to get the best spot in the studio. By paying extra, I could be closest to the step instructor. I was such a perfectionist. Looking back now, it all seems so strange.

At age twenty-four, I had a spiritual awakening. I had a boyfriend who did yoga. He was my inspiration to explore yoga for myself. At that age, I could do every imaginable posture with ease. Because of yoga, I eventually stopped throwing up and going to the gym. But I turned it all into my yoga practice. I became a perfectionistic yogi in a matter of two years.

I took a course at Kripalu with my boyfriend, and during a program break, he decided to meditate. I decided to dance. I had an itch to always be moving. So I went to a dance class that had no mirrors. It was free dance. At one point the instructor had us bow to the earth in child's pose. He said something that changed my life. He said, "You are all so beautiful." In that moment, I burst into hysterics. I lost it. I cried from the depths of my being. It was my big wake-up call. I realized then that the culturally induced perfectionist game that I'd bought into had really hurt me.

That experience inspired my quest for true healing through embodiment. I had already been on a spiritual path of meditation, contemplation, soul travel, and creative visualization. I spent over twenty years learning how to leave my body.

After the pivotal moment with my big cry, I stopped doing yoga. I really loved yoga, but I needed to reclaim my power as a wild free mover and put an end to my quest for perfection. For the next four years I also delved deeply into therapy to end the bulimia once and for all. I went through many therapists searching for someone who wouldn't put me on drugs. I eventually found someone who did gestalt therapy, and it changed my life. I was able to see myself from a more expansive lens and understand why I was using the bulimia, smoking, and exercise as an escape valve.

My wound became my healing, and it inspired me to go to every dance class I could find. Eventually, I quit my corporate job and started teaching dance. JourneyDance unfolded out of my need to discover the truth about the power of the emotional body. In retrospect, I learned that I was an empathic person absorbing unfiltered energy. I learned that if I used the dance floor to release, I felt clear. I felt calm. I felt the same way that I did after a purge.

As I danced more frequently and developed my gestalt-based rituals, I realized that I was on to something. I was learning how to shake off trauma. That's what I teach people how to do in JourneyDance. Dance helps us shift things on a cellular, physical level. In JourneyDance, when we move, we enter a hypnotic state, and the mind takes on a new role. The body can then process our stuff. Our bodies are filled with all of the chemicals we need to be happy. They're also filled with all of the chemicals we need to understand others. The body is full of empathy. It's the perfect mechanism for change, growth, and evolution.

In my JourneyDance teacher training program I inspire participants to be present in their bodies and aware of their own gifts, their own skills, and their own passions. That's my biggest goal.

I believe that emotional expression is essential to life. Releasing grief or anger on the dance floor is very healing. JourneyDance is an emotional journey. I play music that makes people laugh, emote, and cry. I ask evocative questions that do the same. Not because I want people to cry, but because I want them to be able to access the truth of their emotions. I want to provide the space where they feel safe to be authentic and vulnerable. When they finally allow themselves to be real, it's so beautiful.

With greater emotional intelligence and embodiment, people are empowered. They remember their birthright of choice. JourneyDance is about reclaiming the power within.

I've been teaching for over twenty years now, and I've met thousands of people. Every single person is unique. There is no perfect. Each person is beautiful in their own way. This is what must be reclaimed. Once reclaimed, it must be embodied for a return to wholeness.

My main purpose is to empower people. I can't change their lives; only they can do that. But we all have the power to let go of the past. I'm grateful to have created a powerful technique that works. It works for me and I've seen it work for thousands of others. Amazing things happen when we reclaim our bodies. It's really so simple.

Self-Care

I believe that self-care is deeply personal and very necessary. It's about doing what we love and what brings us joy. It's about being excited for each new day. That doesn't mean that we have to search for a special life-purpose. That's not self-care. I believe that we all have many different purposes. What's more important is discovering our true passions. That means embracing the magical existence of life. That's self-care, step one.

There's no point to struggle and misery. If we're miserable and dying inside, we need to make new choices. We're not supposed to be doing the same old, same old all the time. That's a tired old paradigm that no longer works.

So step two is about paying attention to the negative internal chatter that traps us in self-abuse. We need to commit to ending the mental abuse so that we can begin to love ourselves. When we do this, we become more joyful and compassionate.

After that, we do what feeds the soul: walk the dogs, soak in the bath, garden, meditate, dance, do yoga; find a personal practice. The possibilities are endless, but the heart is the driver. Allow your heart to tell you what it needs. Self-care is about getting out of the old mindset and being 100 percent true to the authentic self.

Recharging and Reconnecting

For me, recharging and reconnecting is all about creativity. It's about becoming more empty than full. Expressive dance brings a state of emptiness. Walking in the woods, watching the ocean, and time in nature promote a state of emptiness. When I'm empty, I feel peaceful and calm. Emptiness also frees space for emotion to arise. Wherever there's emotion, there's inspiration. Emotion always leads to inspiration, even negative emotion.

Often, the best songs are written when the songwriter is deep in the throes of passion. We sing and cry along with the artist because we feel something. It's about feeling. When we allow ourselves to feel, we get out of the way and our emotions flow more freely. We make room for creative inspiration. In my own life, that's when I feel the most connected because I'm really in my body. When I'm in my body, I'm naturally more connected with my intuition.

Every human being is an intuitive sensory body. We all have a physical body with an energy field that surrounds us. This is a fact; so if we trust that we are sensory human beings, our feeling intuition becomes a great source of guidance. For instance, we sense and have impressions when we walk into a room with others. We feel drawn to some people and repelled by others. We feel this in our body, in our solar plexus. Unfortunately, most people don't feel safe in their bodies, so they close off this sensory awareness. It's so much easier to reconnect to the intuitive self when we feel safe. To feel safe, we need only connect to feelings of love or gratitude. It's very simple.

Intuition is always working. We just have to feel the body's ongoing signals. If we feel a nagging tightness or agitation, that's a signal to potentially exit a situation. That's something that people forget, because we've been taught to negate our body's wisdom. Let's say, for example, that someone hates their job. Even though they may feel slightly irritated all the time, they stay in the job because they fear change. That's a typical example of the mind shutting the body/intuition down. That's not authentic. That's status quo.

Intuition expresses itself through body. So recharging and reconnecting is about being deeply embodied. This means listening to the intuitive guidance of the body, feeling emotions, allowing inspiration to flow into creative expression, and becoming empty once again.

If You Had a Magic Wand …

The first thing I would do with my magic wand would be to provide clean water for all. I would direct massive resources to sustainably clean up every body of water on this beautiful planet, a worldwide cleanup effort! That's the first thing. Whoosh!

Then my wand would create a world where all children would feel safe and happy. There would be an abundance of smiling, laughter, and play.

Next, I would rearrange the governing powers so that women held the highest positions around the world. I mean real women, wise women: mothers and grandmothers. There would no longer be masculinized women playing out these roles in a competitive world. My wand incites the divine feminine to midwife the world into its next incarnation.

Ultimately, I wish for a sustainable planet where everybody feels safe and has the opportunity to thrive, grow, evolve, and experience joy on a daily basis.

To learn more about Toni and her work, please visit journeydance.com.

TWENTY-ONE

Sharon Gannon

Living Ahimsa, Inspiring Kindness

*"Ahimsa is the highest ideal. It is meant for the brave,
never for the cowardly."*

– MAHATMA GANDHI

Where we stand with the profusion of problems in today's world is of grave importance. We've reached a critical crossroads where the survival of humanity—of all life—ends with a question mark.

Each of us has a part to play within the web of life. But we must first *remember* that we are connected to a web of life. Biologist Jonas Salk spoke a startling truth: "If all insects on Earth disappeared, within fifty years all life on Earth would end. If all human beings disappeared from the Earth, within fifty years all forms of life would flourish."

This statement clearly shows how our separation from the web of life marks humanity as the greatest threat to planet earth. Sadly, it never had to be this way. This is not who we are, and yet we were conditioned to split off and close our hearts. A closed heart is an untouchable mind. An untouchable mind is an ignorant mind. An ignorant mind is a separate mind.

The entire planet is suffering from a crisis in consciousness. We have all the tools, resources, capabilities, and wisdom to shift the paradigm in the blink of an eye. We have the power to put an end to every problem facing the world today, simply by choosing differently.

In our hearts, we all know that we need to change. But change brings up safety issues, and safety issues bring up fear. It takes courage to break free from the psychological fear that arises with change. It means aligning with love and compassion—radical compassion.

What is radical compassion? Radical means "at the root of." Compassion means, "to feel with." Radical compassion is our deepest capacity to feel with others. It is the essence of who we are—our non-separate self, the purest fabric of love within. Radical compassion lives in the heart of each and every one of us. For many, it's a dormant seed. For the change-makers of today's world, it's a tree in blossom. The most powerful expression of radical compassion is to dare to care about others.

Sharon Gannon is a woman who cares, an indomitable change-maker who epitomizes love, kindness, and radical compassion. She's a renowned yoga teacher, author, musician, and the cocreator, with David Life, of the Jivamukti Yoga Method.

As written in the Jivamukti statement of purpose, "Jivamukti Yoga is a path to enlightenment through compassion for all beings. It means to live liberated in joyful, musical harmony with the Earth. The Earth does not belong to us—we belong to the Earth. Let us celebrate our connection to life by not enslaving animals and exploiting the Earth, and attain freedom and happiness for ourselves in the process. For surely, the best way to uplift our own lives is to do all we can to uplift the lives of others. Go vegan!"

Radical compassion is at the core of Sharon Gannon's existence. She's one of few modern-day yoginis who talks it, walks it, practices it, and lives it in every moment of her life. For Sharon, yoga is not just a trendy form of exercise; it's a powerful form of spiritual activism that inspires within others the dormant seed of radical compassion.

Jivamukti yoga is taught worldwide and includes high-profile students such as Sting, Trudie Styler, Russell Simmons, Joan Jett, Willem Dafoe, Madonna, and Michael Franti. Impacted by Sharon's teachings of ahimsa, many of these high-profile celebrities are using their influential platforms to impact others.

In basic terms, *ahimsa* is the Sanskrit word for nonviolence. According to Mahatma Gandhi, who defined his life by ahimsa, "Ahimsa does not simply mean non-killing. Himsa means causing pain to or killing any life out of anger or for a selfish purpose or with the intention of injuring it. Refraining from so doing is ahimsa. Ahimsa means not to injure any creature by thought, word or deed. True ahimsa should mean a complete freedom from ill-will, anger and hate and an overflowing love for all. Ahimsa is the attribute of the soul and therefore to be practiced by everybody in all the affairs of life."

Ahimsa creates connection and dissolves separation. Connection occurs when we transcend our cultural conditioning in favor of the truth that lives in our hearts.

Inside every one of us there exist two heartbeats: the physical beat that sustains our daily existence and the universal beat that plugs us into *all that matters in life*. The greatest moral compass resides within our hearts.

Biologically, humans have evolved beyond the need to consume animal flesh and secretions. Even though we know better in our hearts, some of us cling to antiquated belief systems that trap us in separation.

Through Sharon Gannon's teachings, veganism and yoga are intricately intertwined. Yogis endeavor to live harmoniously with the earth and all beings. By doing so, they actively challenge the separation at the root of our culture of consumption. But we need not identify with the yogi moniker to live a non-separate life; we need only shift our worldview from head to heart.

As Sharon states in her book, *Simple Recipes for Joy*:

> The greatest changes in history (such as the abolition of human slavery, women's rights to education and to vote, the end of apartheid in South Africa, and the fall of the Berlin Wall) have never been instigated by governments or corporations, but by small groups of committed individuals acting out of consciousness for a greater good. We instigate the awakening of self-confidence within

ourselves when we stop blaming others for the ills of the world and instead look at our own lives and ask, "What am I doing to contribute to a more peaceful, joyful, and unpolluted world?" By healing ourselves, we heal the world. After all, the world around us is only a reflection of who we are. And when we make others happy, we become happier too.[8]

We all know in our hearts that we can be better. Sharon says it best: "Each one of us can make a huge difference by choosing not to eat animals. By choosing kindness over cruelty, we contribute to the sustainability of our planet Earth and can even change the destiny of our species and all the species on Earth."

With that in mind, why would we choose anything less?

***

Sharon's Story

Unplugging: Path to Purpose

The moment that changed my life happened in 1982. I was living in Seattle, Washington, as a dancer, musician, and artist. I watched a British documentary called *The Animals Film* that probed into the relationship between human beings and other animals. The film was perhaps the first feature-length documentary to expose the many cruel, exploitive, and inhumane ways that humans treat other animals. It explored the use of animals for entertainment, food, clothing, and as victims of military and "scientific" research. It ended with a scene showing the Animal Liberation Front (ALF) rescuing animals from a laboratory.

That movie woke me up in a powerful way and set me on my path. It caused me to radically rethink art, the purpose of the artist, and what I was doing with my life. I realized that if I wasn't making a contribution in my life to ending this insanity, there was no value in what I was doing.

After watching that film, I became a vegan, then an animal rights activist, and shortly after that a yoga teacher. I knew that yoga would provide me with the best platform to speak up for animal rights and compassion.

The Spiritual Path of Yoga

I've always been a very spiritual person, and my main objective has always been to get closer to God. When I discovered yoga, I knew that it would be the best way for me to get there.

Yoga is about purifying our karmas. Karmas are what our body is made of. Everything we've ever thought, said, or done is carried with us. We incarnate into each lifetime with karmas from the past, unresolved issues that we try to resolve in this lifetime. The Sanskrit word *karma* simply means "action." It doesn't mean good karma or bad karma, bad action or good action. It simply means action.

To resolve a karma means returning it to the source of origin. The yoga teachings say that we originate from love. That's our true nature. Love is our essential heart, the core, the essence of our being—the essence of *all* being. We emerge from this essence and we all try to get back to it. That's why we seek happiness, joy, love, and God. Yoga provides methods, tools—things we can do—to purify our karmas, to resolve our actions back into love.

Whatever we do to someone else, we actually do to ourselves. When we're unkind to others, it stays with us. It's unresolved because it's not love. So to resolve a karma means to bring it back to that place of joy, of love.

Life gives us many opportunities to be kind to others. It's only through kindness that we can resolve our past actions. Ultimately, there are no "others." There's only love. There's only joy. You can call it God, the oneness of being, or whatever feels right.

The main obstacle to perceiving that oneness is seeing others as separate from you. Yoga means to join, to dissolve separation. Through the practice of yoga we let go of anger, resentment, blaming, and complaining. By forgiving others as well as ourselves we begin to remove the armoring around our own hearts so that we can experience the reality of love.

I think the most important thing that any of us can do in our lifetime is to dare to care about the happiness of others. It takes great courage. The yoga teachings tell us that we can have anything we want, but first we must make it happen for someone else. If we make others happy, our own happiness is assured. On the other hand, if we cause unhappiness to others, we can expect more of the same.

One of the major ways that we interact with others is through food. Peter Singer said, "The most frequent interaction most people have with animals is three times a day when they sit down to eat them." "That's a terrible way to define a relationship," adds Ingrid Newkirk, founder of People for the Ethical Treatment of Animals (PETA).

A good relationship is defined by Patanjali in the Yoga Sutra as one that is mutually beneficial. We live in a culture where we're not taught how to interact with others in a mutually beneficial way. We're taught that the world is ours for the taking and that animals exist only to serve our needs. We are not required to feel any responsibility for their liberation or happiness. But yoga teaches something quite different. Yoga teaches that when we care for others, our own happiness is assured. I like the teachings of yoga. They give me a lot to work with for my activism.

Ahimsa

Ahimsa, non-harming or non-violence, is one of the foundational practices of yoga. In the *Yoga Sutra of Patanjali*, it is listed as the first *yama*, or ethical restraint. There are five yamas, ways that a yoga practitioner should behave in relation to others. Patanjali advises that as long as we are still seeing others and not God, then we shouldn't hurt anyone.

In our modern world, perhaps even in the ancient world, extending kindness to others is considered an optional charitable act. It is recognized as a nice thing to do, but not considered essential to one's ultimate success, happiness, or freedom. But the truth is that kindness toward others benefits the one who is being kind as much as, if not more than, the recipient of the kindness.

Another interesting point about ahimsa is that non-harming has been around for a long time. It exists as a foundational tenet in every spiritual tradition and religion. But extending the practice of ahimsa to include other animals and the environment is a radically new concept. By extending ahimsa to include all life, we have the power to dismantle our present culture—a culture based on the enslavement and exploitation of animals and the environment. Ahimsa challenges the status quo.

A Shift in Consciousness

It seems like more and more people are realizing that their actions matter. There are more people doing things to make the world a kinder place. There are more vegans and environmentalists than ever before, and the word "vegan" is now used in mainstream culture. Famous rock stars, actors, and even former presidents are outspoken vegans who are also supporting ecological issues. There are more vegan options in restaurants, airports, and in places we'd not normally expect them to be. Animal rights organizations are on the rise, and animal cruelty laws are making it into the American legislature. That's all pretty amazing.

On the other hand, the global human population has doubled since 1960. World meat production has tripled since 1980. Humans now kill more than 56 billion land animals for food every year. When we factor in the number of sea creatures killed, the numbers skyrocket into the trillions. The human appetite for meat and dairy is voracious. The number of domesticated animals being enslaved, tortured, raped, and killed is increasing, while the number of wild animals is plummeting—many are nearing extinction. The fact is, slavery and violence are still the global trends. Animals and the earth seem to be losing the war being waged on them. What I'm noticing is that as compassion and consciousness rises, so too does ignorance and violence.

Maybe compassion and violence are neck-and-neck right now. But even if violence is winning out, I wouldn't do anything differently. I wouldn't just throw in the towel and give up. Once awake, always awake. There's no going back to sleep. I believe that with awakening comes optimism. By cultivating an unpolluted state of mind, it's easier to believe that truth will inevitably overthrow illusion. So I'm optimistic.

The good news is that speciesism, racism, misogyny, meat-eating, and other forms of violence are not hardwired into us; they're learned behaviors. Anything learned can be unlearned. The ancient teachings of yoga tell us that although there is suffering in the world, liberation is possible. The first step is to take responsibility for everything we see happening in the world and not to fall into the trap of blaming others. If we can free ourselves from being victims, we're on the road to awakening. The truth is that the world we see "out there" has emerged from a collective inner consciousness. To change that, we have to be willing to change what is inside of ourselves. It may take patience and steady hard work to let go of the negativity that has clouded our hearts and minds, but if we believe in the power of love, it's not that hard.

There are numerous dysfunctional cultural programs that our minds have been operating with for many centuries. The most devastating program is the belief that Earth belongs to us. We must challenge this misconception and be willing to experience humility. Humility will be our saving grace. The word is interesting: it comes from the root *humus*, meaning close to the earth. Oddly enough, the word human shares the same root.

We need to support each other in positive and compassionate ways and do helpful, good things together. The time of the lone wolf is over. Even the Hopi elders say this. It's time for community. I feel that our strength is in our numbers, in building unity and community.

When we come together as a group of like-minded individuals, anything is possible. A group of like-minded individuals who are guided by compassion and love are unstoppable. I'm 100 percent invested in building that kind of community, and I believe that there are many more people these days who are on this same path of transformation.

If You Had a Magic Wand …

I would create a kinder, more joy-filled world—a place where love, not fear or greed, motivates the actions of all beings.

Learn more about Sharon and her work at jivamuktiyoga.com.

TWENTY-TWO

Betsy Chasse
What the Bleep Do We Know ... and Does it Matter Anyway?

"The more you know, the more you know you don't know."

– ARISTOTLE

"Spirituality" is a loaded word that evokes many misperceptions. From churches to chakras and sermons to spirit guides, spirituality is so much more than all of that.

The essence of spirituality is alignment with the true sense of self—our authentic humanity. It's not found in holy scriptures, mala beads, or channelers; it's found deep within our own hearts. In the quiet calm of contemplation, in sudden bursts of inspiration, in the rapture of free-flow dance, in the cathartic release of grief, in the depths of meaningful conversation, and in the miraculous beauty of nature, spirituality is the profound sense of connection that we feel to something greater than ourselves. It is awe, it is instinct, it is laughter, it is tears, it is pain, it is peace. It is all of who we are.

Singer Bonnie Raitt once said, "Religion is for people who are scared to go to hell. Spirituality is for people who have already been there." Often, the most transformative gifts arrive in the ugliest packages. Growth is an ongoing spiritual choice.

Spirituality means feeling and healing. It is presence, awareness, self-acceptance, and trust. It means understanding that we are so much more than our physicality, while knowing that the ephemeral nature of the body is a sacred gift. Quite simply, spirituality is about living from the heart—authentically with grace.

A spiritual existence is not about perfection; it's about honesty, integrity, vulnerability, and compassion. It's about the mess, the miracles, and the power of free will. Spirituality is about living the embodied human experience with passion, purpose, and a heaping dose of humility.

Enter Betsy Chasse, a woman who effortlessly embodies spirituality. Without bibles, gurus, or mantras, she gets it. Betsy is an author, screenwriter, speaker, and mom. She's the cocreator of the massively popular 2004 film, *What the Bleep Do We Know!?*—a film that challenges everything that we think we know ... and so much more. It's also the film that inspired Betsy's discovery that she doesn't "know shit."

Betsy has a refreshing perspective on life that is vulnerable, honest, and raw. Her deeply grounded view of spirituality in today's fast-paced world is both humorous and simple. As she states in her book, *Metanoia: A Transformative Change of Heart,* "I am always changing—moving forwards then backwards. I am not what anyone has defined me to be, or even what I have defined myself to be. I just am one little soul experiencing life, stumbling through it moment-by-moment, realizing that finding joy is easy. All I have to do is choose it."

Betsy Chasse reminds us that spirituality isn't hard, because a spiritual existence is just who we are.

***

Betsy's Story

Unplugging: Path to Purpose

If we think about every nine- or ten-year cycle in life, there's a defining moment; a turning point in that cycle. For me, my thirties were defined by *What the Bleep Do We Know!?*. Before I made *What the Bleep*, I knew little about spirituality, and I didn't know how to spell quantum physics. Higher consciousness meant a pair of three-inch high-heeled shoes. I had no clue.

With *What the Bleep*, I had the opportunity to explore these concepts in a way that was truly life-altering. I think that this really came through in the film, because unless you're Steven Spielberg, nobody gives a crap about the filmmakers; they just talk about the movie or the movie stars. But Will Arntz, Mark Vicente, and I each had very genuine transformations that were vibrationally expressed through the film. People became interested in what I had to say, and this was really shocking to me. Because I made a movie about spirituality and quantum physics, all of a sudden I was perceived as a guru who understood it all.

For a while, my thirties were defined by being that guru, that perfect mom, that perfect wife, that perfect filmmaker—the enlightened master. It was a massive ego trip and I really dug it. I loved being treated like a princess and being flown all over the place. But by my late thirties, I started to realize that it was all a load of crap and that I was completely full of shit. I had no happiness. I didn't even know what the hell happiness was.

I had a lot of really cool information and could really talk the talk. I could explain it all logically in a way that was understandable and accessible. But I hadn't embodied it. I wasn't truly living it. I was living the persona of it.

The pivotal moment occurred in my forties when I got divorced. That was when I realized that everything I had created in my life was nothing. There was a time when it all seemed to work and I thought I was happy. But it wasn't working anymore. Something was changing within me. I realized that I was still trying to fit into an old life that I had created, but I wasn't creating a life that fit the changing me.

I ended up getting divorced, which was frightening because all of a sudden I was responsible for taking care of my two kids, not just physically, but financially and in every other way. I realized that I had an opportunity to recreate all that stuff again—find a new husband, find a new house—essentially rebuild the same castle; or I could build something completely different.

That became another defining moment in my forties. It was the first time that I realized I could consciously rebuild my life and that I didn't have to bring in my past if I didn't want to. Except for being a mom, I could do everything differently. I could change my career, I could change where I lived, I could change my hair, I could change just about anything. So the question for me became, "What is it that I really want, and how do I figure out what that is?"

I think the biggest pressure release came from the realization that I'm never going to actually figure it out. I did everything that I thought I was supposed to. I had the husband, I had the house, I had the career, I had the babies, I had everything on the "how to be a proper human" checklist. But I didn't have happiness. I realized that everything that was supposed to bring me happiness didn't. I thought that would be the end game.

But now I realize that there is no end game. When you follow your heart and do the best that you can, things are either going to work out the way you want them to or they're not. Generally, if they don't work out the way you want or expect, eventually something else will come along to lead you in a new direction that can often be better. You are in charge of the yeses and nos in your life. What are you going to say yes to and what are you going to say no to? This is what really dictates life.

Take the concept of the law of attraction, for example. There's a belief that if you just sit there and think positive thoughts, everything will be attracted to you. The truth of the matter is that nothing is actually being attracted to you. You said yes to it or you said no to it. It was always up to you.

There's also a belief that people come into your life to teach you lessons. Not true. People come into your life and you've attached meaning to your experiences with them. The meaning that you've attached to your experiences comes from the belief system or story that you've told yourself.

So it's all about you, which is very arrogant, but true. It is all about you. What are you thinking? Why are you choosing to think that way? Is it serving you? Could you think another way? Super simple, but we like to come up with these magical stories about how if we meditate for six hours a Mercedes-Benz is going to magically appear at our house.

There's a tendency to set up expectations that will supposedly manifest a lot of stuff in our lives. But we don't stop and ask ourselves, "Why do I want to manifest that and what does it mean?" We don't actually do the work. We just think, "I am going to live the law of attraction." But we don't really do the work around what the heck that really means. And then we set up these crazy expectations, and when the Mercedes doesn't arrive, we feel like a shitty failure who isn't spiritual enough. We feel like there's something wrong with us and this is why nothing changes. It's an endless cycle of doom.

The bottom line is that there is no right path. There is your path. Become present to your path and become aware of the yeses and nos that you're choosing in your life and decide to make better choices. Happiness is not a destination. It's a state of mind. That's how I figured out to be happy even in the midst of chaos. It's pretty simple.

Whenever things seem complicated and hard, it's not because of the facts, it's because of the story that has been created around the facts. If we get rid of the story and stick with the facts, everything immediately simplifies. Most of the crazy stuff that we conjure in our lives comes from the crazy thought monsters in our head. We all do it. In my own life, rather than beat myself up over this, I learned how to give myself a break. I realized that we are all assholes with our crazy thought monsters. I decided to give myself permission to be an asshole, but to make sure that I was being a conscious asshole. That means no malicious intent, but a solid intention to live with integrity and impeccability, which is really hard to do. I also decided to look at other people in the same way, so that when they were being an asshole to me, I didn't get caught in the judgment of a story that would cause me to be an asshole in return. I didn't want to get stuck in an asshole parade. I realized that they're not actually being an asshole to *me*. They're struggling with their humanity just like I do. Now if they're harming me in some way, I either eliminate them from my life or deal with it. I no longer worry about whether there's something wrong with me to have invited an asshole into my life.

Sometimes we're just assholes because we're human. Being human is freaking hard. The truth is, most of us haven't ever been taught how to be a real human. We've only ever learned from other humans who don't know how to be real humans either. So we all learned badly. We all had bad teachers. So let's give everybody a break.

Recharging and Reconnecting

I'm a kinetic person and I have a lot of energy. I used to feel guilty about having such a busy mind. Then I realized that if I just started paying attention to all the craziness going on in my head, there might be something worthy in there. When I noticed what was being said, I was able to start making different choices.

I've never been a meditator. If I tell my body to sit down for half an hour, it's going to revolt in every possible way. I'll have to pee, I'll be itchy, I'll get hungry … the list goes on and on.

When people ask me if I meditate, my answer is, "No, not in the traditional sense." Did I spend twenty minutes this morning pulling weeds out of my garden? Yes. Did I walk around and water my rose bushes today? Yes. Those are the things that work for me. My mind relaxes when I do the things that I love. When I'm relaxed, I make better decisions. So if an insecure thought pops into my head, I can choose to discard it. If a creative idea pops in, I can keep it. If an insecure thought persists, then I ask it, "What do you want? Why are you here? Explain yourself. What's going on that you're feeling fear and insecurity around?" When I ask what's up, I can then deal with it.

If we constantly try to push these thoughts out of our heads, they just hide and become our sacred cows. They become our shadows. They become hidden in ourselves and we don't even know that they're there.

So just listening to what's going on in our heads is pretty eye-opening.

Although I don't meditate, I garden and I pay attention to my thoughts. It's a non-practice that works for me. It charges me and it reconnects me. I think if we all just allow whatever works for us—whether it's gardening, or walking, or swimming, or whatever—if we allow that to organically occur rather than trying to squeeze ourselves into a box that may not fit, that's when we more easily connect to ourselves.

An Inspired Life

The most important thing for me is awareness. I try very hard to live my life with awareness of my choices and options. For instance, I don't have to say yes for the same reasons that I used to say yes.

I learn about myself every day and I know myself well enough to make choices that serve my heart. They aren't always popular or well-accepted. But that's okay with me now. I no longer live my life requiring acceptance from other people. I feel like I'm serving myself and humanity better when I'm living from my heart and trusting that the choices I make are what's best for me. Because if I'm happy, healthy, and living from my heart, everyone around me is positively impacted.

There's a Buddhist idea of right living where we ask ourselves, "Will this choice cause harm to me or someone else?" Harm isn't about letting people down if it doesn't feel right. Saying yes when we mean yes and no when we mean no is more important than compromising ourselves. Bruised egos and failed expectations are not considered harm.

It's also very empowering to practice these three words, "I don't know." My honey posted a little picture for me one day that said, "I hate to ruin the ending for you, but it's all going to be OK." I thought that was brilliant. The thing about life that I've come to accept, and actually now enjoy, is that I don't know. Some days are horrible and I feel sad. Other days are great and I feel really happy. And that's the way it's supposed to be. If it isn't then you're either a) in denial, or b) on some serious drugs.

Life is up and down and all over the freaking map. There are no three-step solutions. There are no five-step solutions. But there is a life solution. Just live it.

In the end, just being real is the most inspired way to live.

If You Had a Magic Wand ...

I think the world is fine. God forbid I should say that. I mean, there is a lot of tragedy in the world. There is also a lot of really great stuff in the world. It would be super great to wave a magic wand so that everybody was happy and loved each other, but I don't know that even desiring that is practical, realistic, or helpful. For me, I just have to look at life for what it is and appreciate it. So instead of trying to change everything and fix everything, I just try to be where it is, experience that, take in the wisdom, and move on to the next experience.

The world has always been kind of a mess. Ever since humanity has been on this planet, it has been screwed. We've done a lot of crazy shit. So it's a process.

For more information on Betsy and her work, please visit betsychasse.net.

TWENTY-THREE

Kimberly Carroll
Soulful Activism: Heal Yourself, Heal the World

"He who experiences the unity of life sees his own self in all beings, and all beings in his own self, and looks on everything with an impartial eye."

– BUDDHA

The headlines are everywhere: "Rediscover Your Authentic Self," "5 Easy Steps to Reclaim Your Authentic Self Today," "Learn How to Love Your True Self Now"… on and on it goes. The self-help gurus blast us with uncertainty. From talk shows and personal growth books to blog posts, online courses, and mobile apps (oh, the irony); endless solutions for what we're told we're missing … our true selves.

This begs the questions: why must we blog, advertise, author, and technocize what should be perfectly natural? If we're not being ourselves, then who are we?

"Who are you?" is perhaps the most difficult question for most to answer. "I'm a writer," "I'm an athlete," "I'm a mom," "I'm a teacher," we blithely declare. Our identities sourced from externally accepted social norms rather than from deep internal truths that know that we are so much more than who we think ourselves to be.

Our authentic self lives in our essence. Our essence is the untainted, unchanging nature of who we are—the purest fiber of our being. It is more fundamental and intrinsic than our personality. It is the truth within the feelings and experiences of our lives. It is always present and rising within us.

In the words of psychotherapist Karen Malik:
- Essence isn't alive; it is aliveness.
- Essence isn't aware; it is awareness.
- Essence isn't loving; it is love.
- Essence isn't joyful; it is joy.
- Essence isn't compassionate; it is compassion.
- Essence isn't true; it is truth.[9]

Our authentic self is not defined by our labels, personality, or what we do; it is defined by the essence of who we are.

It is our pain, our peace, our fear, and our courage. It is our grief, our love, our passion, and our joy. It is as much our righteous anger as our compassionate tenderness. It is all of who we are. Our authentic self is the unfiltered expression of spirit moving through flesh.

When we express ourselves from an authentic place, we're rooted in our core beliefs, values, and attitudes. Our lives reflect internal truth rather than external conditioning. We no longer care about the opinions of others because we no longer have anything to prove. We're plugged into our personal power. We're congruent in thoughts, behaviors, choices, and actions. We're embodied—feeling what is real—moment by moment by moment.

Living authentically is about self-trust, self-love, and self-acceptance. It feels good. It feels safe. It feels right.

It is right.

Why then, does authenticity elude us? Conditioning, my friend, conditioning. In a world full of crazy myths that keep us trapped in externally imposed belief systems, we forget who we are. The fastest way to find our true self is to lose who we've been taught to be.

This is the story of Kimberly Carroll, body/mind/spirit coach, life architect, television personality, and passionate world citizen.

In her mid-twenties, Kimberly was struck by a quarter-life crisis that drove her head first into a "wake-up wall." As she tells it, "I was a young, driven woman living a fast-paced, mildly glamorous show biz life. I had gotten so caught up in the chase and proving my worth that I'd lost the connection to the moment, to others, and to myself. Basically, I had become an overachieving zombie!"

This prompted mission "Wake Up," which led her from Manitoba to India to Australia—and many places in between. She reclaimed herself equally in pubs and in ashrams, with life experience leading the way. She confesses, "It didn't happen overnight, but I changed on a deep level, and so did my life. I found my true power and started to grow into a person I love. I became more engaged in the world around me and I eventually became a guide for others wanting to live bolder, more conscious lives." Who best to guide others to bolder consciousness than someone who lives it herself?

I'm honored to call Kimberly a friend. She's a passionate lover of life who fearlessly speaks out for change. She's a fervent supporter of soul awakenings, animals, laughter, the planet, social justice, creativity, human potential, and love. Kimberly Carroll is a beacon of light in a world filled with darkness.

As Carl Jung once said, "The privilege of a lifetime is to become who you truly are." Kimberly Carroll is proof positive that in our hearts, we already know who we are.

***

Kimberly's Story

Unplugging: Path to Purpose

I realized early on in my life that I have the potential to be either very destructive or very constructive in this world. I started my life as a sensitive, scared little being who worked hard to build an ego for self-protection. As an adult, I've been working diligently to dismantle that ego.

I was always a big performer who was really into music. There was a part of me that needed to be seen, heard, and validated. I did everything

I could to achieve that end. I became quite good at it.

As I got older, I eventually realized that this behavior was running my life. I was becoming compulsive and unhappy. I was working as a television host and producer and my life looked pretty good on the outside, but on the inside, it was a different story. I was constantly performing to prove my worth to the world. I'd become an overachiever who moved at a frenetic pace. I wasn't making any space for myself. Eventually, I had a bit of a breakdown. In my efforts to get ahead, I had become completely disconnected from my body and my life. It was at that point that I knew I needed to truly commit to seeking a better way. Interestingly, the seeds for that seeking were sown very early in my life.

I grew up wondering why I was here, what was the meaning of life, what is this thing called infinity. I remember at age six, lying in twin beds at my grandma's place and talking to my cousin about dying. He said that he was terrified of his parents dying. I said that I wasn't afraid of dying, but that infinity really concerned me (you can imagine how popular I was with that thought process with kids my own age). I've always had a curiosity about the purpose of life and what lies beyond.

My family wasn't religious, but I started going to church on my own. It was an outlet for my spirituality, my curiosity, and my celebration of life. It ended up being a good experience for me because I was a very informed kid. I knew what to believe and what to discard.

As I grew older and started expanding my worldview, I realized that religion didn't suit me anymore. The beliefs were too limiting. I ended up leaving the church. For a few years, I struggled because I didn't have a spiritual outlet anymore. When I refer to spirituality, I mean the exploration of self, the exploration of energy, and the exploration of meaning.

It wasn't until I was in university that this all changed. I was in a Canadian literature course reading Leonard Cohen's poem "You Have the Lovers" and was quite struck by it. It really resonated with me. My professor told me that Leonard Cohen was a Buddhist and that the poem referred to the essence of Buddhism. That led me to a Buddhist group where I learned meditation and the fundamentals of Buddhism.

I no longer identify as a Buddhist because I don't call myself anything anymore, but to this day, Buddhism still deeply influences me. The most important things it taught me were non-dualism and that we're all of the same energy. We're all in this together. There is no beginning. There is no end. There are no limits. This informs much of my life to this day.

Because of Buddhism, I started feeling less competitive. I didn't see as much separation. That applied to everyone—people, animals, and nature. I know that a tree or a chicken has as much mystery and beauty as I do. This revelation caused a seismic shift in my journey and inspired the exploration of different cultures, religions, and philosophies—everything from shamanism to new age philosophies to cognitive behavior psychology. I started reading a lot of self-help and spirituality books. I kept what resonated with me and let go of what didn't. It was all wonderful because it opened my mind. But something was still missing. I was trapped in my head and felt like I could go deeper.

I discovered something called the Hoffman Process, an eight-day personal development retreat offered all over the world. It was a game-changer for me because it's so experiential. It transformed everything that I'd amassed in my head by bringing it into my body and being. Knowledge was transformed into wisdom. I still use concepts from Hoffman in my life today.

As all of this transformation was happening, I fell in love with an Australian street performer. I'd been such a career-driven person and I always wanted to travel, but I never went anywhere because I was afraid that people would forget me or that I'd miss my "big break." That all changed in the early 2000s, however. There was a big SARS outbreak, there were big strikes in my industry, and I couldn't get a job to save my life. I dropped out for a couple of years and decided to travel with my boyfriend. I became a street performer and did shows in the squares of major cities around the world. My big finale was lying on a pink bed of nails wearing a skimpy outfit with a 200-pound man standing on my stomach as I sang my grand finale. It was one of the hardest things I've ever done—not physically, but emotionally. It helped break down my ego and the false identity I'd created for myself.

Many people have a perception of street performers as being pretty well homeless. That's not the case. It's actually possible to make decent money as a street performer. I was fully committed to this lifestyle for a while. My boyfriend and I never really knew where we would sleep each night, and we had no idea what was coming next. It was really good for me. It shook me out of the identity-driven life that I had built for myself.

On the heels of that adventure, I spent a couple of months in India. That experience helped solidify my life mission. Up to that point, I'd been living for success and recognition, yet here I was in a country where people were dying of leprosy because the government wouldn't pay for the fifty-dollar cure.

I witnessed horrible suffering. It really affected me. I realized that a huge part of my life mission had to be about ending suffering for both humans and animals. India made me reevaluate my entire life—what I was doing and why I was doing it.

I formed my mission statement while in India. My life mission is: to use soul, style, compassion, and humor to wake up the love, power, and joy in myself and others and create a kinder, healthier, and more vibrant world. When I defined my mission, I got goose bumps. Something inside of me was singing—it still is.

From there, it seemed natural for me to use television to inspire and wake people up to kindness and compassion.

In the quest for doing that, I started collecting many different techniques from inspiring teachers. I gleaned as much wisdom as I could. I studied with the founder of the Soul Coaching modality, Denise Linn, because I wanted more background for the content I was going to be producing on television. It was by pure accident that I became a coach.

Something about coaching really resonated with me. I started doing it on a lark—just for friends—and noticed that I accessed a whole other part of me when I was coaching others. I felt really connected to myself. I decided to let go of television and give coaching a solid effort. My life has never been the same.

When I started doing group coaching, I especially loved it! From there, I began developing more and more of my own content. My signature program is the *Life Reboot Program*. It's a real life-changer for so many people—myself included. It's a body/mind/spirit boot camp for people who are feeling like they want to take their life to the next level by clearing their "stuff" and connecting in ways that they haven't connected before.

The most important thing I've learned as a coach, and in my personal life, is how to hold space for people so that they feel safe and supported. With safety, they can go deep into themselves and discover their own answers. We really do all have our own answers. I've seen it over and over again. By helping people feel safe enough to connect to their consciousness, incredible healing occurs. It's beautiful. I'm humbled every time.

Concurrent with my soulful journey was my journey into animal activism. The two started to interweave a few years ago. When that happened, I began feeling more whole. That's when my activism became more empowered. Instead of being a spiritual being just trying to make myself happy, or just a desperate angry activist, I wove spirituality and activism together, and it's made a huge difference in both.

I didn't become an animal activist because I hate people who exploit animals. I did it because I love animals, and also because I love, honor, and respect all life. This love informs my activism so that it comes from a place of inclusion, connectedness, and empowerment.

There are two places where I'd really like to see people evolve. One place is spirituality. I really respect people who have done a lot of work on themselves and on their own evolution. I think it's so important, and if everybody would make it a priority, the world would be so much better off. But there's more to life than praying, visioning, or meditating for a better world. We actually need to get off our asses and do something about it.

The other place is activism. A huge part of my client base as a body/mind/spirit coach is activists. I love working with activists because they tend to be very sensitive, kind beings. There's often a lot of anger, though. But with a slight perceptual shift, they become unstoppable and readily take on the world in a more empowered way.

I feel really good about the work I've done on myself and how I've evolved as a person. It's a daily journey. I know that I have a natural propensity for being petty and self-centered, but I also have a propensity for beautiful compassion, love, and power. It's a matter of putting more effort into the latter. I also recognize the shadow aspects of myself. I don't deny them. I continually work on them by feeding them with love.

Activism

My theory is that many activists get into activism because they've experienced powerlessness while growing up. They know what it's like to be voiceless, to be powerless. That's why the suffering of the world calls to them. I have a core wound of powerlessness that I constantly work on. People like me are drawn to activism because we can feel the suffering of others so deeply inside of us. We can't ignore it because we're so sensitive to it.

The problem with these feelings is that they create the kind of activism where we're always on the edge of pain, working from a place of deep sorrow, anger, or even hatred. I learned through personal experience that this is not only ineffective, it ultimately destroys our well-being.

The pain of the world is so big and overwhelming. The Germans have a word that represents the sadness of the world; it's called weltschmerz. I think it's very important that we feel the sadness of the world, but in ways that are structured and manageable. We can't just allow the weltschmerz to wear us into the ground each and every day. I believe in regulating the amount of time that we allow ourselves to be in the weltschmerz.

This is where soulful activism comes into play. The most important aspect of soulful activism is learning how to keep the inner fire burning from a place of center—without being taken out by despair. This is where effective activism can be born.

A few years ago, I was deeply involved in "wounded activism." The billions of animals that die every year for food, fashion, product testing, and entertainment took a heavy toll on me. I felt overwhelmed by it all, and it drove me to work 24/7 to make a difference, and I started cultivating a very joyless, desperate life. Fortunately, one of my best friends said to me, "You move mountains because of your energy ... because of your joy, your radiance, and your love. The deeper you fall into the pit of despair, the less effective you are because nobody will be inspired to listen to you." This really affected me because I knew that he was right. He helped me realize the importance of working from a place of love to create radical change.

I totally believe that our denial of pain is the root of all ill in this world. We spend most of our life energy avoiding pain, using food, sex, drinking, work, drugs to run away from it. We fortify our ego against it. Instead, we could take a few minutes and just allow ourselves to really feel the pain. When we wade into the pain, it releases us.

It's a revolutionary idea in this culture, because everything we're taught is about avoiding pain. But we can't avoid pain in this world. It's a deeply painful world. There's no denying it. This isn't a world of butterflies and rainbows. It's a painful existence. Humans have been plopped onto this planet with no idea where we came from or where we're going. We have no idea if we actually serve any purpose. It's quite tragic unless we find a way to embrace it, laugh at it, and be in the mystery of it all.

Recharging and Reconnecting

I have an almost daily practice that includes cathartic work, gratitude lists, and intention-setting. I do yoga and meditation as well. I stay very connected to my body. The body is constantly sending messages for our well-being. When we ignore these messages, they get stronger and stronger, to the point where we end up anxious, depressed, or very sick if we continue ignoring them. I no longer separate myself from my body by living in my head. Being in my body is the key for me to be connected to life.

I recharge with time in nature and with animals. Nature doesn't second-guess, it just is. A flower grows toward the sun. That's just the way it is. Roots burrow into the ground. That's just the way it is. Animals, they live. They're aware. They're emotional beings, but they're not hung up like we are. They're very connected to their bodies and to the earth. When I'm in the presence of animals and nature, I feel very grounded because they remind me that I am also a part of nature.

If You Had a Magic Wand ...

I would create a world where we understood that you are me and I am you. Not just with people, but with animals and nature. We'd respect and celebrate our interconnectedness. We wouldn't sacrifice love and connection for the bottom line. I'd love to see a world where critical thinking and compassion unite as one powerful force. That would be a beautiful world!

To connect with Kimberly, please visit kimberlycarroll.com.

TWENTY-FOUR

Deb Gleason

From Burgers and Bullets to Compassion and Courage

"To become vegetarian is to step into the stream which leads to nirvana."

– Buddha

Heart disease is the leading cause of death in today's world.

With ceaseless wars raging around the globe, one would expect the death toll from this needless violence to top the charts. Instead, our collective mortality is directly related to the war we wage on ourselves through the violence we ingest on our plates. The truth is, burgers (and chicken, bacon, eggs, cheese, milk, etc.) are far more deadly than bullets.

I don't profess to be a health guru, but I'm aware enough to know that from a purely physiological perspective, cholesterol is a leading cause of heart disease. And it's found only in animal-based foods. This simple fact highlights how our bodies are not meant to consume ... bodies. We've been taught to eat bodies to our own detriment—and to the detriment of our planet. The consumption of animal flesh and secretions is directly responsible for exorbitant animal suffering, climate change, world hunger, and preventable maladies such as obesity, type 2 diabetes, cancer, stroke, and ... heart disease.

I find it ironic that the heart—the place of spiritual unity, interconnection, and love—is what fails us most when we make lifestyle choices that separate us from life.

According to Eastern philosophy, the deepest channel of the heart is our essential nature. Our essential nature connects us to life. Our essence can become blocked when our minds attach to hand-me-down belief systems, habituated patterns, or antiquated cultural stories. The way out of these blocks is in—to the heart. When we're aligned with our deepest essential values, we remember our connection to life.

We all have the potential to be incredible vessels of passion, compassion, kindness, and love. So why would we choose to be anything less?

Deb Gleason is a passionate woman who has dedicated her life to bringing more kindness, love, and compassion into the world through the power of food. Her meandering journey has led her down some interesting paths. A former homicide detective turned vegan lifestyle coach, Deb is intimately familiar with both the shadow and the light aspects of humanity.

Born to an alcoholic father and an emotionally distant mother, Deb learned how to cope through externally validated perfectionism. On the outside, she appeared to have it all together; on the inside, she felt misaligned and lost.

Deb's radical transformation from gunslinger to food alchemist was catalyzed by a single question. The answer cracked open her heart and forever altered the course of her life. Deb knows well the effects of both burgers and bullets, and she also knows how compassion is the portal to our greatest courage. Through Deb's personal journey of self-discovery, she uncovered her calling in life. Deb now empowers people of all walks of life to reclaim their health and their hearts through nourishing and delicious whole plant-based food.

I'll admit that I have a particularly close relationship with Deb's story because I've lived much of it with her. You see, Deb is my best friend, my soul mate, and my life-partner. The evolution of her journey to the heart has been a beautiful thing to witness, and I, for one, am deeply grateful for her presence in this world.

Allow Deb to share with you her story of how an awakened heart creates a kinder world for all.

Author's note: there are sections of Deb's story where she refers to "you."
In those instances, she is referring to yours truly, the author of this book.

***

Deb's Story

Unplugging: Path to Purpose

I grew up in a confusing household. My mother was emotionally distant and my father was an alcoholic. There were many times when the foundation of my life would completely fall away. My father would disappear—usually after an argument with my mother—and I wouldn't see him for a long period of time. Although I was told everything was okay, I had no idea what he was doing, and no idea when he would come home.

When I was a little older, I found out that he was holed up in a motel somewhere near his work. He was binge drinking. The length of his absence was always undetermined—varying from a week to a month. When he returned, he was always silent. There was no explanation for his disappearance. He wouldn't apologize or tell me that he missed me. He just waltzed back into my life like nothing had happened. It was all very confusing.

During his absences, my mother would sugarcoat the truth. She would tell me that everything was all right, but I knew it wasn't. As a child, I was dialed in to my emotions. I knew that everything *wasn't* all right. How could it be? My father was gone, and my mother was hiding the truth. It was all very wrong.

I wondered why my father's drinking was more important than his family. I took it very personally when he left. I felt like I'd done something wrong. Because I never found out why he would leave, I developed trust issues. I no longer believed what I was told, so I started relying heavily on my senses. I became so tuned in that just by looking at my father, I could tell when he was about to leave for a drinking binge. I became very sensitive to his energy. I could tell by his voice on the phone if he'd been drinking. I could tell by the tension in my mother's voice when things were going badly. My sensory awareness changed my life and helped me understand what was coming before it actually happened.

Because of this, I developed an intense need for external validation. I couldn't trust what was going on at home, so I started looking to the outside world for my sense of worth. I'm grateful to the teachers and coaches in my life, because they gave me some of what I needed. When they told me that I was okay, I believed them. I worked hard to be at the top of my class and to be one of the best athletes. Whenever I was recognized for my hard work, I felt validated. These accomplishments fed me and made me want to be better. I was always trying to impress people to get that desperately needed sense of self-worth.

My need for external validation had an addictive quality to it. It got to a point where I couldn't get enough. It wasn't good enough for me to get an A on a paper. It wasn't even good enough for me to get an A+. I felt neutral about it. Sometimes I got an A++, and I felt that buzz again, but there was nowhere to go from there. If my accomplishments were anything less than extremely exceptional, I spiraled into disappointment. This became my life—just proving myself over and over again. I became a performer and a perfectionist. It wasn't important to me that my father knew how well I did in school, it was important that my teachers knew how great I was, because they had become my foundation. *They* didn't leave for weeks on end. If they ever did leave for any length of time, they explained it and apologized for it. Even though my father wasn't gone all the time, it felt like he was gone all the time because he was so important to me. He was such a huge character in my life.

I went on to university and got my degree in sociology. I wasn't sure what I would do when I graduated, but because I excelled in my studies, my perfectionist appetite led me to believe that I would continue on to get a PhD and eventually become a professor. I couldn't think outside the box, so I was certain this was my destiny.

But the night before my graduation, everything changed. One of my relatives called my home and wanted to speak to my younger brother about a career in policing. Apparently, my brother had expressed interest, and there were a number of job openings due to a recent series of retirements. At the end of their phone call, my mother asked me if I would consider a policing career. I told her that I was about to become a university graduate and policing was the last thing I wanted to do. But the seed was planted. I went to bed thinking about it, and by the time I woke up the next morning, I had an insatiable desire to pick up an application.

When I looked at the application and read it through, I was hooked. There were so many tests that I could excel at. There was an aptitude test, a fitness test, a psychological test, and so many more. It was all very exciting to me. At that time in my life, I believed that I could do anything, and I was eager to really go for it.

I applied to police college. The first test was an aptitude test, scheduled for the following month. I knew that spelling was part of the test, and spelling was one of the few things I wasn't very good at. I spent the month learning how to spell again. When the day finally arrived, I went into the test feeling pretty confident. The aptitude test was timed. It was one of those tests where you had to do as much as possible, as quickly as possible. When the timer went off to signal the end of the test, everyone waited as the papers were graded. Once that was completed, everyone was told to leave—except me.

I went to the front of the classroom to find out why I had been held back, and they told me that it was because my test score was exceptional. Because of this, they wanted to give me an early interview for police college. I was officially hooked. I knew that everyone in my family would now know how special I was.

I aced the remaining tests and was quickly ushered into police college. Many of the recruits had completed little more than high school or college. There were some university graduates, but overall, the level of education was much lower than what I was used to. Needless to say, it was all very easy for me. I spent a lot of time with my friends at the bar and exploring the natural surroundings. I didn't spend much time studying like many of the others had to.

Police college was very practical. I had the book smarts of university, but police college taught me about street smarts and physical prowess. I made some great friends during that time, and immediately after graduation I was immersed in a new career. Even though I got to intimately know the dark side of humanity, I loved my job.

I was quite naive when I started out in policing. I thought everyone could get a post-secondary education and make something of their lives. I quickly realized that this wasn't the case and that there were many people who, because of their circumstances, had little chance in life. My first year of policing taught me about the harsh realities of life. I had just graduated from university and police college, and I was feeling quite privileged. But there were times when I'd enter people's homes who couldn't afford heat in the middle of a Canadian winter, and I was heartbroken. Their ovens would be turned on with the door open to keep them warm. It was very humbling for me. It gave me a deep sense of gratitude for what I had.

I learned that this was the way a large population of Canadians lived. I had thought that I was in the majority: complete high school, go to university, and get a career afterwards. I realized that I was in the minority. I learned so much about humanity and what makes us tick, what causes our pain, and what I could do to help. There was a lot of suffering, but I never turned my back on it, which would have been really easy to do. The darkness only strengthened my resolve to provide some light for the victims of senseless crimes, especially women and children. After a few years, however, I felt like I needed to do more.

Four years into my policing career, I applied to become a detective. Even though four years was considered a short period in the police force, I was being groomed in that direction by my mentors. It helped that I was ambitious and knew how to play the game. I was so good at that job because I knew what people wanted from me—and I delivered in my typically perfectionist way.

Within a week of getting my detective badge, I was named the lead investigator in a double homicide. I had a team of twenty people around me, many of whom had significantly more experience than I did. It was pretty trippy. Because of my perfectionist persona, however, I dug in with both feet. I grew up very fast in this position, because I loved the challenge. I was also very driven to find justice for the families who had lost their loved ones in such a violent way. I spent the next two years working ridiculous hours on horrific crimes. I was exposed to significant trauma from the violence that my consciousness was exposed to each and every day. It was shocking to me what people were capable of.

By the end of those two years, I was feeling really tired. I wasn't recovering well in my everyday life and I could feel myself heading for burnout. I decided to take some time off. I made the decision to go to Europe for a month to be with a friend who was getting married. I had to book my time off in advance, so it would be another month before I could actually leave.

Around the same time that I decided to take time off, I had a major life shift. I had just connected with you (the author of this book), and we'd spoken on the phone a couple of times. We hadn't yet physically met because we lived six hours apart, but after our talks, I was eager to make that happen. I knew you were a vegan and you told me a little about the lifestyle, but because you didn't say that much, it was still a relatively new concept for me. This is important for what I'm about to share next.

Every Friday night after work, I would treat myself to a movie rental. Often I rented adventure, action, or cop movies. One Friday night, however, after you and I had already spoken a couple of times, I walked into the video store and asked the clerk to recommend something different for me to watch. I asked for a documentary, which was weird for me because I wasn't really interested in documentaries. She recommended a movie called *Baraka*. It sounded interesting enough, so I brought it home.

I made my typical Friday night chicken Parmesan dinner, which consisted of a frozen chicken breast, Kraft American "cheese" slices, and some canned tomatoes—all baked together in the oven. It was definitely not gourmet. I sat down with my dinner and started watching *Baraka*. The movie started with a scene of a couple of snow monkeys sitting in the water of a lake, eyes fluttering as they were falling asleep with snow gently falling on their heads. The movie then moved on to beautiful scenes around the world showing nature, manmade architecture, and brilliant things about our planet. It was all set to music with no words. I was deeply engrossed in the beauty—and then the music shifted. The scene was now showing the inside of a factory.

I had a weird feeling when the music changed. I could tell that something was wrong, but I didn't understand it. It was a scene with factory workers dressed in white smocks sorting yellow objects on a fast-moving conveyor belt. As the camera moved closer to the conveyor belt, I noticed that the yellow objects were actually live baby chicks. I had no idea why baby chicks would be sorted on a factory conveyor belt. I was stunned. The factory workers would quickly pick up a baby chick and look at it, and then it would either go back onto the conveyor belt or it would disappear down a swirling metal tube in front of the conveyor belt.

I had a horrible feeling in my body about the swirling metal tube. Where were the chicks going? Why were some going one way and others going another way? I knew the only person who could give me an answer was you. I was bothered on a very deep level, so I stopped the movie and called you right away.

When I explained what I had just seen, you asked me the most important question of my life. You asked, "Do you really want to know?"

I don't think I even hesitated, because I had to know. So you very gently told me. You told me about factory farming—a term I'd never heard. You told me about how the chicks were being "sexed." How the females were separated out for the egg industry, where they would spend their short lives imprisoned in tiny, dirty, crowded cages pumping out countless eggs until their bodies were spent from exhaustion. You told me that the male chicks were considered useless byproducts by the industry, and that the swirling metal tube was connected to a high-pressure macerator where they were ground up alive.

In that moment I declared that I was vegetarian. I had no clue what that meant, because I'd never considered it before. But in that moment, I knew that I could never contribute to that kind of cruelty again. So I threw out my chicken Parmesan and that was it. I was done eating animals. I spent the next few weeks pretty hungry and confused. I had to learn how to eat again. I was also on the phone a lot more with you learning the truth about animal agriculture. You opened me up slowly because the truth was so painful. Looking back now, it was actually one of the most painful times in my life because I had no idea of the extent of cruelty that I was unconsciously participating in.

In my policing career, I thought I had seen the cruelest of humanity. But I had no idea how much worse it actually was until I learned about the exploitation of animals in our society. The truth is so hidden, and the violence is so normalized. The hardest thing for me was knowing that I was guilty of perpetuating the violence every time I sat down to eat. Through my choices, I was a murderer every single day. As a homicide detective, I had a hard time making peace with that.

By the time I was ready to leave for my European vacation, I was not only burned out from my work, but I was also confused and sickened about how animals were treated in this world. I was desperate to get away.

I had a great holiday in Sweden and Finland with my friends. While there, we decided to take a three-day trip to Russia. Russia was both overwhelming and beautiful. With everything that had transpired before my departure, I had a lot going on in my head and my heart. While sightseeing one day, I noticed a woman standing on a street corner with a little wicker basket in her hand. In that basket were a number of sick little kittens. The woman was selling them, which I'm assuming was to make money for survival, but everything about it felt wrong. I took one look at what she was doing, and in that moment I made a decision to never again participate in the exploitation of animals.

What that meant was that I was now vegan. If I was confused as a vegetarian, I was totally lost as a vegan—especially in Russia. For the next two days I was very hungry and very confused, but in my heart I was the happiest I'd ever been. I knew that I'd found the right way.

With a month away from work and the awakening that was happening in my heart, I had another pivotal moment of clarity. I knew that I had to leave my career as a homicide detective. I knew I had to start again. I didn't know what I would do, but I knew that I'd reached my expiry date. I also knew that I didn't want to become an emotionally vacant old woman with a gun and a badge.

I flew home from my vacation and landed in Toronto, which was two hours from where I lived and four hours from where you lived. We were already dating at that point, and we decided to reconnect over dinner in Toronto. By that time, I already knew that I wanted to be with you for the rest of my life. I didn't know that you wanted the same thing, but what I did know is that when you meet your soul mate it's very clear. I remember sitting at a lovely patio over dinner with you and making the announcement that I had three things to tell you: I was quitting my job, I was now vegan, and I was moving to Ottawa to be with you. You went silent, but you had a huge smile on your face.

I made my announcement on a Saturday, and on Monday I handed in my resignation. It caused a lot of panic and concern in the office and they begged me to stay. They even offered me a one year leave of absence. But I know when I'm done. And I was done. I was ready to move on to whatever was next.

I'm grateful that I got into policing. It was a wonderful training ground that showed me how the world really works. I learned some amazing things and met some amazing people. More importantly, however, I'm most grateful for getting out when I did. I'm a sensitive person, and I can't handle the dark side of humanity without a lot of pain. I wasn't handling the ongoing trauma very well. On the surface I appeared fine, but it was eating at me from the inside. Getting out was the best thing I could have done.

The same day that I handed in my gun and badge, I drove straight to Ottawa to be with you. I cried for six hours straight, releasing the trauma bit-by-bit. Everything that I hadn't processed rushed into my consciousness. I remember stopping in a little community about an hour from Ottawa to buy something to eat. I bought some plums, bananas, and bagels, and I remember biting into a plum and tasting it like never before. I'd made so much space, from all the emotional releasing, that that plum tasted like the best food ever. I was now ready for chapter two of my life.

I took some time off to regroup before finding my way again. I needed to heal and figure out what was next. It was much easier to do that together with you. Although I didn't know what was next, I did know that I needed to serve. I needed to help create a better world. As our relationship deepened and I discovered more of myself, I knew that I needed to be a voice for animals.

My next big leap was a job with the International Fund for Animal Welfare (IFAW). I worked as a campaigner and an emergency relief responder. It was a dream job for me. I was part of a rescue team who responded to disasters and helped animals in crisis situations. I helped in rescues during floods, hurricanes, and various other natural disasters. It was emotionally and physically grueling work, but it was also deeply rewarding. I worked there for a few years before IFAW closed its Canadian office when the financial crisis hit in 2008. I lost my dream job and had to find my way again. I took another high-end nonprofit job after IFAW, but I was feeling unfulfilled. In 2010, I took a leap of faith and finally embraced my calling.

Throughout the years as I learned how to eat again, I started creating recipes. I didn't grow up cooking, so it wasn't innate for me. At first, I adapted recipes and just made them healthier. I wrote my adapted versions in a special book so I could continually fine-tune them. When I'd share my creations at potlucks, dinner parties, and lunches, people wanted to know how I could make a cheesecake with tofu taste so good. They wanted to know where I got my protein and how I had so much energy to do triathlons. They were curious about my vegan lifestyle, and I loved sharing what I knew. I loved sharing how easy and delicious this lifestyle is. As I gained more confidence with my cooking, I started creating my own recipes.

When I went vegan, my life changed dramatically. Before then, I didn't even know that I wasn't healthy. I thought I was doing just fine. But when I went vegan, my skin started to glow, and the whites in my eyes became bright and clear. My energy also soared. I didn't notice this when I was vegetarian, but it was really apparent when I went vegan. Dropping the eggs and dairy helped me come into alignment. I started feeling light on my feet as my body naturally lightened up. I felt like I was connected to the real Deb Gleason—the person who had always loved animals, but who didn't know that eating them was not okay. I just never gave it any thought. But when I made the choice not to eat animals anymore, I experienced a massive shift. I got to see how great my health could be, how clear my mind could be, and how compassionate my heart actually was. Because of my personal transformation, and also because of the curiosity from so many others, I got to a point where I was hungry to learn more.

I went back to school and studied nutrition. I graduated as a holistic nutritionist and was really excited to empower others. I wanted to be the person that I'd needed when I was feeling hungry and confused all those years ago.

I left my job in 2010 and started my own vegan lifestyle company. People immediately responded to my cooking classes, group and individual coaching, online programs, and speaking gigs. Although my work inspired a plant-based diet, in my heart I knew that what I was offering was so much more than food. I was providing the gift of health, clarity, and compassion—the same gift that I'd received.

I saw dramatic changes in people. I had clients who no longer needed drugs for debilitating arthritis. I saw the reversal of diabetes, cholesterol, and blood pressure problems. Symptoms of heart disease reversed. It amazed me. People gained more energy, lost weight, and developed more patience; and many spoke of feeling kinder and more compassionate.

I realized that when people feel good physically, they're able to go deeper into their selves. They align with their hearts and their deepest core values. They're able to drop old patterns of belief and live more congruently with their inner guidance. That's where our unstoppable power resides.

So my work is about helping people break free from their zone of comfort by inspiring critical thought about the truths in this world. I want to empower people to reconnect to their own good judgment. I don't want people to go vegan because I say it's the way. I want people to move toward veganism because they know it's the way.

It was an interesting evolution for me, but this is why I'm so passionate about what I now do in the world—because I've been there.

Love or Fear?

I believe that everything we do—every choice, every thought, every behavior, every action—is driven by love or fear. If we feel jealous, we're fearful. It we feel abundant, that's love. Anything that disconnects us from our inner values is fear-based. Anything that connects us to our values, and to life, is love. It's really quite simple.

Every single food choice we make is driven by love or fear. If we believe that we're not going to get enough protein, iron, calcium, or whatever, we're trapped in fear. If we believe that we need animal products, we're trapped in fear.

The flip side is eating from love. That means first cleaning things up by losing the meat, fish, dairy, eggs, processed foods, and packaged junk. It means eating real, whole foods again. It doesn't take long to feel cleaner. Once that happens, it's easier to hear the ongoing messages from the body and recognize the foods that work and the foods that don't. That's when we can really start eating from love: love for oneself, love for animals, and love for the natural world. Choosing an organic apple instead of one that's heavily sprayed is a choice based in love. This one choice nurtures the body without adding toxins, and it also extends to the farmer who grew the apple and isn't exposed to the toxins. But it doesn't end there. Birds, bees, and other creatures aren't affected by the toxins; lakes, streams, and oceans aren't affected by pesticide runoff; the soil isn't poisoned; and on and on it goes. That is how powerful every one of our choices is. Choosing to eat from love impacts everyone in the web of life in a positive way. Every dollar is a vote, and we have the power to vote for the kind of world we wish to live in. It's very empowering to live this way.

Ultimately, the fork can be the greatest weapon of mass destruction or it can be a beautiful instrument of peace. My work is about empowering people to reconnect to their deepest compassion for all life, including their self. I'm eager to guide people toward choices that nourish both their body and their soul. This means reconnecting to life. We're meant to live vibrantly. We're also meant to feel the good and the bad without numbing out all the time. There is a better way, and it really is so simple. Eat from love. Live from love.

Recharging and Reconnecting

Because of my long history of perfectionism and pleasing others, recharging is an ongoing practice for me. I have the tendency toward burnout because I'm so driven to do everything I can to better the world. I say "yes" far too often, not realizing the consequences until I start feeling worn down. I'm a real giver, but I always pay the price.

I've not yet mastered the art of recharging, but I'm committed to it because I know how much better I feel when I put myself first. I feel a deeper connection to myself and to everyone and everything I love.

What helps me feel the most charged and connected is ample time in nature. I'm fortunate to live in a beautiful part of the world. Living in coastal British Columbia, I'm surrounded by ocean, rainforest, and mountains. I love going for long nature hikes with the dogs. Regular exercise is also really important for me. Running, cycling, and kayaking feed my soul.

I'm also just discovering the artist within. I love working with re-claimed wood that I find along the beach and in the forest. I've built a number of functional projects, such as tables, cat enclosures, and scratch posts, but now I'm starting to create art and allowing my heart to lead the way. It's so freeing and energizing.

I also love adventure, just allowing my instincts to lead the way. For me, this is a true self-compassion practice. I'm getting better at it, but there's definitely room to grow. I have to make a concerted effort to put myself first because it's still not instinctive for me. I can see how far I've come, however. I've evolved from a needy little girl who had to be better than the best, to someone who's willing to let go, change, adapt, and listen to my inner guidance. The inner voice is still small, but at least I finally hear it.

In the past, I had to control my world to get what I needed from it. I had to control my childhood situation so I felt safe and somewhat okay. I now realize that I don't need to control my life; instead, I just need to allow.

In this new place where I stand, I've learned to follow the bread crumbs in life rather than always baking the loaves. This place of allow-ing brings me right back to myself.

If You Had a Magic Wand …

I would wave my wand to create a world full of people who have come alive! I don't know what that world looks like, because we've never lived in a world where people are fully alive. I wouldn't even say it's a ve-gan world, because it would be bigger than that. If we truly connected to our values and our hearts, and we lived an authentic, congruent life, we would create such beauty, majesty, and abundance on this planet that it would be unrecognizable in the most beautiful way.

To learn more about Deb's work, please visit, debgleason.net.

TWENTY-FIVE

Rich Roll

Unlocking and Unleashing Your Best Self

"What lies behind us and what lies before us are tiny matters compared to what lies within us."

– RALPH WALDO EMERSON

There are times in life when we find ourselves in fortuitous situations that seem to be guided by a higher force. A deep sense of calling nudges expansion into the unknown. Perhaps a predestined outcome has been arranged, but uncertainty prevails. Do we answer the calling or play it safe? Therein lies the choice. Such was the origin of my connection with Rich Roll, a man I'd admired from a distance in magazine articles, online interviews, and blog posts for years. Little did I know that he would be such an influential model for my own path to purpose. It began with an inspiring talk in Toronto in the summer of 2012.

Allow me to first set the stage.

Rich Roll is a man of extremes. His story is one of inspired transformation. A former entertainment attorney turned accomplished vegan ultra-endurance athlete, popular podcast host, bestselling author, and full-time plant-based wellness evangelist, Rich would be the first to admit that his wildest dreams would never have conjured this path.

Once known as a promising Stanford University swimmer with Olympic dreams, Rich's outward success masked a profusion of internal pain. Drugs and alcohol were the numbing agents of choice. This self-destructive path proved to be the premature end of an auspicious swimming career. As is common with addiction, it also caused a painful estrangement from the love and support of friends and family. After unlikely forays into jails and institutions, Rich eventually found himself in rehab at the tender age of thirty-one.

This would not be the end of it, though. Despite his subsequent post-rehab sobriety, Rich carried an additional fifty pounds on his once-athletic body. The night before his fortieth birthday, while climbing a short flight of stairs, a sudden attack of chest pain provoked genuine fears of heart attack—or worse. This experience proved to be a pivotal moment in his journey toward wholeness.

As he states on his website:

> The day immediately following my staircase epiphany, I overhauled my diet, became a dedicated vegan, put on my running shoes and jumped back into the pool. It wasn't long before ambition took hold and my quest to participate in Ultraman slowly began. Two years later, 50 pounds lighter, and fueled by nothing but plants, I surprised the triathlon and ultra communities by not only becoming the first vegan to complete the 320-mile über-endurance event, but by finishing in the top 10 males (3rd fastest American) with the 2nd fastest swim split—all despite having never previously completed even a half-ironman distance triathlon.

A brush with mortality can be a powerful instigator for transformation. Fast-forward to the summer of 2012.

The Toronto Vegetarian Food Festival is considered to be one of the largest vegetarian fairs in the world. It's a celebratory weekend that invites people from all walks of life to sample a more compassionate lifestyle. Complete with food, music, workshops, and inspiring speakers, this uplifting festival covers it all. For me, this event is soul food.

The 2012 festival featured many inspiring speakers. Rich Roll was one such person. As a vegan Ironman triathlete on my own inner pilgrimage, I was eager to hear the firsthand account of Rich's transformative journey.

I'd recently read his bestselling memoir, *Finding Ultra: Rejecting Middle Age, Becoming One of the World's Fittest Men, and Discovering Myself,* and I knew that his talk would inspire.

My first meeting with Rich was brief. A few shared words, a photo, and a book signing. What remained was profound inspiration from an indefatigable man who would not allow life's hard knocks to bring him down.

After his talk, my partner was energized in a way that I had not previously witnessed. From this spark, a plan was hatched to bring Rich and his story to the good people of Ottawa, Canada. A mere six months later, Plant Power 2013 was birthed into reality. It would be a day-long event to inspire, empower, and activate athletes and nonathletes alike. The event sold out within days.

On the eve of the event, we shared an intimate dinner with Rich that unveiled a warm, witty, and surprisingly funny man. Endurance athletes can sometimes be a little … stiff, for lack of a better word. Rich's good humor was greatly appreciated. It was this dining experience that inspired a path that I could not have predicted.

Rich had released the *Rich Roll* podcast in late 2012, created to inspire listeners to "unlock and unleash their best, most authentic self." As our evening progressed, Rich enthusiastically shared his podcasting journey. His story stirred something inside of me. I knew little about podcasts— even less about podcasting—but the feeling in my body was undeniable. I was excited … and nervous.

Despite my trepidation, I was inspired to explore more. Rich squelched my fears with ease. It was during this fateful evening that the *Unplug* podcast was conceived. There would be much to learn before I could finally launch, but in the wise words of Marie Forleo, "Everything is figureoutable."

In one brief visit to Ottawa, Rich not only inspired the expansion of my calling, but helped make Plant Power 2013 a colossal success.

Rich Roll is a passionate man on a mission to inspire the pure potential of who we can all be—the plant-powered way. By sharing his story and honoring his calling, he's paving the way for a higher level of consciousness.

As Rich himself states, "Plant-based nutrition isn't just a diet that made me lose a little weight. It was the key that unlocked my heart and made this incredible journey possible for me."

***

Rich's Story

Unplugging: Path to Purpose

I was an awkward child; insular, insecure, and not very socially mature. But I was very internally ambitious and worked really hard in school. I was also an athlete. I was a swimmer, which is a great sport for a socially awkward person because your head is often underwater. It's a very individual sport and you don't really have to interact with anybody.

Because of my work ethic, I was on an achievement track. From very early on, it was instilled in me to work hard. Go to the right school, get the right job, do the right things, say the right things, wear the right clothes, and meet the right people. That was the premise of my entire life.

To make a long story much shorter, I started to derail when I was in college. I discovered alcohol, which seemed to be the solution to my problems. For the first time, I felt comfortable in my skin. I was able to communicate freely, flirt with girls, go to parties, and do all the things that I found impossible when I was in high school.

I thought it was fantastic, but as they say in recovery, it works until it doesn't. It wasn't long before it stopped working and began to erode the quality of my life. The first thing it did was destroy my swimming career. Then it started to erode all of my aspirations. I wanted to be a doctor and go to medical school. I had so many dreams, but they took a backseat to the next party that was happening.

Fast-forward many years. I was in a place where I was hanging on by a thread. My life involved jails, institutions, DUIs, sneaking drinks, hiding empties, and lying to everybody. All the things that a good alcoholic does. I was a broken guy, alienated from my friends and family, essentially unemployable, on the verge of getting fired, living on a bare mattress on the floor of an otherwise pretty vacant apartment, and really at the crossroads of my life.

Was I going to continue living this way, knowing where it was heading, or would I do something about it? I thought there was a good chance that I was just going to have a *Leaving Las Vegas* kind of life and suffer silently for the rest of it. One day I woke up. It was a day not too dissimilar from so many others. The only difference was that I had a willingness to take stock of how I was living and make some adjustments.

It wasn't any big watershed moment. It was more like an internal switch had been flicked on. I decided to make some changes and went to rehab to get sober and change my life. It was that little sliver, that conscious moment where I was able to do something a little bit different. This translated into a quantum shift that saved my life.

In the wake of that, I set out to repair all the damage I had caused in my life—addressing the wreckage and trying to reconnect with the people that I had alienated.

For the next several years, it was all about rebuilding my broken life based on the tools I was learning in sobriety. I was able to return to my career. I was able to repair my relationships with my family. I was able to get married, start having kids, and build a nice home where my wife and I lived. In many ways, I was able to return to the story that I told myself as a young person. You know, achieve, achieve, achieve. Work harder than the next guy. Get the good job, climb the ladder, do all those things, and then you will be happy.

I had actually lost all of that and worked double-time to get it back. I had a really good job. I was making really good money and had all the trappings of modern society that Madison Avenue tells you that you need to be happy.

I was very unhappy. I was happily married. I loved my wife and I had good relationships in my life, but I felt like I was living a lie. I wasn't experiencing the happiness that had been promised to me when I was growing up. It didn't matter if I spent money on the latest new thing, whether it was a car or a gadget or whatever. It wasn't filling the hole. It left me feeling unsure about what I was supposed to be doing with my life, as if everything my whole life was premised upon was a lie. It was like a rug had been pulled out from underneath me, and it left me feeling like I was in some kind of crazy free fall.

It all came to a head on the evening that I had what I call my "staircase epiphany." During this time, I was so focused on climbing this ladder that I overlooked my health and fitness, and I really didn't eat very well. Despite the fact that I had been an athlete in college, I hadn't taken care of myself in a long time. I hadn't exercised and I was really just a junk food junkie.

I ate most of my meals in fast food drive-throughs. When you're young, of course you can get away with that. But by the time I was thirty-nine years old, I'd packed on fifty pounds and had convinced myself, through the incredible power of denial, that I was still a collegiate swimmer. But truth be told, I was really turning into a middle-aged fat guy.

More important than the weight was the poor energy level and low-grade depression that never left. There was a real sense of disconnect from myself and what I thought my life was supposed to feel like and be like.

I came home late one night from work. My family was asleep, and I was watching late-night reruns on television, eating a bag of cheeseburgers on the couch while dozing off. I decided it was time to make my way to bed, but halfway up the staircase, I had to pause. I was out of breath. I was thirty-nine years old and unable to make it up a simple flight of stairs without taking a break. I was bent over, sweat on my brow, the whole nine yards, and it was very scary.

Heart disease runs in my family. My mother used to warn me about it all the time. I was young, so it just went in one ear and out the other. But in that moment, it was like I heard her for the first time. I couldn't believe that walking up those stairs challenged me.

It was the second moment in my life where I knew I needed to make a big change. I was able to recognize the significance of that moment because it was so similar to the moment that I decided to get sober. It wasn't any big dramatic thing. Nobody crashed through the window or anything like that, but it was a little slice of willingness, a door opening. I knew that I needed to act on this quickly or the door would shut and I would return to my old patterns. That's what really began the whole transformative process for me.

It's not like I created a plan over a short period of time to achieve what I have now. It was more like fumbling in the dark not knowing where I was going. Slowly, over time, I developed a more attuned internal compass and a way of living based on faith and instinct. I trusted my internal guidance system to lead me in the right direction even if it didn't make logical sense. It was about trusting that it leads me in a direction that is always in my best interest. That's what it felt like, and continues to feel like.

In the wake of that staircase moment, I knew that I needed to make some changes in my diet. It wasn't like I decided to go vegan overnight, however. There was a lot of fumbling around in the dark, playing around with different diets, and stumbling into a plant-based way of eating almost by accident.

Once I stumbled into it and went 100 percent plant-based, meaning no animal products whatsoever—no meat, no dairy, no fish, no eggs, nothing with a mother, nothing with a face—and once I eliminated all the processed foods from my diet, I had a tremendous upswing in my energy levels and in my mood. The depression went away and I felt an incredible physical, mental, emotional, and spiritual resurgence, simply by changing the way I was eating.

It was so dramatic that it catalyzed everything that followed, from the athletic pursuits that I started to become interested in, to the spiritual development and everything else that has since followed.

Who I am today emanated entirely out of the decision to change what I was putting into my mouth.

Living Authentically

I think that pure authenticity is something that we're always searching for and trying to perfect. I don't know if we ever completely achieve it. It's a life's work, and as they say, it's an inside job.

Not everybody can be LeBron James. Not everyone is going to play in the NFL or the NBA. Not everyone can play golf like Tiger Woods. But I think everybody has something inside of them that they are or can be passionate about, whether they're consciously aware of it or not. I think that we all have the capacity within us. My story is really just a metaphor. In my case it was ultra endurance sports, but it can be anything.

You could be a knitter, an organic farmer, a standup comedian; you could be anything. Unfortunately, I think that most people drift through life just trying to make it through the day. It's become harder and harder to just get by, make a living, and pay the bills. There's no room for the internal work that allows us to grapple with what makes us tick and to discover what our legacy is, or what we're here to express in this short life.

Sometimes it's too painful to look at—especially if we're unhappy with life. It's too disruptive. But I believe that we're here on earth to grow in any given moment with every decision we make, with every action we take. We're either expanding our consciousness and our positive footprint on earth, or we're doing the opposite. We can develop a greater consciousness on a moment-to-moment basis by understanding the impact of our decisions, thoughts, and actions. This is how we move in the right direction.

I think that the more internally focused and honest we are with ourselves, the more likely we are to uncover what it is about ourselves that is underexpressed, which if more expressed would make us happier and more fulfilled. We don't have enough people who are fully expressed in their passionate selves. Occasionally we will see a person, whether it's an artist, an athlete, a writer, a painter, or whoever, who's right there in the moment. They're doing what they love and they're connected. It's almost like whatever is coming out of them, whether it's a painting, or the written word, or the 400-meter hurdles, it's like they're in a different zone and they're channeling something outside of themselves.

I would say that those people are really tapped in. They're fully expressed in their passion and their authenticity. I think that we all have the capacity to tune in to that frequency. We all have our own frequency where we can have that kind of connection, that sort of thing where we're almost just channeling something outside of ourselves. That, I think, is a worthy quest for all of us.

My perspective is that if we want to expand our consciousness—to use *The Matrix* analogy—we need to take the red pill and really see how the world operates and then be honest with ourselves about how we're living, what changes we need to make in order to live more authentically.

That's hard. It's a warrior's path. It's not an easy path to blaze. It takes a lot of mental, physical, and emotional fortitude to say, "I'm not going to live my life the way society tells me to live it." That can evoke the criticism, resentment, and judgments of many, many people. So it requires an extreme amount of strength and backbone to adhere to a sense of what's right for you and to walk that path.

Recharging and Reconnecting

I'm always very busy, but everything I do is something that I'm passionate about. So it doesn't feel draining. It's what I would choose to be doing anyway if I had my druthers. I feel so blessed to be able to get up every day and participate in activities that I don't consider work.

I'm so busy traveling, speaking, podcasting, and writing that I don't have time to train the way I did in the days that led me to this path. It's been a struggle to make peace with that, because now the message is more important than any kind of personal race results.

But I think that in order to recharge I have to stay connected to that physicality. For me, just being able to get on my bike or go on a trail run and go swimming is how I recharge my batteries and reconnect to my source.

Hope For a Better World

I get emails every day from people who provide me with the intimate details of their lives, their journey, and the changes they've been able to make. If all I do is help one person, then that's success. Not a day goes by where I don't get emails like that. That gives me incredible hope that the message is resonating. The podcast that I started in 2012 was just a fun little project. I was feeling creatively stymied. I started it not knowing whether anybody would listen at all, and now there have been millions of downloads. Millions of downloads on a little podcast that I started in my garage tells me that it's not about me. It's because I invite guests who provide helpful information. People are starving for real, sustainable solutions to today's problems. They're sick of the sound bites. They're sick of the sales pitches. They're sick of the get-skinny-quick kind of diet fads.

People want to get well, and they're starting to recognize that it's going to require work. The obligation is on them to become educated and make the right choices. I'm just trying to put the information out there so that people can make educated choices for themselves. I'm psyched. There is real change happening. There is a movement happening right now with plant-based nutrition. It's continuing to build and I think it's really exciting.

If You Had a Magic Wand ...

I would take us back in time and start over. Maybe back to the 1500s or 1600s. I'd send back the smartest, most enlightened people that we currently have on the planet and put them in positions of power. They would create new societies that would be more functional, responsible, and respectful as we matured into the technological age. I know that we could do so much better, but I think we might have to go back in time and think about the way we set things up earlier on before it achieved too much momentum.

To learn more about Rich's work, visit richroll.com.

TWENTY-SIX

Seane Corn

Ignore the Story, See the Soul, and Remember to Love

"Sometimes the heart sees what is invisible to the eye."

- H. JACKSON BROWN, JR.

The face of activism has often been rife with division. Images of anger-filled ruffians belching nasty words (or worse) at the source of their angst are not uncommon, particularly in today's era of secrecy. Transparency has gone the way of the dodo. For those of us who care, anger can feel like a justifiable emotion. There's a problem with this, however. Anger, when projected in an unhealthy manner, creates a chasm of separation that causes the perpetrators of today's problems to dig their heels in deeper. By fighting existing structures from within the box that created them in the first place, we go nowhere. Separation is what traps us in the paradigm of fear. With fear as the prevailing force, there's little room for change; we experience frustration and burnout at worst, incremental progress at best.

It doesn't have to be this way. Activism from the heart foments massive transformation that unites rather than divides. As Martin Luther King once said, "Hate begets hate; violence begets violence; toughness begets a greater toughness. We must meet the forces of hate with the power of love."

This is the essence of Seane Corn, a woman whose work I've admired for many years. Her impassioned activism has bridged the gap between mainstream activism and love. Seane has a way of bringing challenging issues into the forefront of consciousness in a way that unites hearts. Her life is a testament to her unshakeable commitment to a more conscious and loving world. She's an internationally respected yoga teacher and long-time activist for social and political change. Her passion is fierce, her love is deep, and her commitment to truth is steadfast. By bringing the essence of yoga into activism, she inspires union through endless possibilities.

Seane's passion is contagious. There's something about the New Jersey accent and bountiful mane of curly locks that reminds one of a majestic lion commanding respect from the sheer power of its being. In the yoga world Seane Corn has rock star status. It's from this powerful platform that she elevates consciousness in ways that inspire her followers to be so much more. Her workshops combine the physical yoga asana practice with meditation, visualization, intention, prayer, shadow work, and a healthy infusion of critical thought. Seane is an activist at her core. Her commitment to awakening through personal transformation is one that she takes very seriously.

Because Seane is so grounded in her authentic Self, she makes spirituality cool. There is nothing flaky about this dynamic powerhouse. By infusing her activism with the spirituality of yoga, she's influenced positive change throughout the world.

She's the cofounder of Off the Mat, Into the World®, a nonprofit organization dedicated to inspiring conscious and sustainable activism by using the tools of yoga. Off the Mat, Into the World has been instrumental in training over four thousand yogi leaders, initiating more than one hundred ongoing service projects, and raising over four million dollars for humanitarian relief. That's a whole lot of activated love!

Seane was a featured yoga contributor for Oprah.com's 'Spirit' section. She's also been seen on the *Today* show, and a plethora of high-end magazine publications. She's worked with Deepak Chopra, Madonna, Sting, Julia Butterfly Hill, Arianna Huffington, Michael Franti, and numerous other celebrated speakers and musicians. Most recently, she was the co-chair of the Marianne Williamson for Congress campaign in the United States.

I knew that the inspired idea to bring Seane into this project would make life interesting. I also knew that her travel schedule was extensive. Odds were good, though, that she'd eventually make her way to my side of the border. On a pure whim one evening, I perused her online touring schedule. Much to my surprise, I discovered that she would be teaching in Vancouver only weeks from that day. In a fit of spontaneous inspiration, I signed up for the weekend workshop. This would be my ticket to connection.

A couple of days before the workshop, I was on a beautiful rainforest hike with my partner (Deb Gleason) and our dogs. It was filled with massive old-growth trees. I was awestruck. One particular old giant took my breath away. I could feel her ancient heartbeat. As I walked toward her, staring up at her endless magnificence, I lost my footing and went down—hard. A snapping sound deafened my ears. Stars filled my sight as I withdrew into silence. Outrageous pain filled my consciousness. Something was seriously wrong with my ankle.

With assistance from my concerned partner, I eventually stood up. Despite her desperate pleas to head back to the car, I stubbornly pressed on with the hike. She knows not to argue with my impetuous nature. Under no circumstances would I shortchange the dogs from their favorite time of day.

I hobbled over to a waterfall and released my incarcerated ankle from the confines of a shoe that no longer fit. The cooling waters were soothing, but I was shocked by the sundry hues of black, blue, and yellow that decorated my now disfigured ankle. With overwhelming disappointment, I realized that I might not be able to participate in Seane's workshop only days away.

By the time we arrived home, the swelling had worsened. I could barely stand without feeling ill. I was discouraged, desperate to not miss my opportunity to meet with Seane. How on earth could I participate in three days of intensive yoga when standing was enough to evoke nausea? The angst was causing me to spiral out of control.

And then something happened. An inspired thought reminded me that I'm a yogini. In that moment, I stopped worrying and I let go. With surrender came a powerful reframe. My ankle was screwed, but perhaps this was exactly what was needed to ensure that I was noticed. Maybe, just maybe, this injury was my backstage pass for an intimate conversation with Seane. I let it all go with a renewed sense of faith.

The workshop commenced on a cold and dreary Friday evening. As always, I set an intention for everything to align for the highest good. The details were now in the hands of the universe.

Ankle securely taped, I hobbled into the studio. The enormous room was packed. I limped up to the one tiny space left in the room—inches from Seane. I kid you not. To keep warm, I wore a T-shirt over my yoga attire that read, "Go Vegan and No Body Gets Hurt." Seane noticed. With her beautiful smile, she looked me in the eyes and said, "I love your shirt." She proceeded to ask about my injury with genuine concern. I assured her that I would self-limit. Officially connected, I seized the opportunity to explain my vision. Her heart heard mine, and voila—the story that follows.

***

Seane's Story

Unplugging: Path to Purpose

I moved from New Jersey to New York when I was seventeen, where I got a job in a club called Heaven. Heaven was in an old church that had been converted into a night club. In the rectory of this club was an all-male gay sex club. That's where I worked. I was a bartender and the only female allowed in the club. It was a wonderful place to work—especially being so young and underage. Why I was working as a bartender, I don't know. But I was.

I was also drinking and doing a lot of drugs. Every night there was a man who came into the club whose name was Billy. I always remember Billy with red leather pants, a white cutoff T-shirt, and black leather cut-off gloves. Typical '80s attire.

Billy was a gracious, kind, loving man who had a real connection with me. He'd sit at the bar and we would just talk. He had issues with my drug use and would freely tell me so. I rolled my eyes at him, but I appreciated his concern.

There was a three-week period when Billy didn't show up at the club. I found that really odd, but I didn't have any way of contacting him. On the day that he finally showed up again, I was so relieved. As he approached the bar, I leaned over to hug him and noticed that he had open sores all over his neck.

I pulled back and asked him what was wrong. He told me that it was symptomatic of his disease. I asked him, "What disease?" and he replied, "I have AIDS."

You have to remember that this was back in the mid-1980s. At that point, there were only forty reported cases of AIDS. Now there are forty million. Even though I worked in a gay sex club and was as sophisticated as a seventeen-year-old could be, I was still ignorant and fearful enough to recoil when I heard the word "AIDS."

I remember how sad and defeated he looked. I felt really ashamed. So when he asked me, "Do you want to know more about my disease?" I said, "Of course."

He explained to me how he thought he'd contracted it, and I asked a lot of questions; could I get it if he kissed me, or if he sweat on me? He answered all my questions, and then I asked him, "What's going to happen?" Of course he explained that there was no cure, and he said, "I'm dying." Not, "I'm going to die." It was very definitive: "I'm dying." I asked if he was scared, and he told me that he wasn't because he had such a strong faith.

Before I continue, what's important to note is that Billy was born and raised in Ohio. He was married, had children, and was part of the Baptist community. But when he came out with his sexuality, he was ostracized from his church and from his family. Although he was an incredibly loving man, and despite his strong spiritual background, he was still very lonely.

So, back to the bar. He asked me, "Seane, do you believe in God?" I told him the truth, which was that I didn't at that time. I said I was an atheist and he just laughed. Then he asked me, "Do you want to see God right here, right now?" I looked around the club and I said, "Yeah, sure. Show me God here and now." He pointed to Danny the Wonder Pony. Danny the Wonder Pony was a white guy who was naked except for a pair of chaps and a saddle. For a dollar you could climb on his back, and he'd trot around the dance floor and you could hit him with a switch.

Billy pointed to Danny and he said, "God is right there." Then he pointed to a cross-dresser. I'm sure that he was the worst cross-dresser in all of Manhattan. He was huge and he wore a light blue housedress with sensible shoes and nylons that would roll down to his ankles. He wore a pair of gloves and had a pocketbook. He also wore a gray wig with a hat and a veil like my grandmother would wear. Billy said to me, "God is right there."

Then he pointed to two gentlemen sitting in the bar, wearing suits, drinking beer, looking very straight, and he said, "And God is right there."

Then he placed his hand on my chest, and he placed my hand on his chest. He said, "Seane, God is right here. I'm going to tell you something that I hope you remember for the rest of your life. Ignore the story and see the soul and remember to love. You will never regret it."

That was my first introduction to understanding that God is within and that everything else is just a story. We're here to learn, to grow, and to expand our consciousness. We've got lessons to learn and karma to burn. Each of our experiences will be different, but it doesn't make one better or worse. It just makes it life. Our work is to love, and to be really big and bold about that love. We're also to trust the God within ourselves and to know that God is within all beings.

Billy was dead about three weeks after that conversation.

This was my first real introduction to spirituality as seen through a much broader, more accepting lens. It set me off on a trajectory where I was able to embrace spiritual practices with a less dogmatic viewpoint. Spirituality was no longer isolated and patriarchal. It was the idea of ignoring the story and seeing the soul that allowed me to recognize that all experiences are holy.

So I learned about God through an African-American man in an all-male gay sex club called Heaven in an old church. Angels show up in very unusual ways over our lifetime. Billy was a real angel for me.

It became a very synergistic time for me. When I look back, I can see that the unfolding of my life was all very destined. It was shortly after my experience with Billy that I got a job at Life Café where I met David Life and Sharon Gannon. They were my first introduction to yoga back in the '80s.

David and his partner Sharon went on to open Jivamukti yoga centers in the United States. Sharon also worked as a waitress at Life Café, as did Eddie Stern, who was a delivery boy there. Eddie went on to open the Ashtanga Yoga Shala in New York City. All are contemporary forms of yoga that became very popular.

So back in the '80s, I was introduced to yoga by a group of people who would become some of the most well-known pioneers of contemporary yoga in the United States. The universe collided to bring me to the right people. I remember a few years later when I moved to Los Angeles. I was in a sanctuary called the Self-Realization Fellowship Lake Shrine. In the gift store, I asked if they knew of any good yoga schools in the area. The woman said, "Yeah, there's a school called Yoga Works."

That school transformed my understanding of yoga. I started there as a receptionist, so I could get free yoga. I then went on to become a teacher, and from there to become a trainer. It really was the place that catalyzed me as a teacher. That was a very significant time for me. When I pass by the studio today, I still smile at the memories.

There were a lot of teachers along the way who were instrumental in showing up at the right time, saying the right words, and gently coaxing me to more or less accept my fate.

These are a few of the significant moments that were shift breakers for me. Not deal breakers, but shift breakers that moved me from one place in my life to another. When I look back, it seems kind of magical that these people showed up when they did, and that I had access to yoga in a way that supported me in the direction that led me on my life path.

Activism and Off The Mat, Into The World

Off the Mat, Into the World became the "Now what?" in my yoga practice. I'd been practicing yoga for years and learned a lot of different transformational tools. I was at a place in my life where my practice was more mature, present, and open. It stopped being so much about my body and my health. It suddenly started to become about being a collective—about being a part of global change. It became about the collective "we." Service became the natural next step of my yoga practice. It felt wrong for me to be contained to the mat—thus the name Off the Mat, Into the World.

It's easy to practice patience, compassion, and tenderness when you're sitting in a room by yourself on your mat. It's much more difficult when you're out in the world faced with real challenges. Can you still love? Can you still be compassionate? Can you still embrace a larger spiritual picture?

These are the questions I asked myself again and again. It was a natural evolution for me to want to be of service in areas that were important to me. One of these areas was HIV/AIDS, because of Billy. There was also sexual exploitation, any kind of oppression, and gay rights. These are the things that I was drawn to. Transphobia, homophobia, things like that which really get under my skin.

What I realized was that I'd been given a really incredible platform. When I became a yoga teacher, I certainly didn't see it as a career. I didn't know that it would evolve the way it did. I didn't know I would be so successful. I didn't know I would get so much attention. It was always confusing for me because it happened so fast and it was never part of my game plan.

I was uncomfortable with the attention that seemed almost extreme. Would I buy into my own hype? I knew that it was feeding my ego. There had to be a way for me to counteract it. When I finally realized that I could use the platform that I'd been given as a way to raise awareness, it shifted the attention from me personally and redirected it to the things that were important. More importantly, perhaps it would inspire others to step into positions of leadership.

This would then become the focus of my life and the way I wanted my career to evolve. So Off the Mat, Into the World evolved from my own personal practice as a need to make sense of the success and attention I was getting.

It's a nonprofit organization that does a variety of things. Most importantly, it's a leadership training program that teaches people to activate change from the inside out. It starts with the transformational work and moves on to more practical skills.

It's challenging. You have to look at your own privilege, racism, and power dynamics and really be accountable for the ways in which separation is perpetuated in our culture. It exposes the ignorance in our society. It drops deep into the themes around social justice that confront the issues of our times in a way that is radical but loving. It's about no longer perpetuating the sense of "otherness."

The trainings go deep into the mind-body connection. We look at our own trauma, the limiting beliefs that we hold from the way we were raised, and the cultural beliefs that we've inherited. We really examine these themes because it's irresponsible for us to enter any environment where there's trauma, or any culture where there's oppression, when we haven't dealt with our own first.

We do about four trainings per year. We're now branching out and doing online training as well. We're expanding the conversation. It's so important to not be selectively conscious. We inspire consciousness in every level of life, from social justice, to food justice, to how children are raised.

We also do an annual event called the Global Seva Challenge where we invite the yoga community to raise significant funds, meaning $20,000 per person. If they succeed in raising the money, they come with us to whatever country we're focusing on in that year.

For example, we've been to Cambodia, Uganda, South Africa, Haiti, India, and Ecuador. We spend two weeks doing service work, and the money raised is distributed among a variety of organizations. Everything from education to advocacy to building projects that are necessary for the community. We've built an eco-birthing center, a sustainable bakery, and a library. We've done micro financing and micro loans. We've done so many different kinds of projects worldwide with the $4 million that we've raised.

We've been able to support grassroots projects in the United States. We've done a lot of work around youth justice in the US. It has been pretty significant. Off the Mat is like a launching pad for people who are interested in activism but don't know how to do it consciously.

Activism has a name for itself that can often create division—and even self-righteousness or arrogance. It's a word that's really about movement. I can understand why there's sometimes resistance to it. That's why becoming a spiritual activist puts love first. It's about recognizing action, but not at the expense of someone else's spirit.

It's challenging, because when you're a spiritual activist, you get into environments where there's conflict and trauma, and it tests you. For myself, I spend a lot of time around children who have been sexually abused. That means I am also around the perpetrators.

On a personal level, I have a huge issue with perpetrators like pimps and madams. It's very difficult for me to have a compassionate, loving conversation with these people because of the abuse that they inflict on children.

At the same time, it's important that I recognize these people as also having experienced trauma, and that I realize the impact that trauma has had on their psyche, as well as the systemic trauma. So if I want to really elicit change, I have to be able to go into these environments and ignore the story and see the soul and remember to love.

If I'm not remembering to love, then I become part of the problem. I'm the one who's perpetuating the otherness, and therefore I won't be effective. It doesn't mean that I don't get really angry inside. It doesn't mean that I don't feel incredible grief and sadness. I do, but I go home and process that outside of my dialogue with another human being. I go home and I rinse the energy, so that I can show up with love and hold the thread of compassion.

That's what a spiritual activist is. A spiritual activist is someone who sees the bigger picture and approaches service through a holistic lens. It's not about going for the cure. It's about recognizing that the symptoms have to be healed body, mind, and spirit—none can be excluded.

Reconnecting Through Shadow Work

Shadow work has been the core of my own personal practice and healing. In the practice of yoga, we talk about moving toward Samādhi, or enlightenment. I don't know how to relate to that word, because it's truly beyond my comprehension. The only way I can connect to it is through love. That's why we're in these bodies. Through an ongoing process, we're learning what love is. It's an infinite process until we reach a certain level of consciousness that brings us home to our authentic self.

In order to learn what the nature of love is, part of our human experience is to learn its opposite—all that love isn't. How can we truly understand acceptance without understanding loss? How do we truly embrace non-judgment or compassion, or even forgiveness, without also knowing heartbreak?

They go hand in hand, and we can either learn love theoretically or experientially. Once it's experiential, it's embodied. That means it's transformative on a cellular level.

This is what I know to be true within my own experience as a student. Therefore, for the soul to evolve, it needs these experiences. Based on our karma, we're going to magnetize exactly what our soul needs to make transformative leaps. It's not always pretty. It's often challenging, and some of us really get our asses handed to us over the course of a lifetime.

We're in a cocreative process where people come in and out of our lives. Sometimes we're attracted to people based on our wounds. We're meant to learn something from them. They're meant to learn something from us. It doesn't always go the way our ego thinks it should, but we're always on the right soul track—even when we're overwhelmed with emotions like rage, fear, guilt, shame, or grief.

What we're taught in yoga is that everything is energy, and energy is simply movement with information. Energy can't be destroyed, but it can be transformed. It's malleable, and if we're not properly dealing with the vibrations of fear or guilt or grief, these vibrations have no place to go and they become embedded in the body. This can morph into the tension or anxiety that we feel. Our body locks down and contracts. It goes into control mode. It overrides our ability to be available. Very often it overwhelms our ability to cope. This is what happens when we're in trauma.

Our shadow emotions can include fear, guilt, grief, and rage. It's really important not to suppress these vibrations. We need to connect to them, acknowledge them, sit with them, breathe into them, and allow space for them to rise up and release. Unexpressed tension is the reason why so many of us get sick or depressed, and it's also why stress is the number one cause of illness today. A huge part of my healing practice is to acknowledge my shadow emotions, to understand what they're trying to teach me, to see where I'm holding on to a story, and to identify where I've created separation in that story so I can call my power back. I need to see the bigger picture for my soul to transform. I need to take responsibility for the cocreative experience and ultimately forgive. Give it back to God. Let go of the story through a deep reconciliation that often takes time and a lot of big feelings.

The problem with the tension in today's culture is that it's addictive. It's familiar, but it prevents us from moving with the ebb and flow of life. We become reactive, resistant, critical, cynical, and as a result, we continue to create the otherness that is so dysfunctional in the world today.

When things happen in my own life, I first go to the ego place of rage. I feel the feelings. Then I go to judgment and I try to rinse the crazy voices. I acknowledge it and let it out. Once I rinse the crazy voices, I can tap into the energy underneath it all so that I can try to figure out why it almost feels good. Why does it feel so familiar? Why does my body want to go to that place so quickly?

I have to track it and ask myself where the first assault was that taught me to respond from rage. So it's by confronting the deeper shadow of emotions that I'm able to get to what's underneath. I go through a process: "I'm angry because," "I'm scared because," until I get to the bottom of it, which is "I'm sad because." It's through the grief and sadness that we're able to tap into our vulnerability, our child self. It's through vulnerability that we can surrender. Surrender is what allows acceptance, understanding, and compassion. It also helps us to develop empathy. If we can recognize the fragility of our own human experience exactly as it is—flawed and perfectly whole at the same time—we can really embrace the fact that we're on an evolutionary transformational process that opens us through our authenticity. We're then able to recognize this truth in all other beings.

It's ultimately none of our business to judge others. If we can have empathy for ourselves and for each other, it makes life more bearable. It also allows us to bring more purpose and meaning into conflict.

When we are in these challenges, the key is to not be reactive. Instead, we need to be responsive, not from fear but from love. This is how real change is created. This is how I approach my own challenges. It doesn't mean the challenges go away. I'm challenged all the time as I get older. There are just more experiences that come my way—like a parent dying, for example. This wasn't part of my framework. I'm having to learn new emotions as they come up. I'm introduced to a new part of myself that asks, "Can you love *now*? Can you see past the story now?" This is the work that I'm deeply committed to.

Hope

In the past few years I've noticed an urgency on an energetic level. I've seen so many ordinary people who, out of nowhere, are serving or creating their own grassroots organizations—from animal rights to environmental justice. There are so many different ways that people are getting involved and making it their mission to make a difference now. This is happening on such a big level. I see it regularly with Off the Mat, Into the World.

It's happening much quicker than it did ten years ago. It makes me feel like something big is happening. We're on this wave and it's a matter of catching the wave, staying on our board, and being open to how it all unfolds. It's also about being proactive and making things happen.

I think there are a lot of people waking up and realizing that they have a moral responsibility to heal themselves and transform the world. I'm seeing it. People acting from a deep sense of purpose.

I'm very driven with my purpose. It's very clear to me. How it evolves, grows, and changes is kind of nebulous. I know that it will shift, but the engine that drives it is very, very clear. Because I feel so deeply motivated, and because I've watched so many people shift their own consciousness, it makes me believe that we're on to something.

If we don't lose this momentum, if we stay present, if we stay engaged, if we as individuals keep expanding our consciousness in the ways that we're doing, inevitably our children are going to be raised differently. The way that we approach our work is going to be different. The leaders that we vote for, that we elect, that end up making decisions on our behalf, are going to be more aligned with our morals and values.

These are the things that I hold dear to my heart. Whether or not they will happen in my lifetime, I don't know. But I do know that while I'm in this particular life, I have an obligation to make sure that I remain hopeful and enthusiastic and that I believe change from the inside out can happen. As a result, our world would know peace.

So I do feel hopeful. I also get scared. At times, I'm overwhelmed and discouraged. But if I buy into that and allow it to drop me into a place of malaise, boredom, or disinterest, then shame on me. Then I become part of the problem. So I always remain optimistic with what's possible.

Recharging

The nonnegotiables in my life are yoga, meditation, prayer, a good diet, sleep, and therapy. If any of these things fall to the wayside, I know I'm going to be out of alignment very, very quickly. I know my shadow self will rise up. If I'm not staying on my game and ensuring that the nonnegotiables are consistent in my life, eventually I get cynical and reactive.

The way I show up in my shadow is that I get edgy. I'm aggressive and confrontational. I have to make sure that I stay on top of my game if I'm going to commit to this kind of work, because it is very triggering. There are moments that bring me to overwhelming sadness, even despair. I've re-traumatized myself countless times when I've been in certain environments where I wasn't expecting so much trauma. It overwhelmed my capacity to cope. I've got to make sure that when this happens, I check in with myself and make sure that I'm doing my own personal inner work. Otherwise, I will burn out. So I'm very committed to the inner work because I don't want the repression of my own grief to impact my family or relationships in any way.

Purpose and Meaning

For me, purpose and meaning are all about living from truth and authenticity. It's about developing the self-confidence to trust my intuition. In my intuition, my purpose is very clear. The thing that blocks me from intuitive knowing is my self-esteem. If I keep doing the work on myself, calling my power back, and understanding why things happen as they do, my intuition flares so that I'm able to connect to that deep sense of inner knowing. I follow that knowing no matter where it takes me, even if it's scary or uncomfortable. I trust that internal truth. But without self-esteem, it's impossible and I second-guess myself. So for me, living a life of purpose also means trusting my intuitive knowing and doing whatever I need to do to make sure that it stays clear and present. It goes back to that deep inner work. This is why it's a nonnegotiable.

If You Had a Magic Wand …

Of course it would be some sort of a strange, wonderful utopia where all people were equal and free. Where there was first a deep and loving respect for the planet and all of her resources and we cared about the interdependency that engages each soul and each being upon this planet, including all animals. It would be a place where we put the needs of others before our own desires. There would be a sense of support, creativity, ethical respect, and a celebration of diversity.

Love would be the driving force behind all souls. We would coexist with a consciousness and a state of grace motivated by love: love of the planet, love of each other, and a celebration of all souls. We would eradicate oppression, inequality, and fear-based thinking. We would, instead, honor the God within.

For more information about Seane and her work, please visit seanecorn.com and offthematintotheworld.org

TWENTY-SEVEN

A New Beginning

A New Identity. A New Story. A New World.

Another world is not only possible, she is on her way.
On a quiet day, I can hear her breathing.

- ARUNDHATI ROY

This book has been a fervid two-year exploration into the hearts and minds of people who have unplugged from status quo and plugged into *all that matters in life*. In their own ways, they've unleashed the purest expression of their essential nature: courage, compassion, passion, joy, and love. They have all chosen to defy the conditioning of a culture in a trance by living from the wisdom in their bodies and hearts. The results are consistent: a more expansive sense of self; clarity of purpose; vision-ary thinking; a hunger for life, love, and truth; service toward a kinder, more vibrant and compassionate world; and a deeper connection to the natural world, to Gaia.

As we've seen through the stories in this book, there are many cata-lyzing forces that instigate awakening. For some, a tragic wake-up call is the pivotal moment—the savage jolt of a personal tragedy, the outrage of planetary destruction, an unexpected illness, or the loss of a loved one. For others, a creeping sense of unease infiltrates their consciousness in a way that can no longer be tolerated.

Often, it's in the shadowy depths of our deepest discomfort that we discover the truth of who we are. Pain is often our gateway to wholeness. It is the singular force that can shatter a lifetime of conditioning and un-leash the giant from within. Pain is a powerful catalyst for transformation.

I've often wondered why the hunger for awakening—for reclaiming wholeness—is a path that is not well-worn. In a world filled with so much suffering, why do we choose the perdurable coma of samsara: the endless cycle of life, suffering, death, and rebirth caused by ignorance and the subsequent denial of truth? Why do we perversely normalize the abnormal? Why do we choose to sicken our souls rather than befriend our despair? Why do we pathologize our pain and make it a wrong thing? How have we allowed ourselves to forget that unease is what alerts us to what needs attention in our minds, our hearts, and our world?

You see, the more forcefully we deny something, the more power it has over us. What we run from the most is where we most need to go. Buddha taught that the first noble truth is dukkha: "There is suffering." If we are ever to fully open to life, we must face our suffering. When we tell the truth about what we feel in our lives and our world, we are liberated, inspired to follow our calling to make things better. When we open to our pain, we no longer stay there. Pain opens the heart and the eyes so that we see the magnificent beauty of our world. Underneath all pain, grief, anger, suffering, and despair is love. When we renounce our pain, we renounce our love. When we no longer fear our pain, we become potent catalysts for change.

In her book, *Waking the Global Heart*, Anodea Judith writes,

> Mother Nature is going bankrupt and can no longer be depended upon. The fish are disappearing from the oceans; the topsoil is being stripped from the land; urban air is filled with smog; the ice caps are melting. The cupboards are no longer well-stocked; they have not been replenished, and the masses are hungry and still multiplying. Children around the world are crying, with no mother to console them; millions of them grow up with no parents at all. Developing countries long for what the West has squandered.
>
> And what has become of the Father? Ever more distant, his realm is rotting with corruption, getting ready to fall. Christian churches

struggle with priests who molest children and right-to-lifers who commit murder. Muslims blow up themselves in crowds and buses in a desperate attempt to glorify the name of Allah. Israeli Jews treat Palestinians as vermin, forgetting the atrocities of Nazi Germany. Heads of countries, heads of state, heads of corporations, and the news media that tells us all about them, spin webs of illusion to cover their actions. Truth is a commodity, seldom seen or heard. Like children, we are kept distracted from our pain with a constant supply of new toys and gadgets. And, like the many affluent children who suffered a similar fate while Dad worked a sixty hour week, we find that toys are no substitute for love.[10]

Ultimately, we can only create peace and compassion in the world by creating it first within ourselves. We can only transcend conflict and destruction in the world by healing it first within ourselves. There are many people in today's world who speak of adopting an attitude of love and service. In many ways they do so, but then because of their own inner fears, they fail to apply it to the reality around them. It's important to ask, "If suffering exists in the world around me and I fail to address it, am I really in a state of love and service to a better world, or am I simply in a state of fear and denial of reality?"

Philosopher Pierre Teilhard de Chardin said, "We are not human beings in search of a spiritual experience. We are spiritual beings immersed in a human experience." What's important to note is that our spirits want it all—the pain, the joy; the lows, the highs; the failures, the successes; the grief, and the love. When we allow for the flow of life, we are no longer spiritual beings in a human experience; we become spiritual beings in a human awakening.

In order to create a new reality and confront the seemingly insurmountable challenges facing our pain-phobic, anthropocentric world, we must believe in miracles. By now, many of us know that a miracle is required to turn things around on this planet. But what is a miracle? From an old understanding of reality, miracles are thought to be impossible. This is the trap of the conditioned mind. From a new understanding of reality, miracles are not only possible, they are real. This is the wisdom of the liberated heart. Author Steven Redhead said, "We need to make our own miracles, it is a wasted exercise to just wait for miracles to happen; they need a spark of energy and desire to make them come true." To overcome the cultural inertia that traps us in the realm of the conditioned mind, we must return to our essential nature that knows miracles are real. From there, we can create a new story for the world.

Buddhist scholar, author, activist, and eco-philosopher Joanna Macy speaks of three cultural stories currently playing out[11]:

1) The Myth of Separation. The short-sighted, power-based, patriarchal worldview that removes humanity from the web of life. It also holds the dangerous belief that a finite planet can accommodate infinite growth.

2) The Great Unravelling. The accelerated breakdown of the consumptive, medieval systems created by the Myth of Separation. The Great Unravelling also addresses the accelerated rate of species extinction and the breakdown of ecosystems on a human-altered planet.

3) The Great Turning. The transition from an egocentric "Industrial Growth Society" to a soul-centric "Life-sustaining Society." The shift in consciousness that will transform the world from the love of power to the power of love. The miracle.

I write this conclusion in the wake of what has been labeled "the surprise climate change summer of 2015" by the Vancouver Sun. No longer can mainstream media deny what is real. Of course, those of us who tirelessly act for a better world see no "surprise" in the previous statement. Only those who live in denial of the Great Unravelling are surprised when "it" finally knocks on their door. Bearing witness to the ravaging wildfires, drought, red tides, jellyfish blooms, disintegrating sea stars, entangled whales, and endless ocean garbage wreaks havoc with my mind, heart, and soul. This is life in my front yard in coastal British Columbia.

Dramatic earth changes are the new normal. We've crossed the line and there's no turning back.

In her 2012 TEDx talk, *The Green Boat: Reviving Ourselves in Our Capsized Culture* from the book of the same name, Dr. Mary Pipher stated, "We are bombarded by too much information, too many choices, and too much complexity. We have Paleolithic arousal systems, Neolithic brains, medieval institutions, and twenty-first century technology. Our problem-solving abilities and our communication and coping skills have not evolved quickly enough to sustain us. The climate crisis is so enormous in its implications that it's difficult for us to grasp." In our uncertain times, we now stand at a critical juncture. The accelerated pace of the Great Unravelling implores us to decide in which place we will stand: the Myth of Separation or the Great Turning—ignorance or awakening. We have the choice of which story to feed.

The path of awakening, and more importantly, sustained awakening, is the path of the warrior. It is not for the faint of heart. Without strength of conviction, purpose, and the support of like-hearted community, it is easy to fall prey to the impetuous child that the mind is conditioned to be. In Tibet, the meaning of warrior is "the one who cultivates courage." Courage lives in the heart. It is the outer manifestation of internal spiritual strength. The spiritual warrior is the one who courageously chooses the path of awakening and changes the world, not through violence or separation, but through courage, love, and action.

Gandhi once said, "The best way to find yourself is to lose yourself in the service of others." The closer we are to touching our souls, the greater our need to give to others. Spirituality is not just an escape from a broken, ignorant world; it is the very foundation of social justice. It is our deepest connection to the authentic self. It is what kindles our passion for radical transformation. It is our connection to life, love, and truth. It is the integration of all aspects of who we are: flesh and spirit; heart and mind; body and soul. It is our return to wholeness.

In my own life, as I moved through the pain that brought me to my knees, I reclaimed more of who I was meant to be. I made the quantum leap from anger-filled animal and environmental activist to passionate activist for the evolution in consciousness. I realized the important integration of spirituality with activism. I saw the potent results when I connected my inner journey with my outer actions. I realized that the problems in today's world cannot be compartmentalized. What we label climate change, overpopulation, addiction, depression, terrorism, poverty, speciesism, racism, sexism, ableism, misogyny, xenophobia, homophobia, anxiety, or war does not access the roots of our cultural disease. These labels are mere symptoms of a deeper problem. The greatest crisis facing the world today is the crisis in consciousness that traps us in the Myth of Separation.

As long as we continue fighting the fragmented problems in today's world with the same level of consciousness that created them in the first place, we go nowhere. Every time a "wall of oppression" goes down, another, with fear-infected fortification, will simply be built to replace it. There is no room for fighting anymore. There is only room for metanoia and the story of the Great Turning.

Author David Stevens said, "A lie is a lie, even if everyone believes it. The truth is the truth, even if nobody believes it." Collectively, we've blindly accepted an epic lie. But no lie can live on forever. As we bear witness to the Great Unravelling, we are also witnessing the dissolution of the Myth of Separation as the Great Turning begins to take hold. What the final outcome will be is anyone's guess, but the changing tide cannot be denied.

To birth, using the words of Charles Eisenstein, "the more beautiful world that our hearts know is possible", we must remember that we are not humanity protecting the animals, the rainforest, the ocean, and the earth. We *are* the animals, the rainforest, the ocean, and the earth protecting *themselves* through the autonomous expression of our own unique piece of humanity.

We are not separate.

There was a time in history when the collective believed that the world was flat. There were some who believed that the world was round, but with derision they were mocked, judged, and loathed. They were accused of imposing their impossible beliefs on the prevailing status quo mindset—disrupting the stability of a mythical worldview. But what was once considered real eventually fell apart, and a new story was born. This is where we stand today. The transition we are now experiencing is challenging the very roots of our understanding of what is real. This brings up great derision and denial. The status quo attachment to homeostasis is deeply rooted in the fear of change. But Gandhi once said, "First they ignore you, then they laugh at you, then they fight you, then you win." The fight is weakening and the win is around the corner—for the animals, the Earth, and for us.

In a tired old story that tends to abdicate personal responsibility, it is imperative to remember that we are all in this together. The power of salvation lies not outside of us, but within. We are the ones we've been waiting for all along. We are the change that we wish to see in this world. We are in the cocreative process of birthing a new story and redefining who we are, what is real, and what is possible. This is the story of the Great Turning: the story of the heart that weaves us back into the web of life.

The power to make a difference is not given, it is chosen. By envisioning and acting from a different story, we offer alternatives that disrupt the conditioned belief systems that hold the old story in place. As Barbara Marx Hubbard says, "By seeing it, we are being it. By being it, we are creating it." By being in service to something greater than ourselves, we forever alter the world. We reclaim *all that matters in life.*

I end with this book with a question for you: If you had a magic wand and could wave it over the planet, what kind of world would you create?

Miracles happen. They begin with you.

***

Notes

1 http://www.wel-systems.com/articles/Evolution.htm#.Vfo4G3uRLhV

2 Louise LeBrun, *Fully Alive: Awakening Health, Humor, Compassion, and Truth* (Night Colony, Bhopal, India: Manjul Publishing House Pvt. Ltd., 2008), p. 7.

3 http://www.dalailama.com/messages/world-peace/a-human-approach-to-peace

4 Bill Plotkin, *Wild Mind: A Field Guide to the Human Psyche* (New World Library, 14 Pamaron Way Novato, California, 2013), p. 3.

5 http://dlib.bc.edu/islandora/object/bc-ir:102698

6 Barbara Marx Hubbard. *Emergence: The Shift from Ego to Essence.* Charlottesville, Virginia: Hampton Roads, 2001. p. xxi.

7 Sierra Bender, *Goddess to the Core: An Inspired Workout to Maximize Your Fitness, Beauty and Power.* Woodbury, Minnesota: Llewellyn Publications, 2013. p. 33.

8 Sharon Gannon, *Simple Recipes for Joy: More than 200 Delicious Vegan Recipes.* New York: Penguin Group, 2014, p. 18.

9 Karen Malik's website http://karenmalik.com/

10 Anodea Judith, PhD, *Waking the Global Heart: Humanity's Rite of Passage from the Love of Power to the Power of Love.* Santa Rosa, California: Elite Books, 2006, p. 315-316.

11 Joanna Macy's website http://www.joannamacy.net/

Gratitude

There's no way to complete a book alone. As a result, there are many people who deserve my heartfelt gratitude. With so much open-hearted assistance, I've been able to bring my vision into this world with ease.

To Dr. Andra Brosh who saw my message when I didn't. Eternal gratitude to you my friend.

Infinite appreciation to Linda Siversten, the wise mama who created the sacred space for the birthing of this book. Carmel-By-The-Sea will always be special to me.

To Betsy Rosenberg, and Sandra O'Donnell for supporting and nurturing my dream through tears, laughter, frustration, and an ample supply of great food.

To Prexie A. Magallanes, my tireless interview transcriber. So much work completed with so much joy. Thank you!

To my amazing beta readers: Sylvie Gouin, Sean Howard, Karen Way, and Lois Iverson. Thank you for helping make this book great!

To Peter Russell for nurturing my essence and helping me shine more brightly.

To Louise LeBrun for expanding horizons and continually rocking my world!

To Marilyn Burkley, my amazing editor. Thank you for polishing my words and bringing this baby to the finish line.

To everyone who said yes to this project of passion, purpose, and compassion.

I would also like to thank everyone whose names I don't even know. There have been many conversations along the way that have tweaked memories or inspired thoughts that morphed into a passage or chapter in this book. I've learned that inspiration can be found everywhere.

Lastly, I send deep gratitude to every animal, tree, flower, bird, fish, reptile, insect, wind, rain, ocean, river, mountain … to life. My love for life on planet Earth is what fuels my passion for a better world.

About the Author

Deb Ozarko is a passionate activist for accelerated cultural evolution and a pioneering visionary for a new world paradigm. Her hunger for a compassionate world is the inspiration for everything she does in life.

She's an author, designer, partner, dog and cat mom, Ironman triathlon finisher, and indomitable status-quo crusher with a deep connection to animals and the Earth. She's a lover of all things *alive*! Deb is an unapologetic, no-dogma vegan and voracious truth-seeker who lives a simple life of love and inspired action. She's the host of the popular *Unplug* podcast and blogs regularly about connecting head with heart through passion, purpose, and critical thought. She challenges people to defy status quo by breaking free from the fear-based cultural conditioning perpetuated by the paradigm of separation. Deb is a provocateur of inspired and action-oriented living that serves all living beings. Her agenda is love.

When she's not crushing status quo, she can be found in the pool, on her bike, in her kayak, or hiking in beautiful natural settings with her partner and dogs in beautiful, coastal British Columbia, Canada.

You can learn more about her work at debozarko.com.

***

The *Unplug* Podcast

Inspired Living for Critical Thinkers with Compassionate Hearts

The *Unplug* podcast is an inspirational show created for listeners who are fed up with the status quo world of conformity, consumption, compliance, judgment, fear, and indifference and who are ready to shift the paradigm from head to heart by cocreating a more passionate, compassionate, loving, and interconnected world—for humanity, animals, and the natural world. Through in-depth, long-format conversations with inspiring status quo crushers, we journey together into the infinite depths of the human heart to remember, through the power of story, who we all are at the core of our beings. Each conversation inspires you to unplug from status quo and plug in to passion, presence, and purpose. No sound bites, no life hacks, no nonsense.

The ultimate goal: to expand consciousness by opening hearts and minds through critical thought that is well outside the confining status quo mindset, so that you live a profoundly purposeful life that leaves the world a better place.

***

CPSIA information can be obtained
at www.ICGtesting.com
Printed in the USA
LVOW01s1540220816

501365LV00022B/1658/P